A SCENT OF WATER

Adventures in Faith and Science

Jim Parratt

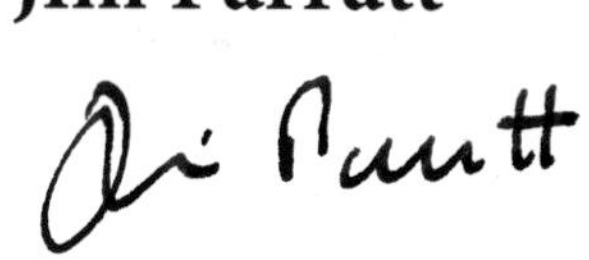

British Library Cataloguing in Publication Data:
a catalogue record for this publication
is available from the British Library

ISBN 978-1-912052-67-7

Typeset in 11.5 pt Minion Pro at Haddington, Scotland

Printed by West Port Print, St Andrews

Dedication

These memories are for my wife of sixty-four years, Pamela who shared in so many of them:

'Dein ist mein Herz und soll es ewig ewig bleiben'

For our three 'international' children:

Stephen (born in Ibadan, Nigeria, now in Scotland)
Deborah (born in Colchester, England, now in Australia)
Jonathan (born in Glasgow, Scotland and now in England)

and for those that follow:

'Things we have heard and known we will not hide,
but tell to the coming generations the glorious deeds
of the Lord and the wonders He has done' (Psalm 78:3-4)

Contents

Part 3 SCOTLAND

Part 4 BEHIND THE IRON CURTAIN

Part 5 HOME AND AWAY

With Thanks

to my grandson Dan Hough for his ideas for a front cover, to Stephen Parratt for many photographs including those for the covers, to Dr Szerdahelyi Péter for the Szeged photos, to friends who commented on parts of the early drafts, to Simon András for the line drawings, to the omnicompetent Susan Campbell without whom the original text could have never have been organised into a form suitable for publication, to my editor, the Revd Dr Jock Stein for so helpfully shaping the lengthy text from what was at one time just a 'stream of consciousness' and for making such a superb job of copy editing. Most of all to my wife Pam for giving me the scope and time to write on memories in which she played such an essential part.

Prelude:
The Scent of Water

A number of people were indirectly responsible for this attempt to remember events from long ago. They know who they are! However, the main reason for writing is the possibility that, one hundred years after the author's birth, our great-grandchildren, as early teenagers, might wonder what living was like during perhaps the most eventful century of all. Also, many children have an inherent curiosity about 'who went before' them – if, that is, they are anything like their great-uncles who were often asking awkward questions about the younger days of their own forebears.

What to call these memories was a puzzle. 'Jim's Jaunts' was felt to be too flippant as was 'The History of (the other) Mr Polly', with apologies to HG Wells – 'Polly' was my nickname by some at school who mistook the 'a' in my surname (followed by two 't's) for an 'o' (and one 't') – a common mistake we find.

What stimulated the present title was the gift to us of two orchid plants, one from family and one from our church fellowship, for our diamond wedding anniversary in 2017. These flowered beautifully for a time but were then abandoned and left for a couple of years with no attention whatsoever. When my wife Pam threatened to throw them out, I tried a little water. They came back from the apparent dead, and two years later, flowered throughout lockdown. Just a little water, just a scent, and revival came!

So, the book title comes from the book of Job chapter 14 verses 8 and 9; 'its stump [of the root] dies in the soil, yet at the scent of water it will bud and put out branches like a young plant'. Flowers too perhaps. This, for me, speaks of new life from the almost dead; spiritually that was my life until, at the age of twenty-one, I first sensed the scent of 'living water' happening to me. And, from then on I have also sensed the hand of God upon me, a pattern for my life. I am reminded of what Paul wrote[1] about the 'all things' in life:

[1] Romans 8:28 (in the translation by J.B. Phillips).

'everything that happens fits into a pattern for good'. An adventure then; and indeed, by God's grace, continues.

How Memory Works

This is a book largely about memories. Mine. It is about things and events that happened to me. Now much written therein can be verified. My ancestry for example. There is good evidence that my maternal grandmother Rebecca Cardozo (or Cardoso) the eldest daughter of Samuel Henriques Cardozo, had married my grandfather Thomas King Parratt at St Thomas' Church, Bethnal Green in London on the 5th March 1887. Of course, I was not present. But it is true and verifiable from records. Like football and cricket results it is factual. No memory is required to determine the truth of that statement, except to remember where to find the facts. It is however not one of my personal memories.

But are my memories true? Do they fit the known facts? Some of my memories are verifiable because for years, since the 1950s, I have kept a diary. And the diaries themselves have also been kept, with one or two important exceptions (mislaid). But is what is written true? Especially as it is my habit, certainly at present, to write up my diary the day after, and, as other folk of my age will agree, short term 24 hour memories are unreliable. This means that there is the question about what I remembered before the diary was written. And, before a diary was kept in my teenage years, how far back, and how accurately, can I remember?

When (and where) are memories laid down? The photograph will clarify. It is of me telling our then youngest great-grandson the rules of cricket. Putting on one side the fact how many of the rules are remembered in that brain beneath the white hat, how much do you think little Oliver James (or 'Ollyjim') will remember of either the rules or the occasion, lockdown in June 2020 when he was three months old? That is, if he was misguided enough to read this book, in say 2033, one hundred years after the birth of the author? However, as he is the latest of the Balfours from Orkney he should have no problem in remembering.

How far do memories go back? At what age do they begin? Certainly not at three months. There are apparently those who say that they can remember their birth. At one time I thought this was also true for me. A dream of being enclosed and trying, struggling to get out. However, it turned out that what I was remembering, at the age of nearly five, was the birth of my younger brother.

We can take it then that much of the first section of this book of memories can be taken with a pinch of salt. Or perhaps more delightfully a sniff of Hungarian paprika. The brain develops of course well before birth, an intricate network of cells and fibres, which is then 'pruned' during the first eighteen months of life reaching about 90% of the adult brain size by the age of five. As far as memory is concerned what increases (with age) must also decrease (also with age). Readers should remember that the author is now 88.

Memory is the particular concern of the hippocampus, the gatekeeper not only of all sensory information but also of other information as well. Once the information enters, it is passed on to the prefrontal cortex where it is briefly held as a working or short-term memory. If this information is repeated (think of learning the five times table) it undergoes a process called long-term potentiation (LTP) which strengthens the synapses, those processes between cells that carry information and where (probably) the memories are stored.

Teaching Oliver James Balfour ('Ollyjim') the rules of cricket. Intense concentration, but how much will a three-month old great-grandson remember?

This process takes place in the hippocampus. Sadly, this shrinks in volume with age after about sixty. Short-term memories then last for just a few seconds or, at most, minutes before they are either rejected (forgotten) or, to a greater or lesser extent, retained. Even those that are retained on the cerebral 'hard drive' can, again probably, be altered on any recall of 'memories of the memory'. This is rather like retyping this manuscript. The original is (hopefully) retained but so also, in a different place are the many later drafts and alterations. So too memories that are revisited may not be the same as the original memory; each revisit may itself modify what was originally remembered. Perhaps! Careful readers will notice how frequently the words 'perhaps' and 'possibly' have been mentioned in this paragraph. That's the scientist in me!

One of my favourite authors is the Australian Clive James. He wrote about his Sydney childhood in *Unreliable Memories* reprinted by the Folio Society in 2010. My memories are also unreliable and as James later wrote 'what you cannot remember you can always make up'. Would it have been 'improved' if I had had more time to remember: as the Austrian poet Rainer Maria Rilke (who died a few years before I was born) once said, no poet would mind going to jail since he would at least have time to explore the treasure house of his memory. One might also say the same thing about 'lockdown', the period during which I have tried to recall my own memories. How much 'treasure' there was in my 'house' in the first place I leave the reader to discover.

One last thing. I repeat, these are my memories. They may, indeed probably will, differ from those of people, especially in the family, who were also 'there', present on that particular occasion. As one famous family said recently of another member of the same family, 'our recollections of that event are not the same as yours'. Read on!

Part 1 EARLY MEMORIES

Chapter 1

Early and Unreliable

I was born at home (as was usual at that time) at number 15 Old Bethnal Green Road on August 19th 1933. This makes me a real 'East Ender', east of the City of London boundary and born within the sound of the great church at Bow, in the next parish – and a real cockney, unlike some today who call themselves 'cockneys' despite being born as far away as East Ham (the birthplace of Dame Vera Lynn), Dagenham or even Southend! Bethnal Green, now populated mainly by more recent immigrants from Bangladesh, was at that time described, by the mainly children's author Leon Garfield, as 'one of the liveliest and most fascinating areas to be found in any city in the world'. It was also one of the most deprived and solidly Labour backing despite the activities of Mosley's 'black shirts'. There are of course other 'east enders', indeed every big city seems to have them. There are, for example Glaswegian 'east enders' coming from places like Parkhead, Calton and Shettleston. But nowhere begins to compare with the 'real' East End of London.

Now, here is my first 'diversion' – you will find many in the book, some in the Appendices (I might have called them 'Endnotes' but I can't resist medical terms). On this same day, but a few years earlier, an important historical event took place several miles north of Bethnal Green. This was the arrival of 'Bonnie' Prince Charlie at Glenfinnan at the head of Loch Shiel. He 'raised his standard' there on August 19th 1745 and the Jacobite rebellion commenced. No sign at Glenfinnan then of a railway viaduct or of a certain Harry Potter.

I have always been a little puzzled by pictures of the Prince's arrival by boat as this is not a sea loch. Artistic and poetic licence? The Jacobite invasion of England got as far as Derby but then turned back. Several interesting reasons for that turn around;

for example, there was a rumour that the final destination was really Bethnal Green and that the retreat was because they then heard about the pugilistic Mendozas who dwelt there. There were certainly important historical repercussions for this 'retreat'. But was our family in some way involved? A subject perhaps for one of the Caryl Brahms and S.J. Simon humorous re-runs of history, like their takes on the Elizabethan and Victorian periods, published in the 1950s, in novels such as *Don't Mr Disraeli, No bed for Bacon* and *You were there*. All among my favourite books.

To bring this story up to date but with reference to an even earlier historical period, the old boroughs of Bethnal Green, Poplar and Stepney were amalgamated into the single borough of Tower Hamlets in 1965. This was not a new name but was revived from much earlier associations with the Tower of London. Men living in the villages (hamlets) to the east of the City of London were especially liable for military service, especially during the reigns of Mary Tudor, Elizabeth 1st and James 1st. One reason was that this area has always been characterised by poverty; at the time my parents were born, at the very beginning of the twentieth century, the employment rate was reported to be as low as 15%. Certainly, this was also well described as a 'tough area' and was the birthplace of a number of prize-fighters in the later part of the eighteenth century. The most famous of these was Daniel Mendoza. Mendoza was, at one time, possibly a family name on my mother's side. Indeed, my brother still uses it as his email address.

The East End was an area of political unrest. Two years before I was born Sir Oswald Mosley founded his 'New Party' (black shirts) attempting to turn it into the British Union of Fascists and appropriating Hitler's antisemitic policies. This part of London thus became a battle ground between fascism and the left- wing labour and communist parties. It led in 1936 to the infamous blockade of Cable Street, situated less than a mile from where I was born. As a three-year old at the time, I took no interest in politics. Certainly, that part of the East End was, in the times of my early childhood, quite unstable.

To turn to my own family. We have at present four greatgrandchildren. Do they remember me, their only living great-grandfather? I think the oldest, six as I write, does. And there are still hugs around the knees when we meet. However, I certainly do not remember my own great-grandparents – or even my grandparents, at all well. No hugs of any kind. So, let me start with a non-memory.

According to the almost illegible family bible my great-grandfather John Charles King Parratt and my great-grandmother Louisa Elizabeth Johnson were born within a year of one another in 1844/5. This was historically a most significant era. It was a time of European ferment prior to the revolutions of 1848 and the breakup of the Austro-Hungarian empire. These revolutionary events were unconnected with the births of my forebears. As for musical history, these years also saw the births of Fauré (in France) and of Rimsky-Korsakov (in Russia) whilst Schumann was composing his piano concerto and his second symphony.

My grandfather, on my fathers' side, William Parratt was born in 1875; there were three elder sisters. The story of one of them (Phoebe) is recounted later. He would have been in his sixties when I first knew him and was, like my other grandfather, a bricklayer or labourer. My own father was faithful in keeping in touch with his own parents and I do remember just one visit to them, even though they lived close by in Shoreditch. A rather morose couple I think, huddled around their fire. I did not know them at all well. How different then to our own grandchildren, now in their twenties and thirties who do know us well: it has been such a privilege to have seen each of the seven of them grow up, as a result of our frequent visits to see them at various stages of their development, even in such faraway places as Hungary and Australia.

I remember rather more of my grandparents on my mother's side of the family mainly because we lived with them for a time during the war at the family home in Old Bethnal Green Road. My maternal grandfather Thomas King (born about 1866) had married Rebecca Cardoso (born 1869) in 1887. My memories of my grandmother were of her always washing clothes in a huge bath tub and then squeezing the water out of them between two rollers ('mind your fingers Jimmy') before hanging them on the line. If she wasn't washing and ironing, she and my mother, were sitting on the front or back steps, depending on where the sun was or who she wanted to talk to, peeling potatoes or onions in preparation for the next meal. She seems to me, looking back, to have been a rather gentle woman in contrast to my gruff grandad in his usually dirty and open neck, white shirt. Why always white I wonder? And the sound of his swearing whenever he was told to get out of bed to go

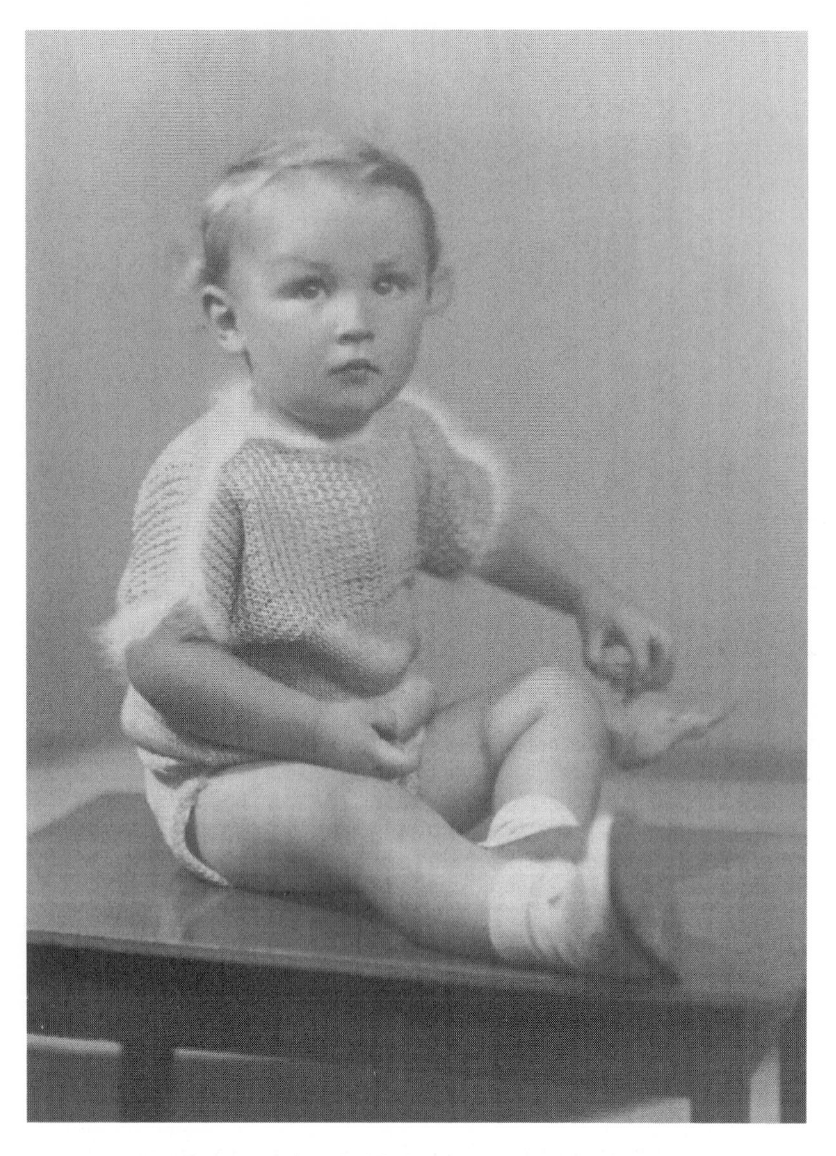

What young 'men' of fashion were wearing in 1934

down to the garden air raid shelter during the war. He died in 1941; my grandmother shortly before the war started in 1939.

Other, more reliable, memories of that time in Old Bethnal Green Road were of the daily delivery of milk in glass bottles left on the doorstep and the visits of the horse and carts with men asking if there were any knives in the house that needed sharpening (we could do with such door to door skills today), and of the 'rag and bone' man – the nineteen thirties equivalent of recycling – except that there was an exchange of money. And then there were the odoriferous visits of the collector of horse dung from the streets; presumably someone with gardens wanted this as manure. You could smell him coming from a distance away! Keep indoors with the windows shut! At the bottom of the back garden and covering the blackened brick wall, was a vine. There was, to my knowledge, no attempt to make wine but the grapes were 'tasty'. Strange that in a deprived urban area of London vines could be grown. The next 'vineyard' I saw was in Hungary in open rural areas.

How things change in just a couple of generations! What would my grandparents have thought of their two grandsons with eight or nine university degrees between them!

Although, of course, I do not remember this, I was baptised (Christened) at the church, St Peter's, just around the corner (of Potts Street and Old Bethnal Green Road) although my father mentioned another church (St Matthews) with which he was somehow associated. As far as I knew neither of my parents attended the church on the corner or elsewhere. But, again, more of this later. However, I did know that my father was greatly influenced by his contact as a young man with the 'Universities Settlement' set up by Oxford University in London's East End in the mid nineteenth century. These clubs (no beer or betting) were set up in the poorer areas of the East End and my father often talked about Oxford House and Mansfield House. It was here that he learnt to box and to row on the Thames or the River Lea and there also seemed to be classes in various subjects, including perhaps on the Christian faith.

It must have been in the mid-1930s that my parents and I moved away from Bethnal Green to Carshalton in Surrey. Being about three or four at the time I remember little of this. Memories at this age are faint. I do remember that we had a garden and that I often met a little girl from the neighbour's garden backing on to our own. My first playmate. Also, I have a vivid memory of the birth of my brother at the local hospital; many years later (June 1960) this same hospital was where our own eldest son had to spend time when he developed a high fever following our return from Nigeria.

The other vivid memory is of a Christmas morning, probably in 1937 or 38, waking up too early and attempting to feel what was in my stocking at the bottom of my bed. Had 'Father Christmas' arrived? Or had I been forgotten? No! There was something which turned out to be a Dinky model fire engine, red of course.

Chapter 2
The War Years

When my father, a sergeant in the Royal Engineers, was in France with the BEF (British Expeditionary Force) it was decided that we as a family should move from Carshalton back to the home of my grandparents in Bethnal Green. This was probably early in 1939. The probable reason for this move was that with two young children (I was six and John my younger brother was just a year old) it must have been hard for my mother to cope on her own. Both my parents would remember WW1 as teenagers and probably remember the difficulties their parents had at that time – and with many more children to look after. I do not know if either of my grandfathers served in WW1. This was probably unlikely as they would have been a little over forty at the time the war finished.

At the beginning of the war years, and my father with the army in France, my mother felt we should move from London 'to somewhere safer'. But where could that be? The first thought was of her siblings. As we have seen she was one of a large family. Was it, as my mum always said, twelve or thirteen brothers and sisters? Were any of these living in a 'safer place'? My uncle John lived with his wife in Bognor Regis on the south coast. Not really such a safe place but my mother, and us boys, would be nearer to her husband (and our father) in France! Would Uncle John and his wife take us in? Certainly not! They had no children and to have a family of three imposed on them, and at the ages 'Lizzie's two boys' were at the time, this was quite impossible. Uncle John's wife was somewhat 'snooty' and house proud, living in a well-appointed bungalow, everything in its proper place. However, they did find us somewhere nearby to stay. This was in an old disused railway carriage placed in the middle of a field; a field in which there was a goat.

I am unsure how long we stayed in this temporary accommodation; certainly, long enough to briefly attend the nearest primary school, a short country walk away. My only memory of this school was the attempt to teach me knitting. I could never get the hang of this. And this despite my mother being a great knitter, which meant I also had some home tuition I could never separate my plane from my purl. Every school day meant a race to the gate in order to outrun the goat, which seemed to regard me as a rival. Sometimes I was not quick enough and those horns were quite sharp. The only other memory from this time was going out shooting rabbits with Uncle John; he taught me how to hold and fire the rifle but, being only six at the time, I was no match for his prowess with a gun.

This was my one and only visit to see this uncle. My family was not very close and it was only on a couple of occasions that I met my other uncle, my mother's other surviving brother, who ran a hotel (or was it a public house) in Yarmouth, a seaside town I have never visited. However, I did once visit, with my mother, the widow of my father's older brother Arthur who had died (aged only 47) in 1945. She lived east of London and was called auntie Min (Maria Noquel) who I remember as a lovely lady; she died in 1979. Apart from a male cousin (Alan Tyson, whose wife Doreen came to my mother's funeral by herself) and whom I remember meeting in my childhood but with whom I quickly lost touch. There are no other relatives, as far as I am aware, on either my mother's or father's side of the family. In contrast, my own family is very close, despite living on different continents.

What do I remember of the London blitz? Quite a lot, even in the absence of anything written down; children of five or six, at least in those days, seldom kept a diary. I remember the 'quiet' period, referred to as the 'phoney war' when nothing much happened after the declaration of war with Germany, except for the preparations for what was surely to come – the blackout curtains, the curfew and the shortened school hours, especially in the winter months. Indeed, it was as though nothing was happening after the initial scare; however, the sense that something was about to happen was very pronounced. My father had arranged, from distant France, for us to travel to the Northamptonshire village of Eydon which we did for a short period. As the village school records show, the first date of my enrolment at the school was on September 11, 1939 a little over a week after war had been declared. But we were soon back in Bethnal Green. Nothing seemed to be happening.

The blitz on London (there were earlier bombings elsewhere including the Orkneys) started on September 7th 1940 – Black Saturday. The same day that seventeen years later was to become our wedding day! About a thousand Nazi war planes (Heinkels, Junkers) arrived over London like, said one observer, 'a black cloud twenty miles wide'. So began twelve hours of horror and the beginning of daily intense bombing that lasted until May of the following year, fifty-six consecutive days of terror. During that period 30,000 Londoners died before the bombing stopped abruptly on May 10th 1941 when Hitler turned east and invaded Russia. My mother and her two boys remained in London through that period until October 1940 when, with the intensification of the raids, we returned to the safety of the Northamptonshire countryside.

Of course, it was dangerous living in London, particularly in the East End, where the bombing was especially severe. The noise, the heart-chilling wail of the sirens announcing the arrival of enemy aircraft, the screeching of the dive bombers, the thud followed by the explosion of the bombs landing, the searchlights seeking out the enemy planes, the raids occurring every day like clockwork. Frightening because a bomb might easily fall on your home.

During the raids the family sought safety in the Anderson shelter, damp and smelly, in our back garden. These structures, small huts shaped rather like a squashed bowler hat, were made up of fourteen pieces of corrugated steel strengthened with girders and home assembled – albeit not by us! They were effective, apart from taking a direct hit. I have since learnt that the cost was between £6 and £10; as we were in a poor neighbourhood our shelter was put in at no cost to us. The Anderson was a tight squeeze – being only six feet long and about four and a half feet across – for a family of three in made up beds, together with Grandma and sometimes various assorted aunts. These aunts, my mother's sisters, had no shelter of their own and often had to resort to sleeping in the underground at Bethnal Green station. My grandfather never came down to the shelter; he always remained in bed, despite my Grandma's protestations, cursing the enemy aeroplanes for disturbing his sleep.

The London Underground was a safe place when the raids came and many slept there; the one at Bethnal Green apparently even had a library of 400 books. However, later on in the raids there was tragedy: over 170 men, women and children were killed when latecomers going down the dark steps in the dark (over-zealous 'shelterers' on earlier nights had removed the lamp bulbs for fear of infringing the blackout regulations) tripped over a woman who had stumbled on the steps, died of asphyxiation or were crushed to death. Although that underground station was only a few minutes from our home we had no need of such public shelters because, having a garden, we had 'our own'.

My own memories include trying to contact the girl in the adjacent shelter by Morse code (largely unsuccessful) and seeing bombed out civilians carrying suitcases and bags, the only possessions they could carry, looking even to my young eyes, confused and frightened. Was this, I wondered, what normal childhood life was like? Being dragged out of bed in the middle of the night and rushed down into the garden shelter? Elsewhere 'normal' life seemed to go on. Later I learnt of the lunchtime concerts at the National Gallery organised by the indefatigable Dame Myra Hess, a renowned interpreter of the piano music of Bach, Beethoven and Brahms, the mighty three Bs of German music. Years later one of her pupils became my own piano teacher.

Outside our own area it was the nearby docks that bore the brunt of the bombing but, because this was indiscriminate, bombs could fall anywhere. I think it was this that led my father, one of the over 340,000 soldiers who escaped from the beaches of Dunkirk in May and June 1940, to arrange for us to return to the comparative safety of Eydon. This we did in late September of that year. By that time Britain was all alone.

However, this for me was far from the end of the war. Much later when we had moved to Chiswick and during the final year of the war, commencing during the early summer of 1944 and as a reprisal for the Normandy landings, Hitler unleased on London pilot-less jet-propelled rockets from sites near to the Channel coast in France and Belgium. These were the flying bombs or 'doodle bugs', the V1 and later the V2 rockets (V comes from Vergeltungswaffen): more than 2000 fell on London over a very short period with at least two reaching as far west as Chiswick. These were especially frightening: one could hear the drone of the engine which suddenly cut out. When that ominous silence came you knew that the bomb was falling. Where would it land? One lunchtime my brother and I were home from school and, when the sirens sounded, we and our mother took shelter in the back room downstairs under the Morrison shelter, like an internal steel table, a replacement for the old dirty, damp and unpopular Anderson shelters of an earlier age. The rocket fell one hundred yards from our house at the corner of Southfield Road and Shirley Road. Huge explosion. The considerable blast blew the windows in and shattered the conservatory, glass and dust everywhere. There were fatalities but we were unhurt although very dirty: as we cleared the debris into Greenend Road a passing lady looked at us and complained how dirty we were. If the rocket engine had stopped a fraction of a second earlier, there would have been no story to tell.

With my younger brother John about 1941

Chapter 3
Village Life - Eydon

It was September 1939 soon after the outbreak of WW2, and then again in October 1940, after my father's escape from Dunkirk, that we moved, to escape the air raids, to the Northamptonshire village of Eydon. We went by car, the first time I had travelled by, for me, such an unusual means of transport. Certainly, for that period and for an 'East Ender', Eydon seemed strange, an out of the way place in the middle of the countryside: it is indeed close to the centre of England. Certainly not a place I had ever been to or even dreamt about before. But why Eydon of all places?

Eydon is an ancient village (recorded in the Domesday Survey of 1086) about nine miles south of Daventry and ten miles from Banbury. Syd Tyrrell surmises, in his first book about the village,[1] that the name is probably Saxon in origin - from 'eye' (meaning isolated) and 'dune', meaning hill, which fits well with its elevated position. If you look for it on a current map (I assure you Eydon is still there!) you may be concerned to find near the village not one but two crossed sword symbols, indicating sites of important battles. These took place just four or five miles from the village. However, if you intend to visit this wonderful village (recommended) there is no need to be concerned because these battles took place many years ago.

The first, in 1469 during the War of the Roses, was the battle of Edgecote (or Danesmoor). This, between the Houses of Lancaster (red rose) and York (white rose), was just a couple of miles from Culworth, one of the nearest villages to Eydon and walkable from there, even at seven years old, the age I was when an 'Eydon resident'. It is uncertain who won this battle between the Royalist and the 'Rebel' armies but the losses were apparently high. Quite a bloody battle then. The war convulsed England between 1455 and

---

[1] Syd Tyrell, *A Countryman's Tale*, Constable, London, 1973 and since reprinted by Readers Union Limited, Newton Abbot, Devon in 1974.

1487 and resulted in the fall of both houses and in the emergence of the Tudor period.

The other battle at Cropredy Bridge on the river Cherwell, a tributary of which flows as a small stream through Eydon, was in 1644 during the (English) Civil War. It was it seems, little more than a skirmish.

Now why these historical diversions? It is to point out that Eydon lies in the English battlefield zone. Nowhere in the country, or in Scotland, are three battles, indicated by those crossed swords, within such a small area; the third at Edgehill, the site of the first (in 1642) major battle of the Civil War, is less than twenty miles from the village. The reason for this small fragment of English history is that one of my enduring memories of my stay in the village during WW2 – between 1939-41, is of yet another battle, this time in the village itself. This took place in the 'Bufton' fields across from where we initially stayed in a house next door to the local inn. This 'battle' was, I think, between two battalions of the Home Guard although, since I remember army uniforms it may have been between 'real' soldiers. Of course, this was a mock battle presumably in preparation for an enemy invasion, but it seemed very real to me at the time. And somewhat frightening. 'Dead' bodies all over the place. However, unlike the earlier historical battles this one ended in a friendly manner with both 'armies' later repairing to the Royal Oak for liquid sustenance.

The reason why my mother and her two boys were in the village, which then had a population of nearly five hundred, not so different from the present (2020) was this: Eydon was a favourite place of my dad's. It was, in his childhood, the home of his Uncle Jim (James William) Gubbins and his wife Phoebe. Great-uncle Jim had been a policeman in the Sudan and had married, by all accounts, a beautiful Egyptian lady, who had sadly died on the boat back to England. Hence his second marriage to Phoebe Parratt (born in 1869) a sister of my paternal grandfather. The wedding ceremony was at St Matthew's Church, Bethnal Green in 1899. She had met Jim Gubbins in London's East End, where the widowed Jim had again become a policeman after returning from Egypt. How they met is unknown. Was she 'lost'? Or had Phoebe committed some felony? Certainly, at the age of about thirty she was 'arrested' by the intrepid William James. After the marriage the couple 'emigrated' (or so it must have seemed to Phoebe) to Eydon, near to Jim's place of birth in the neighbouring village of Byfield. Jim's younger brother Alf had moved to Eydon earlier and lived in a cottage overlooking the village green. I do remember calling on him although the brothers apparently did not 'get on'.

There is an assertion by the famed Eydon historian Syd Tyrrell[2] that this Egyptian episode was a tall story told by Uncle Jim during frequent and prolonged visits to the Royal Oak. This is his quote:

'Oh, what a clever man he was, what he didn't know was not worth knowing. His cleverness, his exaggeration added considerably to the joy of life here, for some of our ways were equally clever in leading him to make the wildest statements imaginable'.

Something here of the 'insider's' attitude to the 'incomer' I think! In fact, they were not 'wild stories' although some exaggeration in the telling is certainly possible especially after visits to the inn! However, the historical evidence is clear from Jim's medals, in the possession of one of my nephews, now resident in Australia and valued at nearly £400 each! It is that Jim Gubbins, the son of a shepherd, was in the Shropshire Regiment that served in the Sudan during the unsuccessful war against the Mahdi in 1885, the year General Gerald Gordon was killed in Khartoum. This was known as the Suakin campaign, Suakin being a city on Sudan's Red Sea coast. Jim then served in the Egyptian police before returning to London where he again became a policeman and met Phoebe Parratt.

My father in his youth used to spend summer holidays with his uncle, cycling all the way from London. Some distance. Although of course there were far fewer vehicles on the roads at that time.

For safety reasons and to escape the London blitz, my father had arranged for us to stay with Aunt Phoebe in her 17th century 'cottage', actually built on three levels: the plaque on the wall is dated JG 1692 although much of the cottage can be dated before 1640. We in fact had two separate sojourns in Eydon; the first was in September 1939 (when we stayed for only a short time) and second in October 1940 at the height of the London blitz when we stayed

---

[2] *Syd Tyrell's Eydon*, Eydon Historical Research Group, Eydon, Northants, 2001.

for just under a year. Not surprisingly, this arrangement with Aunt Phoebe did not work out. Can you imagine an elderly widow (then in her seventies), rather prim and proper, making a home for a rather unruly family including two young boys, John was only two at the time and I was (probably?) a rather mischievous seven year old. Some havoc ensued.

I do remember a few things about the cottage; an old black marble clock (Egyptian?) and my first introduction to music; a contraption, a kind of musical box, that used metal discs with slits cut into the metal and which played a limited variety of music. Almost certainly not Egyptian.

I was given three tasks. The first was to collect water from the pump which, at the front of the residence, also served our delightful neighbour Mrs Bull. This pump, now rather dilapidated, could still be seen in its original place when I last visited the village in 2012.

My second task was to collect milk, still warm, in a metal can, from farmer Gostick's dairy at 'Fir Tree Farm', at the end of what is now known as Lime Avenue. I was quite frightened to make these journeys because it meant passing a large, seemingly uninhabited, spooky dark house 'The Elms'. Syd Tyrrell has interesting things to say about this Grade 2 house, scarcely lived in for any period from that time to this. Ghosts perhaps? Haunted?

The third task, most enjoyable of all was, when in season, to scale the plum trees in the orchard opposite the cottage and pick the gorgeous Victoria plums. This orchard was built over many years ago.

I am not sure how long we, and especially Aunt Phoebe, survived in the cottage adjacent to the Royal Oak but the Headmistress of the village school, Mrs Evans, found accommodation for us in a detached school house on the left-hand side of the playground. It was there that we remained for the duration of our stay in the most delightful, and beautiful of villages.

Mrs Evans was a great teacher, ably assisted by a Miss Marchant to help teach the evacuees from London, who once took us children to pick watercress from the stream (a very small tributary of the Cherwell) behind the village hall. It was Mrs Evans who picked up that I was short sighted and moved me to the front of the class so that I could see the blackboard. At that time, with the increase in pupil numbers, the schoolroom was divided by a non-soundproof glazed wooden screen, into two, with warming heaters on each side. There were outings to 'help the war effort' for example to pick rosehips, an important source of vitamin C and a replacement for that found in citrus fruit, scarce because of the partial blockade by U boats of shipping carrying produce from overseas.

Eydon School

There is one other thing about the village school that continues to resonate. This was the singing, I think at the end of each week, of the 'Blessing':

> Praise God from whom all blessings flow,
> Praise Him all creatures here below,
> Praise Him above ye heavenly host,
> Praise Father, Son and Holy Ghost.

Amen to that!

Another former pupil Helen Doe has written eloquently of her experiences of the village school and, as they are mine too, I quote from them. With permission of course. Helen remembers much about the normal school day with an emphasis on religious education immediately after the register had been taken. This was for 15minutes in winter and 45minutes (!) in summer. This biblical instruction seemed to be related to what was going on in the world. After 15minutes exercise ('drill') in the playground we had arithmetic (10 until 10.45) and then, after 15minutes of playtime, there was writing (composition). At midday we all went home for lunch, just across the playground for me, until 1.15. More lessons in the afternoon until the school day ended at 3.45 in winter and 4.00 in summer. Because of the coal shortage the heating went off on the first of May when Double British Summertime began. Some days that month, as now, were cold! Helen records that there were 32 residents at the school in September 1939 increasing to about eighty when the evacuees arrived, mainly from London and Croydon, centres of the air raids.

As I was with my mother and my younger brother, I did not experience the trauma of the genuine evacuees. These came by train on the, for them, long journey from London through the darkened countryside of blacked out England before arriving at a quiet village. And then the chaos of staying with strange families and getting accustomed to those strange country smells. I came across a cartoon in a Wartime Scrapbook of a group of small, assorted evacuees going to the nurse for their first injections. When the allocation officer asked the nurse 'Have the children been evacuated?', the reply came, 'Not yet Sir, I'm just mixing up the dose'! So, there was also the children's health to consider following such a big increase in the village population.

It was Mrs Evans who, at the end of our sojourn in the village told my mother that 'there was nothing else she could teach Jimmy and that it would be best for us to move back to London' – the blitz at that time being at an end. I am uncertain when it was that we left the village; the school records are unclear but my guess is the summer of 1941, after the blitz had ended and with Hitler turning his attention to the invasion of Russia. And after the plum season!

What other memories do I have of Eydon? Quite a few. At that time there were two shops. One was a combined bakers, grocers, general store and Post Office. Alfred 'Fred' Carter (from London who had come to the village in 1920) was the baker. His wife ran the shop, the Post Office and the off-licence. It was to the bakers that we would bring our Sunday dinner, chicken probably, to cook. Indeed, many of the village Sunday joints were cooked in the bread oven, still warm from Saturday's baking. The shop was, as with most villages, also the source of information both true and 'not verifiable'.

The other shop, unusual for such a small village, was an haberdashery run by two ladies, one or both, were called Tyrrell and related in some way to the author (Syd Tyrrell) of the fascinating books on the village. I am informed that one of these ladies, Annie was Syd's wife. This shop was a favourite because it also sold sweets, always scarce during the war and still needing coupons. I remember on one occasion visiting this shop, to the surprise of the, what seemed to me, rather elderly ladies, in order to purchase, with my severely limited pocket money, a birthday present for my mother. This must have been for May 18th 1941. The gift was a small table runner. I had not realised that 'a gift is for life' and whenever my mother was cross with me (quite frequently) I 'withdrew' the gift until we had again returned to unanimity.

I remember too my first introduction to Sunday School. This was in the Methodist Chapel, opposite the Post Office and shop. I went just once or twice and learnt something about the missionary journeys of St Paul. We went, as a school, at least once to the beautiful village church. I learnt that this church goes back to the 12th Century. The first minister, one Master Philip, was appointed in 1204 and died in 1218. He was followed, two years later, by Master Robert de Hemelden. The minister during the war years was the long serving Robert Baxter Disney (1929-1943) and because, the village school was a Church School, he was a welcome visitor.

Two 'social events' stand out from those years. One was an exhibition by the Home Guard and the (mock) battle, referred to above, between two such 'battalions', presumably one from a neighbouring village, perhaps Byfield or Morton Pinkney. Another occasion was the village sports day. My father, a good middle-distance runner, took part during his leave after Dunkirk. There was some antagonism to 'outsiders', especially perhaps from London and, when in the lead at the halfway stage, he was tripped by a youngish farmer who was clearly the odds-on favourite. He duly 'won' leaving my father to pick himself up. No antagonism from him! Certainly not after the events in France with the BEF.

It must have been the Christmas of 1940 that my father came for a short break during that rather strange temporary period of the war when all seemed to go quiet. He walked me to Woodford Halse, about a couple of miles away. Here there was a railway station, long extinct and a cinema to which some of us children were bussed; my first film almost certainly a Disney. Woodford was the largest of the neighbouring villages and the reason for the visit was to buy my Christmas present. This was a cap of which I became very proud. It was on the way home that it began to snow hard and I was taught carols to help us tramp through the now fast laying white stuff. We eventually got 'home', the house in the school yard, and started to sing these newly learnt (for me) carols outside the bedroom window. My mum was not best pleased. John was very ill in bed with a high temperature and all they both needed was some quiet. I will not describe exactly what my mother said.

There was some antagonism too between the evacuees and the village boys, although my best friend was one of these from the Council houses at the top end of the village. Fights and the occasional boxing match occurred especially at our favourite play area around the pond in the 'big field' with the oak tree at the gate to the field. It was from this pond, now almost dried up, that I first collected tadpoles and took them home to show mum. She was not terribly interested in this, my first scientific experiment. Foretaste perhaps of things to come. Eydon was also my first, or almost my first, awareness of the opposite sex. Dolores O'Loughlin, not a typical Northamptonshire village name, seemed to attract boys as honey attracts bees. She sat at the open window of her dwelling at certain times in the early evening, rather like Juliet in Shakespeare's play. I am not sure I ever spoke to her but on a visit with my wife a few years ago I enquired at the Post Office if anyone of my era still lived in the village. We were told yes – there was a Ronnie Puplett (an evacuee) and Dolores. My wife suggested quite firmly that we beat a rapid retreat so sadly we never really met. Still somewhere about I wonder. Probably well married with umpteen children. On a surprise later visit to the village from her home in Devon she looked much the same albeit, not surprisingly, quite a few years older. News according to my excellent Eydon correspondent David Kench!

One final memory. As a family we were invited for tea (I hope we behaved) at the old Tudor house at the bottom of School Lane facing the Green and the stocks. Here lived a Scottish lady, I think from Aberdeen, called Mrs Newman. She was the widow of the head gardener for Lord Brand at Eydon Hall and became quite friendly with my mother. Little did I know that in years to come I would make my home in Scotland surrounded by accents similar to hers!

I conclude these 'unreliable memories' with a debt of gratitude to the members of the excellent Eydon Historical Research Group (EHRG), founded nearly twenty-five years ago, to Helen Doe and Hope Walker for their own reminiscences about the school, to Sonia Hawes for providing a map of the village and especially to Kevin Lodge and my present local correspondent David Kench for much enjoyable interchange of memories. There are two delightful books about the village written by Syd Tyrrell, and a number of other publications by the EHRG which can be obtained from them. They can be found on: http://www.eydonhistoricalresearchgroup.org/

Chapter 4
Return from Eydon

The date at which we left Eydon is uncertain; although there are two entries in the school attendance register for me arriving at the village school there is no indication as to when I left. My guess is summer or autumn of 1941. The reason is that the London bombing was over by May 1941 and my mother especially was not all that enamoured with country life. Furthermore, my father's work was in London, having been disabled out of the army in 1941. This was first of all at the factory he left to join the army in 1939, a shoe company called Normans not too far away from the family home in Shoreditch. Interesting that their shoes all came from Northamptonshire. Indeed, I still have a pair of such shoes made in Kettering by Loake Bros. Those were the days when Britain actually manufactured things rather than importing them from China! In common with many ex-servicemen and women at that time, things had moved on whilst they were away defending their country. So, my father moved jobs. He became a bookkeeper working with London Transport and the family were now in a position to look to buy or rent their own property which they did, in West London, in Chiswick.

However, before that my parents rented property in Stoke Newington. This was in Palatine Road just off Stoke Newington Road and Kingsland High Street. We lived upstairs (we would now say 'one up'), the lower ground level being lived in by to me, an elderly lady and her attractive, well perfumed, daughter who worked for a drug company, probably as a representative visiting local hospitals and GPs. Maybe there is a link here with what I first became after graduation – a pharmacologist. Maybe she was one too.

Palatine Road consisted of terraced houses; on the front door of each was a black door knocker. These had faces on them such as bearded gentlemen; some were to me quite frightening especially in the dark. A reminder of Dickens and his Christmas Carol. Our flat, like the street, had gas lighting and one had to be very careful when lighting the wick. I think I went through quite a few of these!

My school was just around the corner in Wordsworth Road and I found myself near, or very near, the top of the class. Maybe the result of that village school education. The competition for 'top spot' came from twins belonging to a Jewish family; Stoke Newington was at that time a very Jewish part of London. Sometimes I managed to come between the twins in the class position; occasionally I beat them both! It was here I took the entrance examination to Grammar School. This I must have passed well because, when we eventually moved to Chiswick, I gained a scholarship to St Clement Danes Holborn Estate Grammar School in Hammersmith.

Three experiences that occurred during our stay with this delightful couple of ladies stand out. The first was an invitation to a Jewish household for an evening meal. I was invited to join in the reading and prayers and they were excited when I told them I had myself some Jewish heritage and that my mother's maiden name was Cardoso (Cardozo). Her family were descended from the Cardozos, originally from Portugal. 'Then', said the father, 'you are really Jewish!'. It is true that my mother looked Jewish; my younger brother, especially later in life, even more so. I have since often wondered what would have happened to the family if we had been born, not in England but somewhere in Europe, Hungary for example. There would almost certainly be no story to tell.

The other memory with implications for the future was the discovery, in a book borrowed from the local library, of the story of Wagner's Ring cycle – the story of gods and heroes. Although I have seen various productions of the cycle both in London and Glasgow (when its last production nearly bankrupted Scottish Opera) it is not a great favourite. However, the fanciful story of the Nibelung clearly made a big impression on me as a young boy.

The other lasting impression was the weekly Saturday visit to the newsagent in Stoke Newington Road for the comics; I had become a great reader of comics such as Beano, Dandy, Hotspur and Rover but especially, my favourite, Radio Fun with real characters popular on the radio like Arthur Askey, Flanagan and Allen, Will

Fyffe, Tommy Trinder and, another 'Tommy' – 'Can I do you now sir?' Handley, who kept us amused during the years of wartime with a programme called, *Take It From Here*. I also bought each week 'Hobbies', a magazine that explained how to 'make models', and sometimes the Meccano Magazine. I cannot remember making anything (except attempts at making model aeroplanes, perhaps to help the war effort) but enjoyed daydreaming that I might! What I did not know then, but do now, was that most of these comics came all the way from Dundee. In Scotland!

There was one other unusual incident that occurred whilst living in what was then regarded as north London. One day I followed a crowd of folk walking towards an adjacent street. It seems that a young child actress had come home and a crowd had gathered outside her home to congratulate her. Much applause and cheering. I did catch sight of her but I have often wondered who she was. Who were the famous child actresses of the 1940's? Could it have been Shirley Temple? Or even Petula Clark? Certainly, that was the closest I have ever got to meeting a famous 'film person'. Such persons are now described as 'celebrities', known only to aficionados of the internet or the cinema. Are there I wonder any scientist 'celebrities'? Is there any other word in the language so misused? Well, perhaps 'absolutely' or 'perfect'.

Sometime in 1943 (I think) we said 'goodbye' to that hospitable couple, of whom we had become very fond, and 'moved west'. To Chiswick. 'Go west young man!'

The house (rented accommodation) in which I lived until I got married years later was in Greenend Road, Chiswick. Number 21. My brother tells me that the three-bedroom terraced house cost £5000 (a lot of money in those days) and was sold, when they retired to Kirby Cross in 1965 for over £100,000. What a crazy place London had become! The present value is about £1m.

I must have spent over fifteen years there. How was it that we selected as the family home a house in Chiswick? It must have been because one of my mother's sisters Charlotte, lived in a continuation of Greenend Road – Hatfield Road, at the end of which were 'Playing Fields' (with tennis courts) on which I once scored a century in a game of cricket against about two other boys.

My mother and her sister were never really close. Charlotte, like her sister-in-law (the wife of my uncle John who lived in Bognor Regis in Sussex) was, in my mother's words 'rather stuck up'. Or was it perhaps jealousy? Charlotte's husband worked 'in a senior position' (a salesman) at Liberty's, a (then) high class store at the corner of Oxford Street and Regents Street. I think he was in 'women's jewellery'. I did not see much of my aunt until she, in turn, followed my parents to Kirby Cross in Essex sometime after her husband had died. I was never sure how close my mother had been to any of her siblings, none of whom had children, but I think the question of how and where to look after another sister Lillian, when she had a severe stroke in her sixties, was a major source of family disagreements. Aunt Lil's story will be told later ('A Favourite Aunt').

I think the cost of the rent must have been high because my parents took in lodgers who lived in the main downstairs back room. This led to the small conservatory and the garden at the rear of which, and behind a fence, was an alley, too narrow for cars. I remember a particular couple as lodgers, who both worked during the day. I remember them for three reasons. First, they broke a quite beautiful cut glass set of wine glasses given to my father by a Belgian couple, whom he had met during the war in 1940 and who came to stay. The decanter remains but has never been used. Second, the husband took me a few times to Colchester to watch the local football team. A very poor team in one of the lower divisions. After my usual weekly visits to Stamford Bridge to watch Chelsea play almost every week this was somewhat of a comedown! Then it was the wife who took me up to London to buy my first chemistry set. This I did not like (too childish) and my Mum took it back the following day! But the third memory was that the wife, who seemed to have a soft spot for teenage me, was apparently getting a bit too close for my mother's liking. So, they had to go!

The finances were then boosted when my brother came home from the local primary school one day to say that the headmaster had asked if there was any pupil whose mother would be interested in joining the dinner ladies (with a salary of sorts). My mother applied immediately! Later, she was asked if she would like to become the head dinner lady (now called 'the chef'). She declined.

In those days school meals were provided, presumedly free, to all pupils.

My father's job was at the headquarters of London Transport in Petty France. Free travel of course to all LT employees and, up to a point, to their wives. This did not extend to their children. Many evenings were set aside for my father's charitable interests such as Dunkirk Veterans (of whom he was one) and the St Dunstan's Hospital for the blind. He either acted as secretary or treasurer to a number of such organisations, in addition to other work he could find as a book keeper. This was in order to increase the weekly financial incomings. He taught me many practical things like how to look after my finger nails, how to tie knots, how to polish shoes (his own were always gleaming) and how to box. His handwriting was the most beautiful I have ever seen – I will try to find a sample to include in these 'memoirs' as a stimulus to my greatgrandchildren! One example (shown) is of the card he sent in April 1940 from 'somewhere' (in France) just a month before the evacuation from Dunkirk.

He was a good dad and I came to love him very much. For me, he was 'one of Britain's greatest generation'.

We always had breakfast together, usually beans on toast. As his shoes were always under the breakfast table, he had to make sure none of my beans had fallen into them! In my parent's marriage it was my mother who was the driving force. For example, a problem came when the house was to be sold because the owner of the lease refused to sell the freehold. My mother made many trips to London in an attempt to persuade him to sell. It must have been rather like the parable Jesus told of the importunate widow badgering the judge until he gave in, because in the end the freehold owner did agree to sell, the purchase of which (£1000) added considerably to the price they obtained when number 21, Greenend Road was eventually sold when my father retired.

My mother was not a hoarder, unlike her eldest son. When her last home was cleared there was little to save or throw away; perhaps because she had already got rid of 'stuff'. My father's medals were kept in a kitchen drawer until she threw them away; I am sure she did not know their value to my father. When we were in Nigeria, I returned home to discover she had thrown away my old disreputable track-suit (memories of track 'triumphs' at the White City!) and all the programmes of concerts I had attended, such as those in the 1950s when I had seen Furtwängler conduct in London (1951 and 2) as well as those of the early Sunday evening Amadeus Quartet concerts held at one of the museums near the Royal Albert Hall. Irreplaceable!

What did I do with my days? In those days, except when examinations loomed, there was no homework. That I do remember. I think! But then, do we ever remember homework? Those were days of playing outside in the street or at the playing field. When indoors I loved to play marbles cricket. These marbles were many coloured and I gave them each a name of a famous cricketer. The actual ball was a small ball bearing. So, made up games. I do not remember meeting many of my relations although there was one visit that stands out. This was from a cousin (?) of my mother's – or was it an old friend – who brought her rather attractive daughter along. I was so shy I spent almost the whole visit in my bedroom! Opportunity missed!

Chapter 5
Schooldays

I commenced my secondary education in September 1944 at a school in Ducane Road, Hammersmith called St Clement Danes Holborn Estate Grammar School for boys. When he wrote a history of the school in 1951, just prior to my leaving school, the history master W. Hadley pointed out that the name of the school is one of the most famous in the world because 'wherever the English language is spoken there is known the old nursery rhyme'. It begins:

> Oranges and lemons,
> Say the bells of St Clement's

This refers to the church of St Clement Danes situated at the eastern end of the Strand, which was founded in 1002 and rebuilt by Sir Christopher Wren in 1682 who 'gave his services without payment'. A school was associated with the church as early as 1732 where in the upper churchyard were three schools, one for seventy boys who were taught reading, writing and arithmetic by a master who was allowed £40 per annum (plus candles and coals). The boys were also taught mathematics and singing. The charity itself dates back earlier, to 1552.

The 'old' school was situated in Houghton Street but, because of the necessity to rebuild, the decision was eventually taken to look for another more suitable site and in 1928 it moved west to the site in Ducane Road in Hammersmith. When I attended the school (it has since moved yet again) it was set between Burlington School for girls on one side and the Royal Postgraduate Medical School and Hospital on the other; little did I know that in later years I was to examine one of the doctors there for a higher degree. Next door but one was Wormwood Scrubs Prison. Quite a road then!

When I commenced school I received a scholarship to help my parents pay for the uniform (bright green with an anchor on the pocket, a reminder that St Clement is the patron saint of sailors) and to help purchase books and sports equipment. We were required to wear the school tie; my father taught me how to tie a suitable knot. This procedure later became long-forgotten and, for most an unnecessary skill. Why is that, I wonder, when over the years I have collected so many such ties? Perhaps sometime they will come back into fashion and I will then be well prepared.

I travelled to school on a number 7 bus after first walking over the metal bridge that separated my home from the main road (The Vale) ignoring the taunts (because of the uniform) of the workmen from the factories on the way. I am unsure whether I had a bus pass: I think perhaps that travel for school children up to a certain age was then free. Or whether later I had to pay the exact fare. More about this later.

Some of the teachers at the school were recent returnees from the armed forces, mainly from the Royal Air Force (the RAF) and we were proud to be taught by WW2 heroes. I enjoyed most aspects of school life and seemed to be reasonably good at most subjects, especially history and geography, but was poor in English. Indeed, at the age of sixteen when I took the State examinations for 'matriculation', my marks in this subject were insufficient; one needed a credit in order to matriculate, whereas all I received was a pass. It seemed that this was necessary in order to gain university entrance but, because of higher marks (distinctions) in other subjects, I was allowed to matriculate. The English teacher did his best to encourage me and on one occasion for a class examination gave me 100%; 'gave' is the right word because I hardly deserved it – whoever was ever given 100% for English? He would be surprised to learn that, in later life, I spent my working life writing (in English) several hundred scientific papers. And that in my 80s I even wrote two books. Indeed, at this very moment I am still writing, and in quite reasonable English. Subject of course to strict editing!

What else do I remember about those schooldays? There was the starting of a form newspaper (time consuming and just three issues), giving a short speech in French on behalf of the form to an attractive young temporary teacher from Paris and doing 'quite well at school', as my mum wrote in a book she gave me about Mozart by Eric Blom, which is still on my bookshelves. During breaks from lessons many of us attempted to play football (of the round ball kind) in the 'cage', a space surrounded by a metal fence where soccer skills were hopefully honed. There I discovered I was naturally left-footed. This meant that when I started to walk or run, or kick a ball, it always started with the left foot. There seemed to be few boys at school who were naturally gifted in this way and I soon found myself being picked for one of the school teams. Indeed, I was told one Friday lunchtime (I think I was in only the lower fifth at the time) to check the school noticeboard because 'you have been chosen for the first team'. Very short then of natural left-footers. But I was selected for one match only. Too young and small for the 'big boys'. Later I spent a year in the 2nd XI before promotion to the 1st XI where I remained for my last three years at school. This turned out to be a good team (especially after I had left!) with two (or was it three) future amateur internationals (I was not among them) and we won almost all our matches against other London school sides. Over the years I moved 'backwards' from outside left (number 11) to inside left (number 10) and then eventually to left half (number 6). These are of course the names and numbers of the old positions and are no longer used.

St Clement Danes First XI 1951-2. The outside left is outside right in the front row!

I think my playing declined especially for the final year when, because of my severe short-sightedness, I could hardly see the ball, which is a quite a disadvantage when playing football. My Saturdays were thus spent playing football in the morning, all over London, and after a good clean up, going in the afternoon to Stamford Bridge to watch Chelsea play. And, not only the first team but the reserves as well! That means a real and accredited Chelsea fan!

I think another reason for being chosen to play football for the school was that I was quite fast; indeed, I became the school sprint champion. This ability to run seems to have been passed down to some at least of my grandchildren. The school sports days took place at the nearby White City Stadium and I am proud to have run on the same track as some of the athletic greats like Roger Bannister and Emil Zatopek. Not, however, at the same time.

The other sporting interest was cricket, a game I loved but at which I was quite hopeless. Captaining the 4th XI on one occasion; this was a game we lost and in which I scored a 'duck'. Even in 'house cricket' I was unfortunate when keeping wicket to receive a teeth-shattering blow in the mouth. However, watching cricket was another matter. On most Saturdays in summer I went with two friends (Rattue and Warren) to Lords to watch Middlesex, especially in 1947 when Compton and Edrich were in blistering run gathering form. We would meet outside the baker's shop, owned by Warren's father, in Praed Street in Paddington, opposite St Mary's Hospital. We would collect freshly baked rolls and then walk the short distance to Lord's, the 'home of cricket', in St John's Wood, lying on the ground just outside the boundary ropes. Many years later with our younger son Jonathan, I took our two 'Aussie' grandsons for a tour of Lord's in order to see the urn (the 'Ashes') invariably won by the Australians but, for some reason (too fragile?) never allowed to leave Lord's.

I think the first cricket match I watched was just after the war when the Australian Services XI played England in a series of 'Victory' Tests which the Aussies (captained by the great Lindsay Hassett and with Keith Miller in the side) of course won. I was also present at Lord's at the game in which the England selectors chose, perhaps unwisely, three under-nineteen players including J.G. Dewes, who later became active in Christian work. This Australian side even played two games in Scotland although this was not the occasion when a Church of Scotland minister scored a century against them.

My most memorable match however was at the Oval on the 15th August 1948, the occasion of Don Bradman's last Test match. Great standing ovation for this great Australian batsman and captain when he came out to bat at around 6 o'clock in the evening, almost at close of play. Sadly, he was bowled second ball by the Warwickshire spinner Eric Hollies for a duck. Huge groans around the ground. Could we claim our entrance money back I wondered? I heard later that Bradman was so emotionally affected by the welcome he received that he had tears in his eyes and could not see the ball! That was his last innings for Australia; he did not need to bat in the second innings because the side he captained won by an innings and so Australia was not required to bat again. Bradman had needed only four runs to give him an average of 100 in Test cricket, a record never achieved before or since. You could say then that he was denied this record by his own team (being so good) or by England (being, perhaps deliberately, not very good).

I had to spend three years in the 6th form because in the summer of 1951, I along with so many others countrywide, failed my A level biology. Many complaints. Did nearly everyone mix up the cranial nerves of the dogfish in the practical examination, held in a hall near to the Royal Albert Hall on a very hot June afternoon. What to do? Leave school at that point and forego university? Long discussions with my parents. Could they manage financially? The decision was to remain at school for another year and resit, which I did the following year passing both Botany and Zoology. Could I help my parents financially? I decided to go up to 'town' and look for a job. And, I found an interesting one!

Before I come to that I should describe how I normally spent the long summer vacations whilst at school. We usually went on holiday together as a family, the four of us, to places like Southend, Bognor, Bournemouth, Western-Super-Mare and, my favourite Ferring, a small hamlet on the south coast near to Worthing. I remember little of these times except that on one of these holidays my father bought tickets for a piano recital by a rather ancient pianist called Pouishnoff, who played mainly Chopin I think. It was this that prompted my mother to buy an even more ancient piano and pay for me to have lessons. In this I was most fortunate in that my teacher Kathleen Lane had been a pupil of the great Dame Myra Hess. More of this when I think later about the place music has played in my life. That recital on a rainy evening in, I think, Bournemouth became for me highly significant.

For three or four years I went each summer to a school Harvest Camp in Somerset near Taunton. I seemed to go to the same farmer each year; I later learnt that each summer he had asked for me because I was a 'good worker'; I remember overhearing him (from the top of a haystack whilst having my lunch) telling another farmer that this town boy could manage anything he gave me to do. This included clearing out the cow sheds, the state of which suggested to me that he left them from one year to the next to await my arrival. And, it always seemed to be the time for hedging; again, this had been left from the previous year. There were no flies on these Somerset farmers!

Each year there was the annual cricket match between the 'boys' and the farmers. This was held in a field just after the cows had been moved out of it and, when batting, these 'men of Somerset' seemed to be aiming at the cow pats. Of course, they invariably won hands down; very big fast bowlers. It was in the pub afterwards that we were treated to locally brewed cider, potent stuff for a fifteen-year-old.

Towards the end of my time at school there was my first expedition to another country for which I had to obtain a passport, the first of many. This was to Ghent (Gent) in Belgium. The occasion was an invitation from that city to the citizens of London to send an athletics team to participate in a match against a team from that city. There were the usual races, sprints, half-mile (now called the 800 metres) and a mixed relay of a mile (now the 1500 m) involving four runners. I participated in the sprints and also in the relay team as one of the 200 m runners. This was the highlight (for us) because the Belgian team contained an Olympic athlete who was to run the last leg (800 m) against the captain of the St Clement Danes team. An exciting race ensued in which the Olympian was defeated and we received a trophy of some kind. And chocolates! My only other recollections of that visit were feeling very sick on the

Channel crossing to Ostend and picking up souvenirs (beer mats) from the various restaurants we frequented. These replaced earlier collections of cigarette cards featuring celebrated footballers and cricketers. Probably these too were thrown out (and rightly so) by my mother. However, some of these cards became quite valuable. So I could have become a schoolboy millionaire. Perhaps!

To return to attempts to earn some money during the long school summer holidays. Once, thanks to our next-door neighbour Mr Ferrier, I obtained a job at Walls the manufacturer (now as then) of ice cream and sausages. It was a boring job just watching the ice cream appear from a machine and making sure it finished up in the right place. You were allowed to eat as much ice cream as you liked but after a few days of 'tasting' it no longer held the fascination it held at the beginning. I never took much money home to mum because I spent my earnings, after the Friday afternoon pay out, at the factory shop and so came home laden with sausages, ice cream and other Walls specialities. I think my mother was quite pleased with the produce although I am certain she would rather have had the wages!

My last attempt to 'earn my way' at home came in the last school holiday when I was at last guaranteed a place at university. I told my mother that I would go up to 'town' (meaning the centre of London) and look for work. This I found surprisingly quickly, arriving home that evening with the happy news. I had seen an advertisement in the window of a shop near Covent Garden which said they were looking for a 'bright young man looking for good opportunities'. That, of course, was me! It turned out to be a shop selling ladies lingerie, about which I learnt a great deal in the short time I was there. I seemed to be doing well, with second thoughts about university, when a few days later over coffee I let on that I had that autumn been offered a place at university to study pharmacy. It seemed that lingerie and pharmacy did not go together and they, reluctantly I think, let me go. That glittering career in retail was not to be although, for a few days, I found it a fascinating world! Who knows where I might have ended up! Certainly, a future in lingerie was not for me.

That third year in the 6th form had interesting repercussions. At that time I had taken out a subscription for the Arts Club, also near Covent Garden. This was a private club for putting on theatre productions not normally seen in other West End theatres. I remember seeing (in translation I think) Pirandello's Henry IV and Ibsen's Dolls House (with Mai Zetterling). I also made excursions to the Hammersmith Lyric Theatre (Thomas Otway's Venice Preserved with Pamela Brown) and, especially to see the Donald Wolfit Company in a range of Shakespeare plays, Lear, Macbeth, Henry IV part 1 (Wolfit as Falstaff with a cushion stuffed up his jumper). Everything seemed to be done on a shoe string but the great Sir Donald was the centre of every production. The ladies, including his wife, hardly had a look in! Wonderful acting though! These productions made me a long-term lover of the theatre, greatly increased by many visits to London in the years to come.

There were too during that year the beginning of regular visits to the various London concert halls, with a regular subscription to the BBC series at the Festival Hall with conductors like the three knights Beecham, Barbirolli (an old boy of St Clement Danes), Boult, and pianists like Curzon and, my favourite, Solomon. Then there were the 'Proms' which I attended with my brother; there is a photograph in which we can both be seen at the rail. There was also

Taken at a Promenade Concert in the Royal Albert Hall about 1950. Spot the boys!

my introduction to chamber music. The ones that stand out were those at the Natural History Museum by the Amadeus Quartet, often with Lionel Tertis, Cecil Aronowitz and again, Clifford Curzon. The first hearing of my favourite music, the great Schubert String Quintet, was at one of these concerts. During the interval you could explore the fine collection of Constable's drawings.

I now need to report a strange happening that began during the last few years at school. I developed quite suddenly a speech defect which made it impossible for me to speak in public. Even asking the driver for my bus fare became difficult; I always tried to have the exact fare so that I did not need to ask. The masters at school knew not to ask me to answer questions in class or to give the annual reports as the Temple House Captain. Interviews for university entrance to medical school became both embarrassing and impossible. There was a complete aural block. Much later, after I became a Christian, this changed quite dramatically, as I report later. The next chapter is a digression on speech defects.

In the sixth form during that final year at school two boys in the year below my own (Donald Draper and John Neal) asked permission to organise a School Christian Union. I also write about this later but, although I was somewhat 'anti', looking back it played a significant part in my coming to faith whilst at university two years later.

Thus ended my schooldays. I made one later visit to the school. This was the following year, at the annual athletics match between the school and the 'old boy's' of which I was now one. I participated in the two sprints and won both; there is a photo to prove it! The thrill of leading round the bend of the 200 yards remains a pleasurable memory. Looking back, I was fortunate in that choice of school at which I was happy and well taught. Sadly, political changes in the country meant that a few years later the school left Hammersmith. But that is another story and not part of my educational experience.

Chapter 6
Speech Impediment

If our voices are our 'auditory faces', then speech impediments can have a disastrous effect on our human lives and certainly this was true for me in my later teenage years. Clearly, for a time there was a problem in articulating, or perhaps a defective fluency, and I am still, all these years later, puzzling about the precise physiological mechanisms which were involved in my own case. Because speaking processes are complex, speech can be disturbed at many sites but for me the problem was clearly central in origin. The end of the 'speech chain' was intact; there were few problems with 'ordinary speech', the muscles around the mouth, throat and larynx were in good working order. It was simply that I knew what I wanted to say, in answer to a question for example, but the words just would not 'come out'. The word I wanted was 'stuck'. Somewhere!

If there was time, one way around this was to suddenly substitute the particular word I wanted by another similar word that did not have quite the same precise meaning. This did not result in too many malapropisms; the word chosen was a reasonable approximate but it was not the best word for the situation, not the word I really wanted. Even now, especially when I am tired, I still use this 'technique'. It is kind of 'diversion', I know the way I want to go, the word I want to say, but the cerebral block means I need to find an alternative route (word), a 'diversion', which took time, like the increase in travel time on the Crianlarich diversion on the A82/83 albeit not so long! So, a little time was involved in finding the right word, a verbal hesitancy. People who know me well can sometimes discern this. Anyway, speech hesitancy gets worse with age. So, I find.

Speech starts in the cerebral cortex whilst the cerebellum is also involved. Although, a 'speech centre' can be discerned it is not as simple as that: nothing in the brain is and the concept of a single speech centre is not valid. For example, studies with PET (positive emission tomography) scans show that different regions of the brain are active (and presumably responsible) for generating words and for speaking words. And, mostly thought precedes both! So, for me, the word (the thought) was there but it was just not getting out! As my mother sometimes used to say to me 'spit it out Jimmy'!

Perhaps, for the general reader the above is enough. I never resorted to a speech therapist and would presumably have to live with the defect. However, as we shall see, this was leaving something or rather someone out!

Before coming to that however an excursion into Scripture. Similar speech problems occurred in the lives of some of God's servants. First, there was Moses. When God told him that he had 'heard the cry of the people of Israel and seen the oppression with which the Egyptians oppress them'[1] he said 'I will send you to bring the children of Israel out of Egypt'. Moses' reply (excuse) was 'I am not eloquent, I am slow of speech and of tongue'.[2] God's response to him was 'who made man's mouth? Who makes him mute (silent, dumb, speechless) is it not I the Lord?' In the end although it was Moses' brother Aaron who was to speak the words that Moses put into his mouth[3] it was God who was to teach them (both) what to say. The initiation was from God whereas the expression (the 'speech chain') was both Moses and Aaron. So, what was Moses' speech problem? And, was it permanent? Certainly not since it was Moses who eventually spoke to Pharaoh.

The other example, more extreme, was that of Zechariah, the father to be of John the Baptist. He was 'struck dumb', completely unable to speak at all, by God's angel. But again, not permanent; his first words were full of praise,[4] words still sung today. Even the apostle Paul seems to have had a speech defect[5] yet he 'managed'! With the help of God.

The most embarrassing aspect of my own speech defect occurred when I went for interviews, compulsory in those days, to obtain a place at one or other of the London Medical Schools. I still remember the one at St Mary's in Paddington, where at the time

---

[1] Exodus 3:9, 10.

[2] Exodus 4:10.

[3] Exodus 4:15.

[4] Luke 1:67-79.

[5] 1 Corinthians 2:3, 4.

Alexander Fleming was still active. Sitting before five or six eminent doctors facing questions that I knew the answers to but could not 'spit it out'. Just silence. Of course, I failed to get a place whereas two of my friends, less able academically than I, did obtain places. Later I discovered that they became GPs. Fortunately, that was not for me. My life was to become much more adventurous and a few years later I actually taught, or examined, at the same medical schools! And, I began to see the hand of God in these, at the time, sad experiences. We will think more about this when I write about providence and God's guidance. Did that speech hesitancy disappear and, if so how? Answers please, but 'not on a postcard'.

I now return to this question of my own speech impediment. During the year I spent in membership at All Souls in London I attended confirmation classes taken by one of the curates, the Rev John Lefroy, in preparation for the Confirmation Service taken by the Bishop of London. Two of my friends from the School of Pharmacy, Mike Richards and Malcolm Hooper were in the same class; among the others was a dancer from the Royal Ballet. As part of the 'practical work' involved we were invited to take part in a parish mission to a church in Leyton, at the invitation of the Rector, Rev Frank Food. This took place from October 16th to the 25th 1954, less than a year after my conversion.

For some reason I was asked to give my 'testimony' on the first night of the mission. It was a big barn of a church with a high pulpit reached by a spiral staircase. It took some time to reach the top! I had of course prepared and people were certainly praying. You can imagine how I felt! What happened was quite amazing. I did speak – it was certainly my voice – but it was as if someone else had taken over. The Lord spoke for me. It was almost worth having a speech hesitancy to have experienced such a 'take over' – a feeling like no other! Was it permanent, this cure for aphasia? It seems so as I have spent my life speaking in public, hundreds of lectures to students and to colleagues at meetings all over the world and always by invitation as apparently a 'good speaker'. Then there have been the experiences of preaching, in several countries, many hundreds of times. Like Moses I could say 'I am not eloquent, I am 'slow of speech' (although in my case speech actually stopped altogether) BUT GOD! Paul's experience was also mine. With God's help 'I managed'.

The question is why this experience of a speech impediment happened to me at such a critical time in my education? All those interviews at the London Medical Schools when 'no word came out'? I believe it was not right for me to study medicine and to follow my desire to be a medical missionary. God had other exciting plans. And, later I did gain entrance to medical school and indeed, received, was 'given', an honorary degree (MD) in medicine. For me this experience was an example of 'Providence', of God 'planning' my life; 'I know the plans I have for you'[6] – plans so much better than I could ever envisage, than anything I could have planned for myself.

I have a photo, taken from the local Leyton newspaper, of the mission team. I am still, all these years later, in touch with Professor Mike Richards, whose eventful life, especially in Thailand (initially with China Inland Mission) has been recounted and published, and with Professor Malcolm Hooper, who has been much involved with the Leprosy Mission and is still a powerful Christian advocate for a number of concerns, including adequate provision for army veterans of the Iraq war. Both have remained Anglicans!

As I was revising the manuscripts, we learnt of the death of one of Pam's cousins, David Prior. David was a Church of England minister who had a very effective ministry in Cape Town, London (St Peter's Chester Square) and in the USA. He was also a prolific writer for IVP.[7] As a child, and indeed throughout the rest of his life, he had a severe stammer. He was in good company, King George VI and Winston Churchill for example. Like me he had to adapt when going on errands for his mother (he just handed the shopkeeper a written note) or on public transport. He once preached about this 'disability' and his view, which is also mine, is that God knew what he was about when he created us; we are meant to be here, disabilities and all! And, for a purpose. God's way is that his strength 'is made perfect in weakness', one of my many weaknesses is like David's, a speech impediment. God chooses the most unlikely people!

---

[6] Jeremiah 29:11.

[7] For example, David Prior, *The Message of 1 Corinthians*, Inter-Varsity Press, Leicester, 1985; *The Suffering and the Glory, Balanced Christian Discipleship*, Hodder and Stoughton, London, 1985.

Chapter 7
The Long Chase

In September 1952 I took the tube from Turnham Green station to Holborn on the Piccadilly line to begin life at university. I have often wondered, when my interviews to the various medical schools were so disastrous, how I ever managed to pass any interview to get anywhere. I was certainly just as nervous when, earlier in the year, I had visited the School of Pharmacy University of London (known as 'the Square' because of its position, at that time in Bloomsbury Square) for an interview with the Dean, Professor Berry. I think it was that he put me at my ease, so unlike the long line of academics that interviewed me for entry into a course leading to a degree and career in medicine.

Why at this time was entry to a career in medicine 'blocked'? My view later was that this was a case of Divine intervention. 'In their hearts humans plan their course, but the Lord establishes their steps'.[1] At the time I, and my parents, were disappointed but later I was glad. I could have finished up as a General Medical Practitioner working, as two of my school friends did, within a few miles of their old school. My own training, first in pharmacy and then in pharmacology has taken me all over the world and coloured all of my somewhat adventurous life. If you believe, as I certainly do, that God has promised to guide the lives of those who know him as their heavenly father, even before one comes to faith, then one is to 'expect the unexpected'. I look back with gratefulness and wonder for closing so securely one door and opening a quite different one!

To return to that underground train journey and the start of my university life. The 'Square' stood on the corner of Bloomsbury Square and Russell Street, just a few paces from the British Museum and from Senate House, the administrative home of the University of London. The School itself has since moved to yet another London Square Brunswick, and was later incorporated

[1] Proverbs 16:9.

into University College, at that time one of the top ten places of learning in the world. Number 17 Bloomsbury Square is now part of the German Institute and remains a beautiful building with an Adam ceiling in a room on the first floor used, in my time there, as a pharmacognosy laboratory. Many years later (2014) our youngest son Jonathan came with me to 'explore' where his dad had studied. The room on the left hand side as one enters the building, now an office, seems unaccountably small to have been, in 'my time' one of the main lecture rooms. There were about 30 to 35 students in each of the three years which led to the award of a degree in pharmacy.

First days are always somewhat disconcerting. Will I make friends easily? I reminded myself that, unlike my time at school, students at what was then regarded as the top university teaching pharmacy in the UK (and even the world) came from all over. Most had travelled from other parts of England and Wales; I do not remember any from as far away as Scotland. Many strange accents I had not heard before from locations in the 'the north'; places such as Yorkshire and Lancashire. We were all welcomed by the Dean (who had interviewed me) and by the colourful Professor of Pharmacology Gladwin Buttle, who was later to have a profound influence on my life and choice of career. I am sorry that I did not thank him as I should have done.

There was one other thing about Professor Buttle that impressed me and which has had a lifelong influence, although this has nothing to do with pharmacology. Later, when I was a PhD student in his department, both staff and graduate students were invited to his home for a meal, at the end of which he rolled up his sleeves and washed up the dirty dishes! Since then, I have done the same in our own home to the great surprise, years later, of a guest, himself a professor, who had never seen a professor washing up; something he thought was 'below him'. Later it was something I was to teach him how to do!

Pharmacy is very much a laboratory- based science so we had, as well as two or three lectures each day, three-hour laboratory classes through the week. Except Wednesday, when the afternoon was given over to sport – football or hockey. These practical classes were in chemistry, physiology/pharmacology, pharmacognosy (the study of medicinal plants) and pharmaceutics where we were taught to make (dispense) medicines (pills, suppositories, tablets) as well as aseptic techniques (for injections). Probably our class was the last to be taught how to gild pills and how to make from scratch lotions and ointments. The apparatus for making these is now to be found in pharmacy museums! Now everything is manufactured elsewhere and the 'fun' of making things has disappeared and the main task of pharmacists today is to count pills and tablets; and there are even 'machines' for doing that. I simplify! Pharmacists are equipped to give good advice about drugs; after all they are the experts.

For each practical class students were divided into groups of about eight or twelve. This was done alphabetically by surname. For me this was yet another example of God intervening since I found myself working opposite a lovely, curly headed, blue eyed girl with an unusual surname – Marels.[2] M (for Marels) is of course close to P (for Parratt) in the (English) alphabet. This girl, Pamela by name, became the love of my life, the mother of my three children and my companion and dearest friend for well over sixty years. Indeed, married for sixty years (in 2017) with a card from the Queen to prove it. I think it was love at first sight. If not, it was not very long before I fell head over heels, metaphorically if not physically. There was 'something about the girl', as the song goes. This 'something' I was soon to learn stemmed from her strong Christian faith, the first Christian I had met in my life thus far. However, the 'wooing' took some time as I will shortly explain.

[2] My wife's parents both had unusual surnames. Her father especially so. We had been unable to discover anyone with Marels as a surname (even in Australia) until reading an article in the Glasgow Herald about the 2010 volcano eruption in Iceland. This was written by an Icelandic climatologist named 'Marelsdottir'; '*dottir*' meaning 'daughter of' in Icelandic. An email to Sally Magnuson at the BBC led to the discovery that Marels is a not uncommon surname in Iceland. As Sally commented 'beware, you may have married a Viking'! It gets worse! Her mother's surname was Cuming (with just the one 'm') a Scottish surname from the area around Buchan. Cuming and perhaps Cumming are derived from Comyn, a name of great significance in Scottish history in the 12th Century. The Comyns were pre-eminent pillars of an independent Scottish monarchy well before the arrival of William Wallace or Robert Bruce and in 1296, fittingly led Scotland into the war of Independence. So, my wife presumably has both Viking and Highland Scottish blood. What a combination! Of course, I knew nothing of this when we first met in London in 1952.

I enjoyed university life even though I was, unlike most of my year, still living at home so that change from school to university was not as dramatic as it was for many, including Pam. This sense of 'leaving home' was not there for me; I was still 'tied to my mother's apron strings' and I did not have to think about food; meals cooked when I returned home each evening. Or laundry. Indeed, I wonder how I would have coped with what is today part of student domestic living. Both my parents were working and my younger brother, now at the school I had just left, were all still at home. My room was the same. As was the piano. Advantages perhaps but not as developmental as living away from home for university education, as our three children and our seven grandchildren have done. For their benefit I think.

I must have been reasonable academically because I was somewhere near the top of the class. This was certainly true in pharmacology, except for one examination close to finals when the lecturer did not even attempt to mark my paper because of the illegibility of my writing. No marks. And so close to finals. A good (and some would say a well-founded) lesson. Whether I have learnt it is an open question; certainly, with the years my writing has got progressively smaller so that at times even I have difficulties reading it.

At this point it might be helpful to attempt to explain what is involved in reading for a degree in pharmacy; I am reasonably sure, there are few if any, of my readers who have themselves taken such a degree. For one thing it is a wonderful university education for doing something else! A good 'jumping' degree into disciplines like pure and applied chemistry, engineering (an option leading to employment in the pharmaceutical industry), physiology (a famous physiologist at University College started in pharmacy) and medicine: a visit to my own GP surgery a year or two back led to the discovery that I had once taught the locum doctor cardiovascular pharmacology when she had first studied pharmacy at Strathclyde. She still possessed my lecture notes! Then there are the various branches of pharmacy itself – working in hospital (clinical pharmacy), retail or industry. A broad-based scientific degree then. A well-trained pharmacist knows much more about the mechanisms of drug action and the side effects of medication than any other health professional, a fact that is becoming increasingly recognised.

As the 'centre of excellence' the 'Square' had, as one might expect, excellent teachers. This was especially true of pharmacology. A published history of the school shows that some of the most illustrious pharmacologists of the twentieth century once taught at the 'Square' including future heads of the pharmacology departments at the universities of Oxford, Cambridge and Edinburgh; all Fellows of the Royal Society. Indeed, it was a lecture by one of them, J.H. Gaddum that led me to wish to be a pharmacologist.

Chapter 8
A Scent of Water

If you were to ask professing Christians how they came to faith you would usually get one of two answers. One would be that they were influenced by their parents, or grandparents, who took them to church or Sunday School and that sometime after those, often prolonged, experiences they became sure that, at some point, they had received the gift of faith. They believed; they were sure they were Christians. We could describe this as imbibed faith, faith almost by osmosis but nevertheless very personal. They perhaps could not identify a definite time when the exchange happened but they were now sure that they were Christians. On the other hand, others could point to a definite time at which a transaction was made with God. They could even identify a time and place, when and where this took place. Often these transactions were sudden, a kind of 'Damascus Road' experience such as happened to Saul. This kind of experience is also quite common; it was the means by which, for example, such different people as Augustine, John Wesley and Spurgeon became Christians. My own experience accords with theirs for I had no meaningful religious background, let alone a Christian one, before my conversion.

What occurred then, at the beginning of my second year at university, was sudden and was to have a profound effect on my life; indeed, it changed the whole course of it. What happened was this.

In November 1953, just a few weeks into my second year at the School of Pharmacy, there was a mission to the University organised by the London Inter-Faculty Christian Union (LIFCU). These missions occurred every third year, so giving every student an opportunity to hear the Christian message at least once during their university career. This one ran from Sunday to Sunday (November 15 to 22) and took place mainly at All Soul's Church in Langham Place, next to the headquarters of the BBC. You can see a picture of the church on most days at the beginning of the BBC

TV News. I was clearly being prepared for this event because of my contact with the School of Pharmacy Christian Union: I had started going along to their weekly meetings from the beginning of my second year; one of the student speakers was later to become my wife and another was in the same football team. There was a pre-mission conference, at which Revd John Savage, of the South American Missionary Society was the speaker, but it was the first Sunday evening of the mission that most affected me. The preacher was William Nagenda, a colleague of Festo Kivengere of the African Revival Fellowship.

Much has been written about the revival[1] and, indeed, about Festo himself, but not very much about William. As he was so influential in my life (through just that one sermon!) I have since decided to learn something about him. Like Festo he was from Uganda, a government clerk in Entebbe, who one day met with a team of evangelists and, 'because of their faces' ('so happy, so alive, so fulfilled') had, by midnight of that same day, turned to prayer and faith in Christ. Always talking about Christ, not revival, he had a world-wide evangelistic ministry – including that evening in London in November 1953. I owe him much: the first time I really heard the good news of the gospel in a way that really 'hit home'. Interesting perhaps that later I too spent time as a Christian in Africa. A debt in small part repaid?

The main weekday mission meetings were held in the Chapel of King's College, the first on the Tuesday evening of November 17th at which Dr John Stott spoke. John spoke about the Cross of Jesus from John 3:14 – 'As Moses lifted up the serpent in the wilderness even so MUST the Son of Man be lifted up, that whoever believes in him may have eternal life'. MUST, it was a categorical imperative. It was as though Jesus himself was speaking to me from the Cross and I realised that he died for me (in my place) and bore my (many) sins. I realised too that it was important that, when the invitation to respond came at the end of the service, I was to get out of my seat and go forward, so declaring my decision to follow Christ: as I wrote in my diary (one of the few entries in it apart

---

[1] Patricia St John, *Breath of Life*, Norfolk Press, 1971; Anne Coomes, *Festo Kivengere*, Monarch, Eastbourne, 1990; Richard Bewes, *Under the Thorn Tree*, Christian Focus, Fearn, 2017.

from football scores and concert programmes) 'I have nailed my colours to the mast'. I shook John's hand, took away a booklet about 'Becoming a Christian' written by him (and which I still have) and took a friend along to the next meeting two days later praying he too would respond. He did not.

My own experience can be described (inadequately) in different ways: I had come to a living faith in Jesus; there was a sense of his personal presence. But was it sustained? Is such faith just a fad? Well, today I write nearly seventy years after the event. For me then it was life-changing.

Many years later and after meeting the Revd Dr John Stott on several occasions (including in Nigeria) I decided to write to thank him for leading me to Christ. A late response; the letter was written on the 10th August 1996, forty years after the event! When Bishop Timothy Dudley-Smith was writing John Stott's biography in 1998,[2] he came across that letter in John's meticulous filing system and wrote to me asking what I remembered about that London Mission. There was almost nothing about it in his files, despite the fact that it was only the second of John's university missions. I found my diary, and the mission programme; my account of it is recorded in the book. Incidentally this commenced a correspondence and friendship with Bishop Timothy that continues to this day.

That evening on a November night in London thus began for me a relation with Jesus that means more to me than anything. He is not only my Saviour and my God but my friend – 'I have called you friends, for all I have heard from my Father I have made known to you'.[3]

The above sounds like a sudden, perhaps some might say rash, decision but there was preparation for it. C.S. Lewis described his own conversion as like being pursued, by being manoeuvred into a position by a chess master with the inevitable 'check mate' to close the 'game'. Pursued by the 'Hound of Heaven'. And, like that great author, certain events led up to the decision day.

This sequence of events may sound as though there was no alternative, that no free will was involved. But, even in such

---

[2] Timothy Dudley-Smith, *John Stott. The Making of a Leader*, Inter-Varsity Press, Leicester, 1999.

[3] John 15:15.

circumstances we are given a choice. Let me illustrate very simply. Every year at Christmas, and on our birthdays, we receive a parcel from Australia, where our daughter is a doctor working among 'native Australians', work that over the years has taken her across the Northern Territories, some of the islands situated to the north of that great country and at present into New South Wales. When the parcel eventually arrives, from that great distance, it needs to be 'received', to be accepted, to be signed for; even on one occasion, a fee was payable! We could, I suppose, refuse such parcels. But, of course, we never do that simply because we know from whom they came. It was sent with love and is received with love. Perhaps God's gift, for surely it is that, of friendship with Jesus and of salvation in him is to be received with thanks because we know that it comes from God and is a sign of God's love for us. This makes it 'easy' to accept it. And very hard to refuse. It has come a long way!

Many years ago, also in Australia, there was the visit to that country of a high-ranking churchman, in fact Pope John Paul II. He was interviewed over the radio by some of the pupils of the 'school of the air', set up to teach children in the isolated communities in the 'outback' by radio. They were allowed to ask him questions. One question, highly perceptive I think, was about the most difficult task he had to undertake in his influential position. He said this:

'The hardest thing is to see so many people do not accept the love of Jesus, do not know who he really is and how much he loves them. He is the Saviour of the world and offers them his love and leaves them free to say yes or no . . . it saddens me to see that some people say no'.

It seems at least to me, that this 'chase', this seeking of us by God, is gentle, it does not 'overwhelm'. It is gradual, it often takes some time - as in my own case. Above all, it is a gift. And, when we make that choice, when we receive that gift, it is often, certainly in my own case, largely unemotional. It involved for me simply accepting the gift, getting up from my seat and going to the front as a practical way of acknowledging my acceptance of that gift. However, although the reception of the gift may be sudden there was, behind the scenes as it were, also much preparation, a kind of pre-evangelism.

Perhaps one can liken this 'process' to having a surgical operation, of which I have had four already in my lifetime. First, comes the diagnosis, something is wrong, 'not quite right', a feeling of pain warranting an appointment with your GP and then a referral to the hospital to see a consultant. Yes, he agrees, something does need to be done; perhaps in some cases urgently. When admitted and prior to the operation itself, you meet with both the consultant and the anaesthetist who explain the procedure, give your pre-medication (and later an anaesthetic!) and then you are well prepared for the operation itself. Of course, hopefully at any rate, the surgeon is also prepared. He has had a long training and especial expertise in the particular operation you are to undergo. So, there has been already much preparation. Then comes the operation, whilst you are unconscious. Or awake, screened from the surgeon and listening to music, best of all Mozart. Then, if all goes well with the operation, there is the very important post-operative care. Exercise perhaps (if you have had a hip or knee replacement) gentle at first. During which period you are well cared for by nurses, physiotherapists and wives.

Each of the above events (pre-operation, operation, post-operative care) has spiritual parallels, counterparts in the 'operation' of conversion. The pre-operative phase can be short but it has to happen; it is necessary. My own pre-operative phase would have included that visit to the Sunday school in Eydon, the singing (and religious instruction) in the primary school there, the unobtrusive witness of the next door neighbour going each Sunday morning to church, the witness of those at secondary school of whom I took little notice, the welcome of the miniscule Christian Union at university. And falling in love with one of the members: albeit not always a requisite! And, also an unconscious sense of need, of wanting 'something' not possessed. All leading up to the 'decision' itself.

Then there was the post-operative care from the Christian Union members and the church. In my own case, church conferences on witnessing, daily bible reading[4] and prayer, and also preparation

[4] I discovered, during a garage clear out, a copy of *Newness of Life*, a booklet published by Scripture Union, designed (successfully in my case) as an introduction to daily bible reading. This should be reprinted.

for Confirmation. There too was 'practical work', participating in a church mission to Leyton Parish Church in October 1954 and in Scripture Union (CSSM) camps for children during the summers of 1954 and 1955 on the Norfolk coast. In other words, practical outworking of what should have been learnt in theory: all part of the long, hopefully continuing, journey of following and serving Christ.

How does the above experience match with scripture and especially the well-known account of the conversion of the apostle Paul on the Damascus Road recorded in Acts,[5] the pivot on which turned the future of the church?

Was there, for example, any evidence of 'preparation' of Saul by God for that Damascus event? I think there was. Earlier in the book of Acts, in chapter six, is the account of the martyrdom of Stephen[6] where Saul is mentioned twice.[7] Presumably the author doctor Luke, obtained this information from Paul himself. So, Saul was a witness; he both saw the stoning and heard what Stephen had said. He heard his prayer for forgiveness for those killing him, he heard him talking to Jesus - 'Lord, do not hold this sin against them' and he also heard Stephen say, 'I see the heavens opened and the Son of Man (Jesus) standing at the right hand of God', indeed words Jesus himself had said at his trial before the High Priest.[8] Was his conscience pricked by these events, as well as by his own brutal savaging of the church, dragging men and women off to prison? As Jesus said to him 'it is hard for you to kick against the pricks', against the 'goads'.[9] To resist a power altogether superior to his own was a profitless and perilous experiment, to fight against the warnings he had resisted and defied in his frenzied zeal against those who were willing to go to prison and to death rather than denounce the name of Jesus. These surely raised misgivings in his mind which became part of the 'preparation' for his encounter with the Lord.

[5] Acts 9:1-9.

[6] Acts 6:8-15.

[7] Acts 7:58; 8:1.

[8] Mark 14:62.

[9] Acts 9:5 KJV.

When Paul later looked back on what happened on that road, almost like a subtle process of self-analysis, he saw how God had been preparing him, had taken the initiative – 'it pleased God to reveal his Son to me'[10] and had 'arrested' (taken hold of) him, just as his intention was to arrest and take hold of the disciples of Jesus; Jesus had 'seized' him.[11] He too 'saw' a light from heaven[12] as Stephen had seen the glorified Lord.

On that November night at King's College, I did not see any light from heaven, nor did I hear with my ears a voice from there, but to my prepared mind, my prepared heart, Jesus had clearly spoken and, as with Saul who became Paul, my life too was changed.

There was a slightly later occasion that bears some relation to this passage in Acts 9. It was days later when in the company of Ananias, that Saul was 'filled with the Holy Spirit';[13] so then a later, post-conversion experience of the Spirit. A few days after the events at King's College, it was in my bedroom late at night and whilst praying, that I had an overwhelming sense of the presence of God. So much so that I had to place a handkerchief in my mouth to stop me calling out loudly in praise – and waking my parents! An experience I think of the Spirit – and after conversion. Perhaps the belated welcome of the angels into the kingdom of God? Or, a 'seal' or 'pledge' of that welcome[14] and a guarantee of the gift of the Sprit of Jesus in my heart.

---

[10] Galatians 1:15,16.

[11] Philippians 3:12.

[12] Acts 9:3.

[13] Acts 9:17.

[14] 2 Corinthians 1:22.

Chapter 9
Still Chasing!

At the end of the second year, students needed to decide which two subjects they wished to specialise in for the final (third) year. I chose pharmacology (my favourite) and pharmaceutics. Because of accommodation difficulties (number 17 was quite confined) both of these subjects, apart from the lectures, were taken outwith that lovely Georgian building. Looking back, it was a privilege to have studied for two years in one of the most attractive buildings in London. Pharmaceutics (the predominant subject in any pharmacy course) was taken in a new building, later to house the whole School, in Brunswick Square, still situated there sixty years later. Pharmacology practical classes were taken in laboratories at the Veterinary School of the University in Camden Town. This was also where I studied for the PhD degree from September 1955 to May 1957.

During my final year it was suggested to me that, if I wished, I could continue in the School and study for a higher degree. I decided, albeit seeking the Lord's will but not in the right way, that if I obtained a first-class degree in pharmacology I would do that, finances permitting. This was rather like putting out a fleece and I had to learn that there were other, more scriptural ways of discovering God's will for me.

Probably you could guess what happened! I did get a first in pharmaceutics but not in pharmacology and it took kindly counsel from Professor Buttle that decided me, with my longsuffering parents support, to nevertheless commence research in pharmacology and study for a PhD degree. I was fortunate, again with the support of Professor Buttle, to receive a scholarship from the Pharmaceutical Society of Great Britain to enable me to do this. Buttle (who regaled us during lectures with tales of his experiences of driving a bus during the 1930's General Strike) was a quite wonderful man with a very characteristic non-vulgar guffaw. Sometimes he forgot who he was lecturing too, thinking we were medical students. When he realised, he would stop in mid-sentence and let out this huge laugh. He was also incredibly generous and years later offered to dip into the 'Buttle Trust Fund' to help support me through medical school.

Here I backtrack and continue the saga of 'chasing' Pamela Marels! At the end of our first year I had decided that Pam was the one for me! One way of getting to know her better and aid my (limited) powers of persuasion, would be to travel to and from College with her. However, she travelled for that first year on a different Underground Tube line to me. At the beginning of my second year I changed my season ticket so that we could, or so I thought, travel together. Only to find that she had changed her accommodation and was, in fact now travelling on the line I had previously been travelling on! Much teasing from the rest of the class.

Of course, the main reason why Pam took little notice of me was that she could never marry a non-Christian. I would not say that the reason I became a Christian was to marry her (!) but there was more interest shown following God's intervention in my life after November of our second year. Indeed, she was a great help in the early days of my Christian life.

To abbreviate the story of the 'chase', we did become engaged at the end of our degrees when she became a hospital pharmacist (and later, at another hospital, a senior pharmacist) whilst I commenced research for a PhD. This involved, before I was 'accepted', being taken around her family; they were concerned for her – not surprisingly because our backgrounds were rather different. This involved, of course, meeting her parents and obtaining her father's permission. He was a most impressive big man and, on the surface, quite frightening. As a bank manager he wanted to be sure of my 'prospects'. These were uncertain as I was still a student. Years later, when 'Gramp' (as he was known in the family) was in his 90s we had the privilege of sharing in his evening prayers on a number of occasions; we were impressed by the list of people he prayed for – names written on the back of an old envelope!

There were then the introductions to a variety of countless family cousins. One visit was quite alarming; the uncle was someone 'big' in the City and there were four boys in his family, two around my own age. After the evening meal, where I just managed the correct table manners, I was challenged to a game of Scrabble, which requires you to know the Oxford Dictionary almost by heart. When I put down a suspect word, our host the uncle, challenged the word. He was right, it could not be found in the body of the dictionary. Tongue in cheek I suggested it might be found in the Supplement. And indeed, there it was! After that, there was no difficulty about entering the family. Here was someone who knew not only the dictionary but the Supplement as well!

That summer of 1955, after we had graduated in the July at the Royal Albert Hall in the presence of the Queen Mother, we were both staying at Frinton-on-Sea, the home of Pam's wonderful Grannie Cuming (note again just the one 'm'). On the famous 'greensward' I asked Pam to marry me. No immediate decision. Not surprisingly she needed time. A night of prayer I think. But, in the morning she said yes and the following year, the year of her 22nd birthday, we became engaged. There is no indication on the 'greensward' at Frinton of that significant event but, the last time we were there we discovered a bench, set up to commemorate 'years of the family holidays spent in Frinton'; very near the spot where I had gone down on my knee to propose.

In September 1955 Pam commenced working as a hospital pharmacist whilst I started my research. However, by Christmas my research was not making much progress and I thought of giving up and returning to pharmacy. Dr Monica Mann, that same Monica who had refused to mark my examination paper when I was an undergraduate, persuaded me to persevere. Good counsel!

My supervisor Dr Geoffrey West had returned to London from Dundee on his appointment as Reader in the University and I was his first PhD student. He later wrote,[1] 'I was fortunate with the first of my London students (Jim P.) who turned out to be the most conscientious I have ever known'. However, accommodation at the Veterinary College was not the best; his office doubled as his laboratory and at one time there were three, often four, of us crammed into a really tight space. Dr R.K. Sanyal was one student who worked next to me; he was later to reach high office in the Indian Medical Service. He taught me the elements of pathology

[1] G.B. West, *A Handful of Luck*, The Book Guild, Lewes, 1986.

and introduced Pam and I to curry – a life-long gastrointestinal delight.

Geoff West had taught at the evacuated School of Pharmacy in Cardiff during the war (alongside Dinah James who I was later to get to know in Ibadan) and, whilst in Dundee, had worked with James Riley to discover the presence of histamine in mast cells.[2] When, at the end of my first term as a research student I found in a scientific publication that another important body amine called 5-hydroxytryptamine might also be present in these cells, the research took off and resulted in a number of publications and oral communications given to the Physiological and British Pharmacological Societies. We traced the development in mast cells of both these important biological substances. I surprised my mother once by bringing home for the weekend on the underground a family of baby rabbits needing attention; she allowed them to play on the green dining room carpet, I think they thought it was grass! Geoff was a friendly supervisor and took the trouble of introducing his young research students to the eminent scientists of the day including the two 'Sir Henrys', Dale and Barcroft. Years later (1994) I was asked to give a memorial lecture in Geoff's honour.

Important was the discovery, at the end of my PhD studies, that these amines, histamine and 5-hydroxytryptamine, were involved in the development of shock. This became an important area of study later in my career. The result of all this work was that the experimental part of my research was completed in just fifteen months: I can remember writing up my thesis at home in the heat of July 1957 whilst listening to tennis from Wimbledon on the radio and the exploits of the Australian doubles pair Hoad and Rosewall.

As many of you reading this would not have experienced life in the 1950s, and more particularly the years 1956 and 1957, when I was writing up my PhD thesis, perhaps some observations on life in those, for most readers, far off days might be appropriate.

---

[2] These are heavily granulated 'wandering' cells found throughout the body. Riley showed the granules contain histamine. They are concerned with allergic responses and may play a role in defence against infection, producing the typical signs of inflammation (reddening, swelling, pain).

The 1950s were just a few years after the end of WW2 and Britain was only very slowly recovering from the consequences of winning the war. It was badly in debt, especially to the United States, there was poverty, austerity and the rationing of food and clothes was still in place; this only ended in 1956. London remained a dismal place with bomb damage still very apparent and the pollution was such that it led to days of severe 'smog'; sometimes it was difficult to see where you were going. And, this was the London where I lived and worked.

The year 1956 was an especially critical year. It was the year of Suez and of the Russian invasion of Hungary. This meant that there were many Hungarian refugees in Britain. Their impressions of the country give some idea of what that period in this country was like. It compared unfavourably with those in the country they had just left. Indeed, Britain was a culture shock to those Hungarians who had decided to leave their homeland after the crushing of the Revolution by the Russian army. 'The trains were grimy and the upholstered seats seemed dirty and I refused to sit down' . . . 'The toilet would not flush and the heating did not exist' . . . 'How will I ever be able to live here?' They were dreadfully disappointed to find a poorer and dingier nation than the (communist) one they had just left; and, with their liking for rich food and sophisticated culinary tastes, the limited food options were traumatic. No earthly paradise then. Those who, like us, lived in Hungary during the final days of communism, can understand what they meant! For many, Britain became a transit to somewhere else. Indeed, the 1950s was a period of considerable emigration of many UK citizens to former colonies like Canada, Australia and New Zealand. Even the Prime Minister Harold Macmillan once joked that he would be open to that himself! However, I have never been tempted to emigrate to another country, or even to live in London, the city of my birth. Years later I received a letter from a Nobel Prize winner inviting me to become the Head of a pharmacology department in London. I declined; not normally what one does to such an eminent scientist!

To return to the London of 1957, I completed my thesis and spent the next few months having it typed and preparing for the oral examination and for marriage later that year.

So, there were plans to be made. After marriage what? What did God have in mind for us; we did believe He had a 'plan' for our lives together. It is what God had promised.[3] Many meetings and much prayer for guidance, which God had also promised. We both felt that God might want us to go somewhere as missionaries. This had been in Pam's heart for many years. My desire was to retrain in medicine and serve, perhaps in a mission hospital in East Africa. Pam's heart was more towards Asia. The plan was for me to gain entrance to a medical school and help pay my way through another four years of study by teaching pharmacology. Through Gladwin Buttle's influence I was accepted at Bristol University. Pam very bravely offered to support financially, carrying a huge burden, by working as a pharmacist. As we shall see this was not the Lord's plan for us. Something surprising and considerably better was!

I passed the PhD oral examination; I am sure that the illustrious examiner Wilhelm Feldberg had only read the Introduction to the thesis! Feldberg was one of a group of gifted German scientists who fled their homeland when Hitler came to power in 1933. He came to London at the invitation of Sir Henry Dale and together they provided the final proof that acetylcholine is one of the mediators of muscular transmission. When I first met him at the National Institute of Medical Research, introduced by Geoff West, he was tapping on the work bench to bring the lever down during a histamine assay on the isolated ileum; anyone who has attempted this will understand what I mean! Before the viva examination for my doctorate, Geoff had put on the table a selection of Feldberg's favourite cigars! Was this I wondered a Scottish tradition discovered during his days in Dundee? How much this contributed to my success I leave the reader to decide.

My favourite story of this brilliant scientist is of an invitation he received to be the guest of honour at a dinner. He turned it down with the comment 'I am taking my grand-daughters to Covent Garden to see Cosi fan Tutte.' A scientist with the correct priorities; in a similar situation I would have made the same choice and indeed, have been known to do so. Music before official dinners every time!

---

[3] Jeremiah 29:11 (NIV), said of God's people – us!

Chapter 10
Change of Plan

Pam and I were married at Caterham-on-the-hill Methodist Church on September 7th 1957. My brother John, who was best man, and I travelled by car, a rare experience for us, from Chiswick to Caterham with our minister John Caiger and his wife. By then we were both members of Gunnersbury Baptist Church in Wellesley Road. My brother and I had moved there as, being more local than All Souls, it was easier for our parents to attend church with us.

John Caiger, later to be chairman of the Keswick Council, gave the address. I found it interesting that I had first heard John preach at All Souls, as it was the tradition there at that time to have an 'exchange of pulpit' with a free church minister on the first Sunday of the New Year. He had preached from Psalm 133 – 'how good and pleasant it is when brothers dwell in unity'.

Many of Pam's family were present at the wedding, as were my own parents, and a number of colleagues from the pharmacology group, including Geoff West and Monica Mann. Sixty years later we still use the very practical presents they gave us. I seem to remember I gave my 'testimony' at the reception. There was no alcohol and no dancing! Afterwards we went by train to Frinton-on-Sea to stay for the weekend with Pam's wonderful Granny, who had been unable to travel to the wedding ceremony. Our first Sunday morning service was at the church which had sent out the Rector's daughter, Joanna Ashford-Smith to Nigeria. Little did we know then that we would meet her there in just over a year's time!

On the Monday we started our honeymoon after the long train ride to Helston in Cornwall where we had booked a farm cottage on the Lizard Peninsular. Very relaxing with walking in the Goonhilly Hills and along the coast of that beautiful part of England. It was when we returned to stay at Pam's parent's home in Caterham that a big surprise awaited us. It was to completely change the plan for me to study medicine in Bristol.

The unexpected surprise was an official letter from the people responsible for National Service. At that time every male had to complete a two-year period in one of the armed forces; we were only ten years from the end of WW2 and the armed forces needed to be built up and prepared for emergencies. 'Your Queen needs you'. The rule was that one could delay national service by completing a university course and preparing for a profession. This had allowed me to complete a PhD but did not allow me to change to another profession such as medicine. However, I was given exemption to complete my training as a pharmacist, which required a further one-year practical 'apprenticeship'. The dream of becoming a medical missionary fell by the wayside.

There was another problem. We were now looking for places for Pam to continue her profession as a well-qualified hospital pharmacist whilst I needed to find a hospital looking for a studentship (apprenticeship) in pharmacy. The latter was particularly difficult because such places were very competitive and most would have been taken up in June or July, soon after the degree results had been announced. Mid-September was very late to start looking. We then turned to the vacancy columns in the Pharmaceutical Journal to discover to our surprise, that the two positions we wanted were to be found in the same place – Brighton. The applications went in and we were called for interview on the same day, Pam for a position as pharmacist at Brighton General Hospital whilst, for me, a vacant postgraduate studentship at the Royal Sussex County Hospital situated near the seafront. The two clearly intrigued Chief Pharmacists had been in contact with one another, the interviews went well, we were invited to tea with one of them and started looking for accommodation. Albeit not on the same day!

The story of the studentship is interesting because one had already been appointed. However, unusually the chief pharmacist at the Sussex County had decided they could manage to look after two apprentices. Hence the late advertisement specially designed for me! Of course, God was in control of the whole situation, closing the door to medicine (for the time being) and preparing us for something we could never have envisaged. On reflection, we wondered how we would have coped in our early marriage with Pam being the bread winner for a four or five-year period, whilst

I studied. She, wonderfully, had been prepared to do this in order for me to prepare to be a medical missionary. God's plans for us are perfect, over-ruling our own quite reasonable plans for Christian service. God knew what was best for us – and for his work.

That year in Brighton was a special one. We found accommodation in Lansdown Street, on the border between Brighton and Hove, with a Jewish immigrant widow from Vienna called Mrs Trebitsch-Tree. She kept lodgers, our 'flat' being on the ground floor. We bought furniture from our good friends Michael and Joan Richards, who were about to go to Thailand with the China Inland Mission; our paths have crossed at various times throughout almost the whole of our lives. We even managed to move my piano down to the flat and being from Vienna, Mrs Tree was not averse to my playing. Vienna (Wien) was later to play an important part in our family life; one of our granddaughters now works with a church in that city and one of our great-grandsons was born there.

We were happy during our stay on the Sussex coast. The flat was just a bus ride from the two hospitals and during the summer months I cycled to work along the sea front. We were happy and fortunate in our working conditions and the Royal Sussex County was certainly a great place to be an apprentice. With two of us we were able to make many of the required medicines from scratch, although that took our joint arguments to persuade the chief, Mr Helyer, to allow us to do this. He claimed to be an atheist and I remember one day over dinner, before an evening meeting, he told me that in his view the bible was unreliable. I asked him for examples, placing my pocket New Testament on the table beside him. Somewhat taken aback, he was unable to do so. He knew of my Christian faith and of our desire to become missionaries but I'm not sure that particular approach to witness was helpful!

There was one other factor that encouraged us during our ten months in Brighton and that was the church. In the next street to our temporary home was Holland Road Baptist Church, a very lively place of worship and outreach. We had an immediate visit from the pastor, Ernest Rudman. There was also a very active and ably conducted Male Voice Praise (MVP) Choir. This was a fine group for fellowship and we both made many friends in a short time. Indeed, we were much encouraged; good preparation for what was to come.

The choir took part in outreach events around the area. One or other of us would preach or 'testify'; sometimes just two of us would go to some of the outlying villages, one to sing, usually not me, and one to preach. This too was good experience. Even more so was this introduction to the MVP movement started by Jim McRoberts from Maryhill in Glasgow years before: I was to get to know Jim well when we unexpectedly came to live in Scotland. Each year the choirs from all over Britain would combine and meet in the Royal Albert Hall in London. On the one occasion when I took part (June 1957) it was recorded and a 45rpm recording made, which I still have (somewhere). If you look carefully on the cover with a magnifying glass, I tell people that you can pick me out. Possibly – there were another 999 men in the choir. Jim McRoberts was one of the conductors on that occasion in a packed Royal Albert Hall.

One member of the choir was an Anglo-Indian (as such folk were then called) who was, of course, very keen on cricket. We had a team that played against other churches in the neighbourhood. What I remember most about Mr Toomey-Wilson was something he said to me just before I was about to preach at an outreach event. 'Jim' he said 'tell us about Jesus'. I think of those words often before I preach. Preach Jesus.

There was one other significant event during that stay in Sussex. We were both baptised as adult believers. Ernest Rudman preached frequently on 'believer's baptism' and in May 1958 we really felt God calling us to take this step. Our parents were present, which greatly encouraged us. Afterwards Dr Cochrane, famous for his work on leprosy, came to talk with us because by that time we knew we were going to Africa where he too had worked. Our friend John Stott was not too happy that we had been re-baptised but it was something we believed we really had to do. Since then, we have become convinced that baptism is for believers: all our children have been dedicated to God until such time as they felt they wanted to demonstrate their commitment to Christ by believer's baptism.

Much later, when our youngest child Jonathan was born in Glasgow, we were members of St David's Church of Scotland. I asked our minister (Revd Dr J.G.S.S. Thomson) if he would dedicate Jonathan rather than 'christened'. The 'doctor' with a background as a former missionary in North Africa, readily agreed, borrowing the order of service from the local Baptist pastor! Some in the congregation thought he had 'forgotten the water' since Dr T was noted for his forgetfulness. It is interesting that members of the congregation present that day were quite moved by the occasion. Later baptism became an issue within the Church of Scotland and a dear friend, a minister and army chaplain, had to leave his position when he and his wife felt it right for them to be baptised as believers.

Holland Road Baptist Church had a strong concern for overseas mission and each Easter Sunday afternoon there was a service at which a number of missions were represented. I remember one of the speakers over Easter that year was Saroj Arambam from Manipur State in India; Saroj was later to become my brother's wife. Perhaps this church concern for mission re-emphasised our commitment to seek to serve God in another country and indeed, we still had conversations with the China Inland Mission (now the Overseas Missionary Fellowship) about going to Asia. These came to nothing; they could not see how they could use two individuals with our backgrounds and qualifications. So, more than half-way through our year in Brighton we were unclear as to what our next step should be. We were learning that God does guide (our move to Sussex had shown us that) but it was to be 'one step at a time', as so many others have proved. Then came an incident which took us to quite another destination – and which became our 'call to Nigeria', of all places! This is how it happened.

We were still wondering what our next step was to be: one possibility for me was to return to the 'Square' at the suggestion of Dr West. Then one lunchtime, I was reading the Pharmaceutical Journal, that same journal that had been the means of introducing us to our then present positions in the two Brighton hospitals. This was not my normal lunchbreak reading but in it I 'happened to see' an advertisement for positions vacant at a new school of pharmacy in Ibadan, Nigeria. Nigeria was the last place I had on any list of places to serve God for two quite silly reasons – I knew it had more missionaries per head of population than any other country in the world (so why were we needed?) and because I did not get on too well with the only Nigerian I had known at university! He later became a colleague and friend.

We first wanted to know what 'opportunities' as Christians there might be if I took up such a position. During discussions with Dr Oliver Barclay and Freddie Critenden at the IVF office in London, I discovered the 'Nigeria initiative'. This was a vision for placing Christians from Britain in secondary schools and other places of education in that country. They put us in touch with Christians in Ibadan. The response was to 'come'! Plenty to do. To us it felt like the call Paul had to go to Europe! So, I applied.

The interview in London was very relaxed. I knew it was in God's hands. When asked what I did in my spare time I explained that I was a Christian and that how I spent my time was governed by my faith. The Chairman Dr Rowson, who was to become my Head of School, told me he was a Methodist local preacher! The outcome was that instead of the lectureship I had applied for they appointed me a senior lecturer with responsibilities for organising the whole department of pharmacology. Starting in September. I came back to Brighton somewhat elated. This was a quite unexpected turn of events; Nigeria was the last place we had expected to go to. But we felt this was clearly of the Lord.

The final few months before leaving were spent in attempting to plan the first-year teaching syllabus and ordering the equipment. And there were many things we needed ourselves; the Crown Agents had an exhaustive list which included mosquito boots (hardly worn, we were to discover, in Nigeria by anyone else) hairdressing equipment and other things we never used in our eight years in Africa. Perhaps the list had not been updated since Dr Livingstone's time!

I did not complete my one year to be fully qualified as a pharmacist but this, and my national service, were waived as I would be teaching in a pharmacy school in one of the colonies. We sold most of our furniture, put the rest into storage and looked forward with excitement to the travel, our first by air, and to all those new experiences that lay ahead.

Appendix 1
The Parratt Family Name

Where does the name Parratt come from? It is a relatively uncommon surname more often adulterated by changing one or other of the two 'a's to an e or an o' as with a famous snooker player and a choral conductor, Andrew born in 1947. These Parrots, Parrotts, Parretts and Parratts are presumably derived, a long time ago, from a common group of ancestors. Possible explanations are they came from Somerset or Devon (where there is a River Parrett) or from the French Pierre, a frequent forename of the many Huguenots, the French Protestants of the sixteenth and seventeenth centuries, who fled to England as a result of persecution. Many settled, like so many emigrants, in London's East End.

There are Parratts in Scotland and indeed it is classified, in the standard book on the subject, as a Scottish surname. For example, there is one other Parratt in 'Who's Who in Scotland', an eminent lawyer, born in Dundee, a specialist in 'Written Pleadings in Scots Civil Procedure'. This Dundee connection also includes another Parratt, David a bacteriologist and fellow member with me of the 'shock team' founded at the Western infirmary in the 1960's by Iain Ledingham, the first UK Professor of Intensive Care Medicine. Both are now working in, or retired from, Ninewells Hospital in Dundee.

Many years ago, when driving to a conference at St. Ninians in Crieff, we passed a saddler's shop owned by a Parratt family since the eighteenth century. When next we passed the shop had disappeared. Had it closed or moved? Could this be another case for the fictional Dr Gervase Fen who, as readers of the crime novels of Edmund Crispin may recollect, solved the mystery of the 'Moving Toyshop'. With fading memory, I wondered if I had mistaken the place: could this have been Dunblane and not Crieff when making our way to another Christian conference centre, Churches House? On enquiry the oldest Dunblane inhabitant denied any knowledge of the existence of such an establishment anywhere near Dunblane.

But then, how much could she remember? Sadly, when we had seen the shop, wherever it was situated, we had failed to stop and investigate. What happened to these 'saddler Parratts'? Are any of them still around and are we related? Enquiries continue!

Other Parratts we have come across on our many journeys worldwide is the Essex 'clan' based in Colchester, the oldest Roman town in England. We came across one of the Essex Parratts when purchasing our first furniture in 1959 (Ercol, still beautiful and functioning). The owner of the furniture store was also a Parratt; so, the cheque was from one Parratt to another; no special discount. This story raised the possibility of a Roman connection since Colchester was an important Roman army base. The Romans and their army have long gone, but could they have left one of their descendants behind, the start of a Parratt dynasty?

The most disturbing connection however was in Australia. Always interested in meeting others of the same 'flock', we checked the name in the Sydney telephone directory. Quite a few. Should we make contact and introduce ourselves? I am reminded of the story Révész Arpad told me about his moving to Szombathely to pastor a church plant. One of the things he did was to introduce himself by phoning all those with his surname and offering to visit! Interesting contacts. However, when we examined the addresses of the Sydney Parratts my wife dissuaded me from doing the same; most of those addresses were at or near Botany Bay. For those not in the know, this was one of the first convict settlements in the eighteenth century. One wonders how many of them came from London's East End. But why had they not moved further away from their place of origin? Although the Museum of History in Sydney has a good record of the names of such convicts (and why they were there) we decided not to follow up this line of enquiry. One never knows what one may find. This reminds me of the story of an American lady, keen to trace her ancestors, only to discover one of these was sentenced to death in the electric chair for murder. How to put this into her archives? She came up with the following: 'he held the chair of electrical engineering in a well-known national institution'.

However, for my brother John and I, the most interesting possible connection is with Sir Walter Parratt, a celebrated organist and Master of Music to no less than three monarchs (Queen Victoria, Edward VII and George V). He was also a composer (sadly few of his compositions have been recorded) and a gifted chess player. He once played chess blindfolded with two opponents whilst improvising on the piano and, for fun with his children, playing simultaneously, 'God save the Queen' with one hand and 'Rule Britannia' with the other. With a prodigious memory he could play Bach's 48 Preludes and Fugues at the age of eight and his early musical genius, apart from composition, was compared with that of Mozart and Mendelssohn at a similar age. However, it was his organ playing and his ability to improvise that were his greatest achievements. What intrigued John and I, who could both be described as somewhat musical, was his ability to play the viola in a string quintet (John's instrument) and, for me, his considerable expertise on the piano (I was taught by a student of the great Dame Myra Hess). Of course, we are not comparing the musical abilities of a past Master of the Kings Music, with our own! But then there was also his ability to 'run fast'; I was sprint champion at school. Are musical interests and abilities gifts that are handed down? Where do they come from? Could they have come down, very greatly diluted, to us from such a 'Master'? One can only dream. Any real connection is under investigation!

So much then for possible but unlikely family connections. What can now be proved, rather than dreamed about?

What we know for certain about the Parratt lineage can be dealt with briefly, although there is an intriguing family mystery with my great-grandparents marriage which I will explore later (see the appendix about jams . . .). This great-grandfather, John Charles King Parratt, a baker, married Louisa Elizabeth Johnson at Christ Church Spitalfields on June 5th 1864. His father was Charles Luther Parratt, also a baker, who married into the King family. This Charles was the son of Thomas Parratt, a coach builder from Aldgate. This East End family connection thus goes as far back as at least the end of the eighteenth century because Thomas was recorded as being baptised, again in Aldgate, in 1797 just six years after the death of Mozart.

William (my grandfather born in 1875) was the third of their four children. He and his wife (Elizabeth Bartlett) whom he married in 1895 at St Peter's Church in Hackney, had three sons, the youngest of these was my father James John Parratt. Of the other sons, the eldest, another William, died as a teenager in 1902, whilst the middle son Arthur died childless in 1945.

My Parents' Wedding in 1928

What I learn then from this brief history of my father's side of the family is that the Parratt family had a long connection with London's East End and that they did not move very far from their place of original settlement. Their trades included bakery and coach building. We have not explored further back in time and especially with any possible French Protestant link with the Huguenots. It is however of interest, certainly to me, that one possible derivation of 'Parratt' and 'Parot' is that the latter is a diminutive form of Pierre. I was once in contact with a Dr Parot from Paris during my post-graduate years in London who did wonder if we were 'connected'.

The family background on my mother's side of the family is more interesting and, for this, I am indebted to my brother John who continues to explore this. But, where to start! Perhaps with a remote ancestor who was born in Lisbon in 1692 or 93. This may mean that we could claim Portuguese, and hence EU citizenship, if ever this was needed! My niece is exploring this.

Closer to our own generation, my parents were another James John Parratt (born in 1900 and died in 1977) who married Eunice Elizabeth King (1901-1990) in September 1928 at St Matthew's Church, Bethnal Green. My grandparents on the maternal side of the family were Thomas King (son of Henry Francis King, born about 1866, a sawyer) and Rebecca Cardozo (born about 1870). They would have been in their late 70s when I knew them when we, and they, resided together with us for a time, at 15 Old Bethnal Green Road.

It is possible, because of the accuracy of synagogue Sephardic records (and through the Chief Archivist, Spanish and Portuguese Jew's Congregation) to trace our ancestors on our grandmother's side of the family back to the 17th century. My brother John has done this as far back as Abram (ben Jacob) Henriques who married a Sarah (probably a Cardozo) in Lisbon in 1716. Henriques was the name of the first king of Portugal (he reigned from 1139-85) and liberated Lisbon from the Muslims, securing the independence of Portugal. Several Jewish families adopted his name because of his friendly relations with them. Later, migrants to Britain continued this tradition hence the name Henriques Cardozo appears quite frequently as a family name.

I write elsewhere of the influence my parents had on me. Do I, or my children, resemble them in any way? Certainly, their influence on me was always for good. All of us are made in God's image but we are all wonderfully unique. They wanted the best for me and did not interfere in any way with what I wanted for my life. They were happy that I was reasonably good at school, that I went to university (the first in the family to do so), that I married and had children – their grandchildren, of whom they were very proud. They had a deep interest in all that concerned us as a family. And, I learnt much from them both. More of them later!

Only one descendent, now living in Sydney Australia, will have the onerous task of carrying forward the family name. This is Alex, the son of my nephew Timothy Parratt, who is himself the second son of my brother John. On my own side of the family, one of my five granddaughters (Kirsty) decided, when she married, to add her surname to her husband's surname. She is now Kirsty Ebadi-Parratt, works with a church in Vienna and recently had her first child, Leon who is also be an 'Ebadi-Parratt'. My two grandsons (Australian citizens) have their father's surname (Hough).

Appendix 2
A Favourite Aunt

Although my mother was from a large family, seven siblings all of whom survived through childhood; the eldest Charles was killed at Gallipoli during WW1. My mother (born in 1901) was the only one to have children. Of her four sisters my favourite was aunt Lily (born in 1893). A family legend is that she lost a boyfriend (fiancé?) during WW1. When I first got to know her, just before the beginning of WW2, she was always 'in town' (meaning the centre of London – the 'West End') on Saturday evenings with her friends from work, dancing and visiting theatres – she was especially fond of the Victorian Music Halls, from whence she picked up (and sang) some of the lyrics. I can still hear her and my parents singing about 'My old gall'. This popular song continues something like this:

> We've been together now for forty years,
> An' it don't seem a day too much
> There ain't a lady livin' in the land
> As I'd swop for my dear old Dutch.'

As sung by Albert Chevalier, whom I am sure had a more melodious voice than Aunt Lil. This song introduces us to Cockney rhyming slang (of which my aunt was an expert). 'Dutch' coming from 'Dutch plate' (mate), crockery common in households at the time.

Aunt Lil was very fond of her two nephews. Another memory is of her wheeling my younger brother's pram around Woolworths. My younger brother, who must have been about two, picking things up from the lower shelves and hiding them in the pram! Not many readers will remember Woolworths: the one in Glasgow was near the 'highwayman's umbrella' by Central Station. Long since gone – Woolworths that is, not the umbrella.

After the war Aunt Lil lived near Shepherd's Bush but sometime in the 1950s, during my schooldays, she had a stroke which left her very disabled. Sadly, her friends seemed to abandon her, she had little or no pension and no other member of the family was willing to help take care of her. My parents took her in and she lived with them until she died, which was after they had retired to Kirby Cross. Today perhaps she would have gone into a home of some kind or some other institution caring for the frail and sick but this was in the immediate post-war years: in the 1950s the National Health Service was only, and very slowly, getting off the ground. Better by far to live with relations, although this was clearly a financial hardship for my parents. But who else was there to look after her? Certainly, I have a great admiration for the way my parents cared for her over many years. But then, that is what they were like.

A favourite aunt, a lovely gentle person with a sense of humour, dealing with her disabilities with great fortitude and just getting on with life. We did manage to bring her up to Glasgow and, when staying in Kirby Cross, would help to wheel her down to the beach hut. She regained reasonable movement in her hands and the very colourful rug she made over a long period of time, and gave us as a wedding present, is still in our possession – a real work of art.

She died in January 1973 aged 80, in those days a good age for a stroke victim. The funeral was taken by a very pastoral missionary who worked with the 'caravan mission to children in rural England' and whose name was Brooks; his friendly, talkative wife was known as 'Babbling Brooks'.

Part 2 THE AFRICA YEARS

Chapter 11

Nigeria - Early Days

We arrived in Lagos by a BOAC plane from London in September 1958, just a year after our marriage. There were in those days three legs to the journey. The first stop, for refuelling, was in Spain (or North Africa), the second, after the long flight over the Sahara, always inspiring but somewhat frightening, was in Kano in Northern Nigeria, and then on to Lagos. We travelled comfortably in First Class! Why First Class? Because in those days, when Nigeria was still a British colony, this was standard procedure and part of the contract for those working under the Crown Agents, a British Government institution. You could opt to travel home on leave (after a nine month 'tour') by various somewhat circular routes, such as by way of the United States, so long as the cost of the first class fare was not exceeded and was spent only on travel. So, for us, on our first 'leave' we were able to travel home by way of Lebanon and Israel. More of this later. Later, most of those working in the University opted to waive this generous provision and travel home by standard class.

It was good for us that we travelled, on our initial trip to Nigeria, in the company of Dr Rowson, and his wife. Dr Rowson was the first Head of the new School of Pharmacy, a Yorkshireman well experienced in all things pharmaceutical.

The first thing that hits you when you arrive in West Africa is the heat and the humidity; just like a hot shower. And the animal life with lizards scurrying over the tarmac. No problems on that first visit with immigration and customs, although on the many future visits there could well be problems because of 'dash', the expectation by some immigration and custom officials for bribes. This is not the place to debate something that was, perhaps still is, almost indigenous to countries where wages are low, and where the income differential between rich and poor is enormous. Except perhaps to say that in Europe 'tips' or a 'service charge' are 'given' for service rewarded after the deed is done, which a Nigerian would consider repulsive, whereas 'dash' is given before the deed is done. This is like paying the bill before you have seen the menu.

View of Lagos about 1959

The distance from Lagos airport in Ikeja to Ibadan is roughly one hundred miles and must be one of the most dangerous roads in the world. This was especially so when, later in our stay, the Government decided to change from driving on the left, said to be a remnant of colonial Britain, to driving on the right. Best, at the time of the change, to stay at home. Of course, for 'mammy' wagon drivers, displaying names on the front of their vehicle like 'God is with us', 'While I breathe I hope', 'Your kingdom come' or 'No telephone to heaven', it made little difference. They invariably drove down the middle of the road. There are few things more frightening than, when driving carefully on the correct side of the road (with a sharp edge to the tarmac on the passenger side) one is faced by a heavily laden, swaying mammy wagon called 'Do not fear' coming toward you in the middle of the road! In fact, mammy wagon drivers are well trained: not to be overtaken, never to park in the dark with tail lights showing, never to give signals and always to abandon their vehicles in the middle of a traffic hold-up. All part of their driver's test. Which always involves 'dash'.

On this, our first experience of this later well-travelled road, everything went smoothly; there was even time for a stop halfway for a cold drink. Eventually we arrived at the Nigerian College of Science and Technology, then (in 1958) the only such college in West Africa.

For the first two nights, and to enable us to settle, we were housed in the Principal's House, a rather impressive building in the 'Colonial' style. There were other colonial habits, unusual for us, like cocktails each evening before the dinner (for which one dressed formally) and the introductions to various high-ranking members of the campus. Two other things stand out; first the noise. At night by the army of various insects and at dawn by the chorus of birds; then the evening habit of the College Principal, Mr K.O. Williams, of checking the inside of the many windows of the house for the tiny, almost transparent, green tree frogs. These were 'captured' under a glass jar and returned to the garden. This habit we too cultivated.

Our home on the large and well-kept compound was a two-bedroom bungalow with a garden leading at the foot into the 'bush' – tropical forest with a small stream. This stream provided a good source of toads and frogs for the class physiology practical class, collected in a bucket the evening before. These tropical amphibians have large hearts, so easy for students to perfuse, and are also good for nerve-muscle studies beloved of budding physiologists. The garden was good for growing bananas, used for our first Nigerian scientific experiment as well as for eating, and pineapples. There was also a resident mango tree. Sadly, this produced inedible, stringy mangoes said by the gardener 'to come from the West Indies'. Genuine Nigerian mangoes were delicious.

We quickly made friends. Rowland and Sheena Moss from Aberdeen lived almost opposite. We had first met them in London. Rowland, a geographer, later became Vice-Chancellor of the new University of Salford, a Vice-President of the UCCF and the author of an early book on the environment published by IVP. In Scotland they were members of Gilcomston Church of Scotland in Aberdeen and, on Sunday evenings, we listened together with one or two students, to the sermons of the illustrious minister the Revd Willie Still. We also invited students to our home, initially for games, later for what were termed 'squashes', food, game and an epilogue about some aspect of the Christian life. These 'squashes' later became important in the growth of student witness.

At the beginning of our stay in Ibadan we would drive the hundred miles down to the noisy, smelly (open drains) city of Lagos to shop. The main shops were along the Marina, a spacious avenue alongside the busy harbour. Here were also situated the imposing cathedral, numerous warehouses and dignified colonial buildings all alongside parks and fine gardens. There too was the sprawling warren of slums, houses walled and roofed with rusty pieces of corrugated metal, traversed by narrow alleys cluttered with debris, chickens and the occasional goat. The venue for us was Kingsway, a source of almost everything including long playing records some of which we still have; I listen to one as I write. We also still have left just one piece of a large, but incomplete, dinner and tea service, made of porcelain in Germany and sold at Kingsway. This was all that was left of several such services, many pieces of which had been broken in transit from Europe. However, one was allowed to put together an almost complete service from these various pieces which could then be bought at a knockdown price. Later we found almost all we needed (including gramophone records!) at the Lebanese store called Leventis. This store was in the centre of Ibadan. Outside, in the carpark, there were several greatly disfigured beggars, all 'parked' in their set places, a reminder for us of one of the beggars at the poolside at Bethesda recorded in John's gospel. Just waiting.

Lagos was then, and even more so now, a great sprawling place and, on our first visit we found it impossible to find our way out of the city and back onto the road to Ibadan. 'If you ever want to know the way ask a policeman' says the old song. So, we did. This one ordered Pam out of the front passenger seat, took her place and gave directions all the way to the outskirts of the city and on to the road we needed. He then jumped out, hailed a taxi (free to all policemen) and was taken back into the city centre. Courteous and kind.

In the pharmacology laboratory at Nigerian College 1958. In those days contractions of smooth muscle preparations were recorded on a revolving smoked drum. This is now a museum piece.

The Nigerian College (of Science and Technology) including the newly founded School of Pharmacy, was situated in an attractive, well maintained compound. My responsibility was to organise the teaching of pharmacology and to initiate research. This involved setting the syllabus and ordering all the necessary equipment and chemicals from the Crown Agents in London. These needed to be ordered well in advance since the journey by sea took three weeks after which, a process which usually took even longer, it needed to be cleared through customs and then arrangements made for the journey up to Ibadan. Good practice in thinking ahead then!

As with comparable Pharmacy Schools in Europe, it was important to commence research and to begin post-graduate studies. Two main lines were inaugurated. First, comparatively easy to start, was the continuation of some of the research arising from my PhD degree. This had been on the function of a chemical found in the human body called 5-hydroxytryptamine (5-HT). We had discovered that this substance occurs widely in nature. For example, it could also be found in bananas, readily available, in various stages of growth from our garden. For some reason the enzyme responsible for the synthesis of 5-HT is present from a very early stage. Later, when I moved to the University Medical School, Dr Ojo and I, with the help of students and staff, examined the possible involvement of 5-HT, ingested in bananas, in endomyocardial fibrosis, an unique form of cardiac disease found almost only in Africa. These results were published in *The Lancet*.

For a period, before becoming a mother Pam, as a qualified pharmacist, helped in the teaching of pharmaceutical chemistry. One of the exercises involved identification of a chemical precipitate by colour. The standard textbook referred to this as 'flesh coloured'; but, as one of the brighter students asked her – 'your colour or mine'?

During our three years at Nigerian College some rather unusual things happened. Here are some of them.

A highlight of our first year was a visit to the Drama School of the University by the theatre group based at the Crucible in Sheffield. Shakespeare's great play Macbeth was one of the plays performed. Full house! This was almost certainly Ibadan's introduction to our national dramatist. Now Nigerian audiences are very vocal and involved and whenever Lady Macbeth came on stage there were boos, whistles, shouting in Yoruba and much gesticulating. Judy Dench never had such a reception and I wonder if this has ever happened again during her illustrious career. Not surprisingly there is no mention of this reception and of the audience participation in her autobiography!

Another theatrical performance of a quite different kind followed the Shakespeare. Returning from the play, as our car approached the end of the road in which our bungalow was situated, there were more whistles, this time from the resident 'night watchman'. When we got home there was a rumpus, a lot of activity and commotion. We had been burgled! However, there were a few anomalies to a 'normal burglary'! Piles of our clothes were laid (very neatly) on the grass in the rear garden. This signified a very careful burglar. Then strangely, although one window had been broken the glass from it was outside the bungalow on the veranda. One did not need to be Sherlock Holmes to ascertain that this was an inside job. Of course, the houseboy, who had the key (and who came out of his quarters nearby looking as though he had just arisen from sleep) was responsible for the theft; the carefully piled clothes meant that he did not need to rewash – or iron them again. Money belonging to Scripture Union was stolen. Houseboy dismissed with no reference.

We had spent the first evening of our marriage in September 1957 in Frinton-on-sea visiting Pam's granny, her one surviving grandparent who, through age, had been unable to attend the wedding ceremony. Our first church service as a married couple was at the local Anglican church. It so happened that the daughter of the Rector, Joanna Ashford-Smith was a CMS missionary in Nigeria. 'When you are there look her up' was the suggestion, as though Nigeria was a small place (like Frinton). In a country with a population of millions and many times the size of the UK we thought this rather unlikely.

On our first Christmas Day, and a long way from family at home, we were invited to a rather special wedding. It was between Dr Ishaya Audu, a Hausa from northern Nigeria and Victoria, a Yoruba from the South. In those days such an intertribal marriage was very unusual. We will write more about Ishaya in Appendix 4. A few days later, during the New Year break, we decided that with friends we would explore a little of the country. We set off for Akure about sixty miles northeast of Ibadan. Again, more of Akure later! What surprised us, staying in the Government Guest House, was the temperature; at that time of year there is a cool (we thought cold) wind, the harmattan, blowing down from the Sahara. A blanket was needed.

We had heard that there was a Christian Centre (the Vining Centre) in Akure and discovered there was to be a service at midnight to celebrate entry into 1959. And, as you can probably guess, who was responsible for that service, of all people, but Joanna. But especially moving, feeling somewhat homesick, was that when we picked up the hymn book, inside was an inscription that it had been purchased with a gift from a Mrs Cuming of Frinton, Pam's granny!

Another of our excursions from Ibadan was one of several to Eastern Nigeria involving a ferry trip across the massive and very long River Niger. At the ferry point, meat was available on an open-air stall with vultures sitting on the roof waiting for pickings. Ugly birds. This Eastern Region later declared itself independent, becoming Biafra thus starting the Civil War in 1967, a few months after we had left for Scotland. We made our first visit to a leper colony, at Uzuakoli where there was a famous, very good leper choir in their blue robes and singing in Ibo. We still have their recordings. At yet another leper colony we met Dr Stanley Brown later known as Mr Leprosy.

Not far from Umuahia we had a narrow escape. Driving along a narrow laterite road with tall elephant grass growing up on either side I suddenly saw a face in the grass on the driver's side. Just a face. Suddenly the face was joined by a body. A body with horns. Then we were charged by a bush cow. These extremely dangerous animals, like a small buffalo, stand about four to five feet tall and which have been known to charge and kill farmers. This one pushed the mud guard of our Morris Minor Traveller into the front wheel, shreds of tyre rubber spinning off before the car was brought to an abrupt halt. Here we were, on a quiet lonely road with dusk approaching and several miles from help. Thoughts of spending the night in the car surrounded by dangerous animals! What to do? First, pray! Second, get out of the car, very tentatively, because an injured annoyed bush cow would be in front, to assess the damage. This I did. No sign of the bush cow which seemed to have continued its journey, presumably to look for the cow's equivalent of an aspirin.

The car was undrivable, because not only were we incapable of levering the mud-guard off the wheel to change it, but one of the animal's horns had pierced the radiator with water already dripping out. Stuck. Far from help. However, after only a short time we heard singing coming from behind us. It was the sound of foresters coming home from their days work in a truck that had all the equipment for removing the damaged wheel. Not only did they change the wheel for us but they had some kind of sealant for the radiator. With thankfulness to them and to the Lord, our prayer answering God, we continued to our destination and next day to

Onitsha. Waiting for the ferry (before the bridge had been built). This is the crossing of the Niger to the Eastern Region

the nearest garage. But what happened to that bush cow? Probably awoke next day with a terrible headache.

Either on this trip, or another such (we made more than one visit to the 'east') we visited Calabar, the home of the famous Scottish missionary Mary Slessor, to stay with another Aberdonian who later became a Church of Scotland minister. This again involved a ferry, this time without the car, which we had to leave safely (?) parked for our return. This also meant taking a mammy wagon to the ferry point, the first, and fortunately the only time, we had occasion to do this. First class seats are at the front next to the driver and known as 'death (entry to heaven) seats'. Hair raising! Here I should again explain what a mammy wagon in Nigeria is. These are lorries designed to transport anything and everything. Besides people this includes animals (especially goats and chickens) cloth, mattresses, all kinds of fruit, meat and fish. They are always well named; some of my favourites include 'Go straight' (!) 'God rules' and 'Keep left' (when they now drive on the right). Mammy wagon drivers and their vehicles 'own' the roads.

In colonial times the 'rule' was to drive on the left. Earlier in the chapter, I mentioned the decision of the Government to change this to driving on the right. The argument for this change was to reduce the number of accidents when travelling from Nigeria to the surrounding countries to the east, former French colonies. Before this change in the law I once had to drive to Ghana through Togo and Dahomey and it was true that there were rather more observed crashes on the road than even in Nigeria itself – which is saying something. On this occasion, taking my life into my hands, I drove from Ibadan to Accra (Ghana) and discovered that it is always advantageous to be on good terms with the police, wherever you are. This visit to Winneba in Ghana was to a Christian conference for students from all over West Africa organised by PAFES (Pan African Fellowship of Evangelical Students). Near the end of the programme I was asked if I would take the main speaker, Tony Wilmot, to the airport. We were accompanied by a Ghana resident whom I did not know. In the middle of Accra, a sprawling city even more confusing than Lagos, I took a wrong turning and drove up a one-way street in the wrong direction, to the accompaniment of shouts of 'one way' from the various stall holders on each side of the road. What to do? 'Drive on' said the voice from the back seat. He turned out to be the Chief of Police of Accra. No problem then. I remembered that when I first took my driving test in Brighton I was failed because the instructor had told me to take the next turning on the right which I did, only to discover it was also one way. No friendly policeman at the back.

1960 was not only the year of Nigerian Independence but, even more importantly for us, it witnessed the birth of our first child on March 14th. Nigerians are fond of children but boys are more valued than girls. If it is a girl the comment from passers-by is 'sorry oh'; if a boy it is 'congrats'. So, for us, in the University Hospital it was congratulations!

When we brought Stephen home from the hospital among our first visitors were three students who were regular at our 'squashes'. They had come to 'greet' the new born. Of course, they had seen many small babies before but not this colour! They saw this tiny white baby sleeping in his cot under a mosquito net and did three things. First, they prayed for him, then they gave him a copy of God's word and then they named him. Typical African custom. They named him 'bandele' which means one born a long way from home.

Three years at Nigerian College was, from the viewpoint of 'future prospects' for when we eventually returned to the UK, enough. I had learnt much as a young scientist and as a Christian; how to organise teaching, plan the syllabus, order goods from faraway Britain and to begin to understand how to live in a tropical environment and to discover opportunities for serving the God we loved and had come to know. But now, it was time to move on to a situation where it would be easier to undertake scientific research in a university environment which I hoped would be my career. Late in the spring term I heard of a lectureship becoming vacant in the university 'next door' (the two campuses were physically connected). This was in the Department of Physiology, one of the pre-clinical departments of the Medical School. I met with the Head of that department, Professor John Grayson and, in the absence of other candidates, I was appointed; it was only a year later that I took another degree, this time in the subject I was about to teach. More about University College Ibadan, Nigeria's first university, in Appendix 3.

Chapter 12
Ibadan

Ibadan was the town where we spent the best part of nine years during the 1950s and 60s. It was, at that time, the largest town (or should it really be called a city – it has two cathedrals) in West Africa and, with about 600,000 inhabitants, the largest indigenous population of any town in the whole of Africa: at the time less than 0.2% of the residents were non-Nigerian, mainly British colonial officials or traders from Lebanon. The name Ibadan is derived from the Yoruba *'Eba-Odan'* meaning 'by the side of the field', lying as it does between the dense coastal forest belt ('bush') and the more open grassland to the North. We once had an audience with the ruler of the local chiefs, the Olubadan, or Bale. Unusually, in Ibadan this office is not hereditary, unlike the usual institution of kingship, where the kingship (Oba) is kept within the immediate family.

Ibadan lies on a series of hills (the highest point is nearly 750 feet above sea level) and 7 degrees north of the equator. This means it is hot with average temperatures between 70 and 95 degrees. This, with an annual rainfall of nearly 50 inches, means humidity is high especially during the 'wet season' (from May/June until October). University teachers from 'overseas' went home on leave during much of this rainy period; however, as you will see, we once remained in Ibadan for the whole year (1966) and so experienced this uncomfortable, but quiet, time of year.

Ibadan is an untidy, ramshackle, odoriferous, town made up of mud or brick dwellings with tin or aluminium rooves – the photo gives some idea of what it looked like when we were resident at the university just a few miles away. Ibadan itself was always a bustling, busy place, being the commercial centre of Western State and the nodal point through which agricultural produce passed south to Lagos and through which imported goods passed north (by rail or road) to the other main regions of the country. We often 'hosted' missionaries travelling north to the areas in which the

Sudan United Mission (SUM) worked or to Ekiti country. We were reminded recently that one of our present Africa Prayer Group, Elizabeth Deeks, called in, after leaving the train, 'to greet' – and for refreshment – the date in our visitors book is September 4th 1965. She was on her way to work with CMS in Ondo and Akure, where she served for many years.

Some visitors chose to spend the night in Ibadan, staying at the local Government Guest House; cost of a single room 27 shillings, breakfast 5s 6d, lunch 7s. 6p, dinner 8s. 6d! We rarely needed to use Government Rest Houses in which one special article of furniture was always present. This was a 'high stool', about five feet in height. When I first saw such a stool I wondered at the very tall people who would sit on it, until I realised that it was there to put the lamp on since often there was no electricity available in the Guest Houses, even when it was connected. I am reminded of those 'high stools' when I read in the New Testament about letting your light shine, 'not hiding one's light under a bushel' or, as the chorus goes, 'lift Jesus high'.

We seldom visited 'town' apart for shopping, for visits to the British Council library or to one of the city churches. Congregations in these were large, colourful and noisy and the services often (always!) very long, folk arriving (and leaving) at any time and with the front row given up to mother's breast feeding their babies. One such church visit was to meet the 'chief of chiefs' of Ibadan. This was for a rather unusual reason and story requires retelling!

In 1960 the American evangelist Billy Graham paid a visit to Nigeria, including Ibadan for a huge open-air meeting on the racecourse. Prior to his coming he had sent members of his team to 'prepare the way'. Nigerian College had a visit from an associate evangelist called Roy Gustafson who preached at the College Chapel the Sunday previous. I decided to attempt to record what he said so that we could use it when some of the students came to visit us in our home. This, with a small portable cassette recorder was not too difficult.

After the meeting a small and not very imposing elderly man came up and asked if it was possible for me to make a duplicate tape for him. I had no idea who this man was until someone took me aside to say this was the king of Ibadan! I said this would require a second recorder. His response was that he would bring one round the next morning to our home. I made sure I was 'on seat' (which means 'at home' or 'there' in Yoruba!) and at the set time a police cavalcade came sweeping around the drive followed by a big Mercedes car out of which stepped the 'king', an influential member of the Apostolic Church. He and his entourage were entertained with cold drinks, some chat and the signing of our visitor's book. So that was 'the day the king came'! This later became a much-used children's talk! The tape was duly made and next day I drove into town to deliver it.

We thought Roy's talk was so good we would like to hear him again so we took a number of students to hear him later that Sunday elsewhere in town. What we heard however was the same sermon we had heard him preach that morning. Disappointing. A warning for all preachers!

The first part of the infamous Lagos-Ibadan road, on which we travelled each year from Lagos airport in Ikeja to our 'home' in Ibadan, goes over the swamps connecting Lagos island with the 'mainland' and the several bridges across the various tributaries of the Ogun river. This is the most attractive part of the almost hundred mile journey. Small riverside villages in the dense forest or 'bush'. Perhaps a little frightening; not a good idea to be stuck on this particular part of the route.

The photo, an original painting by the artist Moukoko in our possession, gives some idea of the terrain. It is easy to imagine what it must have been like for the early missionaries just over one hundred years before we arrived. In those far-off days the journey was by canoe, first across the Lagos lagoon and then (with a change of canoe) up the Ogun river to Abeokuta, the scenery changing from mangrove swamp to more open countryside, with a preponderance of cocoa and cotton trees and, outside the numerous villages, banana plantations. In those days, and little had changed by the 1950s, the river was so shallow that those on board had often to get out and push the boat over the sandbanks, keeping a lookout for crocodiles. Later came the two to three-day journey from Abeokuta to Ibadan. This was on foot (lady missionaries carried by hammock) or, for the men, the back of horses. That journey which we often made by car took, barring accidents (no guarantee) less than an hour.

Abeokuta, the site of the first Church (Anglican) Missionary Society (CMS) mission compound was founded by Bishop Samuel Crowther. At the age of just twelve Crowther was a Yoruba boy named Ajayi, captured by Fulani slave traders and rescued (in 1826) from the hold of a Portuguese ship by a Royal Navy anti-slaving patrol vessel outside Freetown. These RN vessels were active all along the West African coastline until the late 1860s. Crowther was ordained in 1846 and became the first native bishop in West Africa: he was responsible for translating the bible into Yoruba.

The Ibadan (CMS) mission was founded by David and Anna Hinderer in the Kudeti region of the city. There is an interesting novel[1] by Ellen Thorpe, the wife of a Senior British Government official in Lagos in the 1940s. It is a fascinating read outlining, in some detail, the traumas of early missionary activity in the south of Nigeria. So many of these early heralds of the gospel succumbed to disease; the many graves confirm this. Some would - be missionaries died whilst still on the boat once the West Coast had been reached. Once the boat had dropped anchor off Lagos island they had then to travel on by canoe, followed by sharks, across the Atlantic rollers and sandbanks to reach their destination. Slaves made the same journey in reverse, the sharks still waiting for a canoe to upturn. As I re-read these stories of the early missionaries to Yorubaland in the middle of the 19th century, I am both moved and challenged by their commitment to the spread of the gospel and the feeling that even after so many years, so little had been done.

Then, as much later during our own time living in the same region of Nigeria, there were wars and rumours of wars, the major one (the Biafran civil war) starting just a few months after we had left. Previous to that, many were killed or injured during the two military coups that took place during our final tour of the country in 1965-6. Back in the 1860s, during the long-lasting wars within the Yoruba kingdoms between the cities of Ibadan and Ijebu (Lagos), there were road blocks, the pillaging of crops, armed bands, the kidnapping of young men and boys, the child soldiers and the resulting isolation, poverty and hunger. For us, as for them

[1] Ellen Thorpe, *Swelling of Jordan*, Lutterworth Press, London, 1950.

a century earlier, the Lagos Ibadan road was also often closed with many 'roadblocks'. People were advised to remain in their homes; sometimes even these were not completely safe. On the University campus we were in a kind of lockdown with armed guards at the gate.

At one time we were worried for our friends the Bennett's of the SIM (Sudan Interior Mission) whose compound, where the church used for the Sunday afternoon student services was situated, was a few yards along the Ibadan to Lagos road. It was felt that they should not remain in that potentially dangerous place so I drove, by a very roundabout route to avoid the centre of the city, to 'rescue' them and bring them to stay with us in the comparative safety of the university campus. What I remember about that particular journey was the strange quietness everywhere. No one about. And the fact that I drove over a huge snake, probably a python: without stopping!

Our usual place of worship during our years in Ibadan was the University Teaching Hospital, a 'Chapel in the Nurses School'. There was a morning service organised by a group, mainly expatriate, within the hospital, with a committee which I later chaired. Some idea of the composition of this committee in those days can be judged by the number of white faces in a photo – a 'farewell' for the hospital treasurer Jeff McLachlan when he and his family returned to Scotland.

Each Lord's Day there was a morning service, a Sunday school (crowded) where Pam was sometimes one of the teachers. There was also a weekly bible study and time of prayer. Dr John Mills from the American Baptist Mission acted as part-time Chaplain. All faculties in the hospital were represented – David Trew, who with his wife Barbara later moved to Canada, was in radiology, Jean Patterson in pharmacy and Dorothy Harrison was a sister in the labour ward. Dorothy cared for Pam after our first child Stephen was born in the hospital in 1960. After leaving Nigeria, Dorothy became a missionary with the Africa Inland Mission.

We joined the fellowship in 1958, a year after the hospital was built, a mile or so from the university campus. The services officially began in 1959 but for two years previous to this there were gatherings for prayer and bible study and a Sunday school, held in various homes around the hospital compound.

How did these regular Sunday services commence? They started following the death of the three-day old son of one of the doctors, Ralph Schram a lecturer in public health and his wife Enid, a nursing sister on the maternity ward. Their small son was buried following a ceremony at the Sudan Interior Mission (African Challenge) compound on the Lagos Road. After the memorial service some of the hundred or so people who attended asked Ralph if there could be regular worship services on the hospital compound. Permission was granted, and these were organised a few weeks later. They continue to this day. The grave of the Schram's son had to be moved after the Challenge (a prime site) was bought and built over by the Ibadan Authority; the memorial stone could still be seen learning against a wall.

The Schram family played an essential part in the beginnings of Christian witness at the hospital. SU work also started from their home as did witness among the clinical medical students and nurses. When they left Ibadan in November 1962 the Christian witness was well established. Ralph, like Jean Patterson, then came to Scotland and was an active member of the Broughty Ferry Baptist Church before being appointed to a senior position at the London School of Tropical Medicine. He wrote the then standard textbook on public health in the tropics.

Sixty years later we wondered if the hospital worship services, that had meant so much to us, were still functioning in a very different Nigeria. They are! David Trew sent me a video clip of the sixty year Jubilee celebrations. It is clear that the fellowship has grown enormously. The video shows a full, colourful (and noisy) congregation, Yoruba ladies in their multi-coloured cloths, a great sense of joy and enthusiastic thanksgiving was evident together with African informality – mothers arriving (and leaving!) at various times during the service with their small children in tow, the Chaplain (now a fulltime appointment) resplendent in his deep red cloak with a huge metal cross around his neck. In the congregation not a white face to be seen. The weekly activities now include a Sunday school service for the children (probably a very messy church), a weekly bible exposition and prayer meeting, 'life cell' meetings, choir practice and 'teen challenge' on a Saturday afternoon. All evidence of growth, joy and outreach. A vibrant fellowship of believers. This was a celebration, as only Africans can, of God's faithfulness and goodness. All from a tiny seed, the tragic death of that small baby so many years ago. 'To God be the glory great things He has done'.

A typical Yoruba wood carving probably depicting the capture of young boys during the slave trade in the mid 19th century. Everything crammed into the available space, the head of the horse larger than the man riding it!

Chapter 13
Living in the Tropics

As probably few reading these words would have lived and worked in a tropical colonial country in the 1950s and early 1960s (since you would need to be, like the author, in your late 80s) perhaps a few words are appropriate about what daily living was like in those, now far off days. Remember that Nigeria was at one time part of what was described as 'the white man's grave', that is the West coast of Africa.

With the British deep and daily concern for the weather, this should be first on the agenda. Ibadan is 7 degrees north and, being so close to the equator, there are just two seasons. Wet and dry. The dry season is very hot, perhaps over 90 degrees in the shade and 120 in the sun, especially at midday; 'only mad dogs and Englishmen go out in the midday sun'. This heat is alleviated by the coming of the rains, the timing of which corresponds roughly to what in more temperate zones is usually called summer, June to August. Because we were normally back home in the UK during this period, for the long university vacation, we were only in Nigeria during this wet season once, in 1966, for a few months before we finally left the country.

Most folk welcome the coming of the rains: it brings a welcome coolness and that characteristic smell of wet earth. Soon everything becomes damp; there is a musty, mildew odour especially on clothes and books; even fifty years later the smell on certain of our books brought back from that time still have that 'odour of reminiscence'. The coming of the rains begins, off stage, with the 'sound of a mighty wind' (as Elijah described) the wind blowing initially a cloud of red (laterite) dust that covers everything. Then the lightning, the rumblings of thunder still far off, an eerie, uncanny stillness, the darkening sky which makes the colours of trees and shrubs sharpen, making them stand out. And then the steaming wall of water and the noise of it on the metal roofs; all unearthly noise and water. Once, during one such storm we were in the Africa Challenge chapel on the Lagos road. The missionary speaker, very American, not to be undone, tried to compete. As the noise of the rain on the tin roof increased so did the volume, the loudness of his voice. All noise and water. And, nothing from him was heard.

There is a certain joy that comes with the first rains. Once, again in Akure when the rains arrived, we put on our swimming costumes and put out all the containers we could find to collect this so valuable water. Perhaps only those who live in the dry places of the earth can really appreciate the coming of water. 'I will pour floods upon the dry land'[1] and 'the dry ground into watersprings'. After that the damp earth and the steam arising from the ground when the sun came out. And the smell!

Often during the dry season there is a brief spell, which Nigerians call winter, when the cool harmattan wind from the Sahara reaches south to cover everything again in the 'red dust'. Then you need a sweater and a blanket on the bed. We were caught out by this welcome coolness during another visit to Akure during our first New Year in the country. Unexpected. As too is the 'small dry' that sometimes happens during the wet season, making this a good period for farmers to plant, a favourable time for action. 'There is a time to plant'[2] and the 'small dry' is one of them.

There were good reasons for describing the west coast of Africa in bygone days as the 'white man's grave' due to the high incidence of tropical diseases such as malaria and dengue. Stories of missionary endeavours during the nineteenth century are full of the deaths of many visitors to Liberia, Ghana and Nigeria, some even before they landed. Died at sea and buried there.

Ellen Thorpe writes dramatically in a novel[3] about the initial days of missionary activity in Nigeria around the middle of the nineteenth century, about the early attempts to preach the gospel in countries where there was little (apart from quinine) to counteract the deadly effects of malaria. Would-be visits to this part of the world, as to many others, was made much easier with the later

[1] Psalm 107:35.

[2] Ecclesiastes 3:2.

[3] Ellen Thorpe, *Swelling of Jordan*, Lutterworth Press, 1950.

discovery of antimalarials. At that time there was little resistance of the malarial parasite to the standard antimalarial drugs then in use, at least in West Africa. We were prescribed pyrimethamine (daraprim) advertised as the 'Sunday Sunday' medicine because it only needed to be taken once a week. So, it was placed on the table for the Sunday lunch to enable us to remember to take it. If, that is, someone remembered to put it on the table in the first place. Late in our final tour I did forget and promptly went down, at a most inconvenient time, with malaria. Not a pleasant experience but easily solved by a short regime of chloroquine given, not as a prophylactic but as a curative, a remedy.

The unpleasant symptoms of malaria are a profound increase in temperature (the hot stage) followed by a cold stage and sweating. Malaria is caused by parasitic organisms of the Plasmodium genus, usually in Nigeria, Plasmodium falciparum. The organism is injected into the bloodstream when one is bitten by a mosquito of the genus Anopheles. Repeated infections in the days before the advent of the available drugs, led to recurrent fever (ague) and an enlarged spleen and eventually to some degree of immunity. In communities where these drugs were unavailable (or simply not taken when they were available) this enlargement of the spleen becomes clearly visible; if such an enlarged spleen was fractured by a blow (sometimes intentionally) death was due to rupture and a fatal haemorrhage. Clearly, this did not happen in my case!

Even more dangerous was dengue, an infectious disease again resulting from a mosquito bite. This is an extremely debilitating condition with extreme nausea, vomiting and fever. It can be followed by disseminated intravascular coagulation and bleeding from a variety of sites. It is not a situation I would welcome again. Good that it is rare in Scotland; certainly, at the moment but with global warming? There was an interesting repercussion to this. When we came to Scotland we had more than the usual health checks in view of where we had been. The blood results led to one interesting finding such that the army became involved to use me as a blood donor. Nothing came of this, but I have wondered if there may have been elevated antibodies or some other protective factor present. If these could be raised and used then it might have helped those serving in situations in the world where dengue is prevalent.

We were able in our various tours of the country to visit leprosy settlements and to see at first hand the effects of this terrible and ancient disease. The gross disfigurement of limbs and face. Isolation or living with other sufferers not the only consequences. Few people at that time were cured and the surgery, so intricate, was demanding. Only a few brilliant surgeons were capable. It was in Nigeria that we got to know Dr Stanley Browne ('Mister Leprosy') who also later visited us in Glasgow. An excellent book,[4] and earlier ones by that doyen of leprosy research, Paul Brand[5] give vivid examples of all that is involved in the treatment and research into this still debilitating condition. Dr Robert Cochrane, another famous leprologist and a member of the same church we attended in Hove, was a great encourager to us as a young couple setting out on an adventure to the tropics where he had worked for many years.

Apart from the bush cow incident mentioned above, there were other encounters with animal life of various kinds. One of such encounters face to face although thankfully, as with the cow, with metal between, was an early meeting with a bush rat. These can grow to an alarming size. On one occasion Pam was about to run a bath (showers had at that time not been invented, at least in Nigeria) when a face appeared with huge front teeth at the metal grip covering the exit hole for the water. Quite frightening even though there was no way for it to get to us. It had managed to climb into the exit pipe from the garden. I am unsure with the progress of time whether we simply washed it away or if the garden boy managed to extract the animal and take it back to his quarters for 'chop'; apparently the meat is quite good.

A gentler creature we discovered in the garden of our friend Richard Childerstone in Akure. Chameleons have the ability to change colour as part of a defensive mechanism. We put this one to the test. Finding a multicoloured umbrella we moved it round from one colour to another timing how long it took to change colour. This was probably five-year old Stephen's first introduction

[4] Phyllis Thompson, *Mister Leprosy*, Hodder and Stoughton, 1960.

[5] Paul Brand and Philip Yancey, *Fearfully and Wonderfully Made*, Hodder and Stoughton, 1981.

to a 'scientific' experiment. Probably, since this experiment took time, it put him off a scientific career for life.

Geckos are also interesting. How is it that they do not obey the law of gravity, walking upside down on the ceiling? Although take care they do not descend (perhaps when they fall asleep?) onto the dining table and into your soup!

A more prevailing presence were ants. These amazing creatures were everywhere and we were in constant battle against them. Huge numbers, whole brigades of the ant army, were always on the move and formidably alert to the smell of sugar and the sticky taste of jam: they were willing to commit mass suicide for the sake of just a taste. The refrigerator had to be protected by placing the legs in tins of water and any food enclosed in tightly packed jars. To sit in the garden, or anywhere else outside, was impossible for they would be in your clothes, crawling up your legs, biting as they went. Worst of all were the white ants (termites) that had an appetite for anything (thatch, mud walls, books left outside) and could destroy everything in their path – except concrete.

Although we saw scorpions, fortunately we never made contact with them. The sting in the poison-barbed tail could be very painful and a shock to the system; slash the wound and cover with potassium permanganate. We never had the need ourselves to test the efficacy of this 'remedy'. More common were cockroaches. In our first home a large colony were resident between the panels of a wooden kitchen door which had to be removed and burnt. It turned out to be a very large colony indeed.

Apart from the big stores buying anything required 'bargaining banter'. Nothing is bought without a haggle; it is an essential part of the process. There are no price tags! If you have the time, which most of us had then, the process is enjoyable and well worth it. Some of the things brought round by tradesmen, mainly from the north, or from visits to wood carvers are quite exquisite and beautifully worked: we still use, fifty years later, a carved, ornate bread board and a small table originating from the village of Awka. There is, of course, a very long tradition of metal work (Benin bronzes being the most famous example) and wood carving in Nigeria. When we eventually left the country in December1966, my university colleagues gave me wood sculptures (see below) carved by a local (and now world famous) artist, Akin Fakeye. The Scripture Union gave to us an ebony carving, the story about which is told later.

A frequent visitor to the house was a Hausa trader, tall, erect, slow moving who travelled from several hundred miles north of Ibadan. Everything was carried on his head in a wicker basket that was so heavy we had to lift it off his head to enable him to spread out his wares before the bargaining could begin. Most of the morning gone!

A leaving gift from the University department, December 1966. The carving is by Akin Fakeye

Bargaining is an art which is in an African's blood; maybe there is a special bantering gene? The 'rule' is for the seller to estimate how much the prospective buyer is likely to afford (newcomers and visitors are most vulnerable) assess the top end, add fifty percent and start from there. The buyer starts at 25 to 30% of the price first demanded and then comes the cut and thrust, the haggling, the arguing (hotly but gently!) the leaving, involving a return visit, feigned or real, to another similar trader. The process, for something you really want, can last all day until some sort of compromise is reached. But, of course, it is the seller who is the 'victor'. But why bother? There could be a set price, like most western merchants. But this would be the equivalent of eating yam without salt. Insipid, uninteresting.

A visit to the market is another unique experience; a crowded labyrinth of open-fronted stalls. The excitement, the noise, the smells; the whiff from the open cement gutters, a couple of feet deep, carrying filthy, odorous fluid, merging with the smell of fish, peppers, oranges, meat on open stalls (watched from nearby by vultures), the variety of the cloths, bursting with colour, the prints in gaudy designs, these perhaps the result of the uninhibited fantasies of designers in rainy Lancashire. One could find patent medicines for every known (and not yet known) ailment – stomach and headache cures, tonics for 'stirring up the blood', for expelling worms, for rejuvenating the body. Almost anything can be found here or, if not, easily obtained 'tomorrow' from somewhere else. Nearby are shacks, the dwelling places of 'lawyers', with signs like 'Batch. Law' London (underneath, in smaller letters, failed') to sort out, at unrivalled cost, any market disputes, or 'doctors' able to cure anything – at a 'small small' price, just in case any of the market traders came to blows. Not unheard of.

(Note – advice when buying eggs. 1. Shake – if there is no liquid 'gurgle' it was surely bad. 2. Squint through the egg at the sun – always present. Opaque? Bad. 3. Put it in water. If it floats it is suspect. If it sinks, buy.)

You could also find in the market hairdressers, one of the essential professions. Even in the tropics one's hair needs to be cut, maybe more often than in temperate zones? Among the essential items on the long list provided by the Crown Agents to would be travellers to West Africa were hair cutting implements and, at the beginning of our first tour, Pam tried her hand at this. Although unusually gifted, this particular skill did not come naturally to her and we eventually resorted to a barber who came once a month to the house. However, she did not feel that this particular barber, although skilled enough to cut my hair, was of the quality to give Stephen his first haircut; so, I had to take him into town for the real experience. His hair, before cutting, was very special, very wavy and very blond. Not so after this first haircut experience; I had picked up a magazine, paying little attention to what was going on in the barber's chair. When I looked up, Stephen had had what was called in those days a 'crewcut' (I think, now referred to as a 'number one'?) Pam was horrified. One husband in the 'dog house'.

Chapter 14
Israel 1959 – a Place of No Return

Both Nigerian College (where we were from 1958-1961) and University College Ibadan (from 1961-67) had similar educational systems. This involved returning to your place of domicile, for us the UK, at the end of each academic year, usually in June, and returning for the beginning of the new academic year in September. This amount of annual leave may sound excessive but there were good reasons for it. The first reason was health. For those working in the Colonial Service the usual tour of duty in West Africa was eighteen months; missionaries in contrast did tours of three to five years! An eighteen-month tour would have caused havoc with the university teaching system; it would have meant returning for home leave in the middle of a teaching term. The alternative was to return home every year; two years was felt to be too long to stay in such an unhealthy climate.

The second reason was to allow staff to maintain contact with their home-based colleagues in the UK and to attend academic congresses the main ones, certainly in science, being in July of each year.

So, at the end of each academic year staff and their families were given fares in order to return home. For the first five years of our stay these were first class fares for the whole family; staff later, after independence, requested that this privilege be rescinded. Return flights were still paid for but at the usual economy class rate. However, during those first five years it was also possible to 'take' the equivalent of the first - class fare in cash and use it to travel home by routes other than the direct one, by way of the United States for example. But only so long as the money was used solely for travel.

For our first home leave, and with no children at that time, we decided to visit the Holy Land, a long-held ambition. This involved considerable preparation. For example, there was no Israeli Embassy in Nigeria at the time (1959); the nearest office was in Ghana. Fortunately, for this and the other necessary visas, we needed four in all, there was a postal service. This took considerable time.

We knew that two of our Ibadan friends had visited Israel previously and had kept diaries. They made important suggestions – where and with whom to stay! One of them, Francis Foulkes even loaned us his own extensive diary. All this planning was important because entry to Arab countries was not allowed if you had your passport stamped with an Israeli visa. For us, this was stamped into our passports as we entered the country and meant that for the next nine years, until we renewed our passports, we were not allowed to enter certain restricted Arab countries. For example, on the return leg to Nigeria one could not fly on a BOAC flight that needed to stop in North Africa to refuel even though passengers were in any case not allowed to disembark.

We flew from Lagos to Khartoum, right across the Sahel of Africa, by an airline we would not choose to fly with again. From there our journey took us to Beirut in Lebanon, at that time a lovely city with good walks along the promenade overlooking the Mediterranean Sea. Here we stayed, by kind invitation, with Hazel St John, the sister of Patricia, a missionary in North Africa for many years and the author of numerous books especially for children. Hazel was the headmistress of an Anglican school for girls and a great source of advice about the country.

One of her suggestions was to take a taxi ride to Baalbek in the mountains about an hour's drive east of Beirut through the Beqaa Valley. A quite frightening experience. The drive that is. Choose your Lebanese taxi driver carefully. Baalbek is a fantastic place; one of the wonders of the ancient world dating back 9000 years, a magnificent World Heritage site, a huge complex of temples (one to the god Baal) but at that time quite deserted. Not now apparently.

We then flew to Amman, the capital of Jordan. Not quite so interesting but our best route into Israel. The entry was over a long bridge. On the Jordanian side the soldiers took our luggage to the centre of the bridge (without looking straight ahead) put it on the ground, turned their backs on the Jewish border guards and returned to safety; no love lost there. When they had completed their journey to their side of the border, Jewish soldiers came to collect the luggage and take it to the Israeli side. As they knew we were coming our visas were stamped into our passports at the border crossing.

In Jerusalem, we stayed – again by invitation! – at Christ Church, a good centre to explore the fascinating old city. This included the 'pavement', where Jesus had been tried, which was then just being excavated. It is not easy to explain the sensation of being in the city where Jesus had taught and healed, was crucified and rose again! Literally walking in his footsteps. Our Sunday service was held at the Garden Tomb, which is one of the possible burial sites. A most moving experience. Later we visited Bethlehem. The church, said to be built over the historical birthplace of Jesus, is very ornate with different 'denominations' worshipping in their separate corners within the church. An ornate stone covered the supposed birthplace. For us, the most memorable experience was the small opening into the church itself; one had to bend to enter. Most appropriate.

We took the opportunity of visiting the Dead Sea. The route took us through the arid mountainous 'wilderness' and I asked the taxi driver to stop in order for me to take a photograph. He refused, saying it might be dangerous and that there were 'brigands' waiting. We thought back to Psalm 121 where the psalmist, on a journey to attend the festivals in the city, travelled through those same mountains. He looked up at those hills and asked the question - 'where is my help coming from?' In order to pass through those dangerous hills with those 'brigands' the traveller needed help. His testimony was that help came only from the Lord who had indeed created that frightening wilderness.

At the Dead Sea itself we swam – or tried to – the buoyancy made swimming difficult. There is a picture Pam took of me 'sitting' on the water reading a newspaper. However, the newspaper was in Hebrew and I was holding the paper upside down!

I have used this experience for a children's talk at church. Why is it dead so that nothing lives there? Because there is no outlet for the water. It just stays there, the water evaporating in the heat and the salt concentration increasing. What a difference to the Sea of Galilee! Full of life, full of fish! Why? Because the Sea of Galilee has both an inlet, from the River Jordan, and an outlet. What it receives it gives out again. As Jesus said – 'It is more blessed to give than to receive'. Then expand!

The highlight of the whole visit, a bus journey from Jerusalem, was to Galilee. Here we stayed in Tiberias, at the hospital set up by the Church of Scotland. Now, I think a hotel for tourists. And, perhaps pilgrims. What a delightful spot! Getting up early to watch the sun rise over the Lake, the boats coming in after a night of fishing, other fisherman beginning to mend their nets. Such happenings seem to have changed little from Jesus' time. James and John, Peter and Andrew could have been those fishermen not far from where I was sitting – 'in simple trust like those who heard, beside the Syrian Sea the gracious calling of the Lord'. Such calm. The hymn writer, John Greenleaf Whittier, was right – 'O Sabbath rest by Galilee! O calm of hills above'. And it was those calm hills that for the two of us was the most special memory of all. 'Before the winds that blow do cease, teach me to dwell within Thy calm'.

We took a bus to a convenient place on the road around the Lake where there is the chapel of 'the loaves and the fish'. From there we walked around the Lake to Capernaum, the synagogue, not apparently the same one as in Jesus' day; it is now a ruin. No one in sight the whole journey. And the silence: 'the silence of eternity interpreted by love' – wonderful words but what do they really mean? We felt we knew. There was just one other person at Capernaum, a priest who came to the gate of his 'compound' (as we would say in Africa) to 'greet' us. Conversation in French in which, so he said, he recognised fellow believers by *'les yeux spirituelle'*. He welcomed us into the garden and gave us a flask of water, a melon and a list of the New Testament references of the times Jesus had been there. It was the highlight of our visit: to sit by the Lake eating our lunch and looking up in our bibles those visits the Lord Jesus had made to that, now quiet and lovely spot. I think one of our ten all-time life experiences. Never to be forgotten and never to be repeated.

There was a rather humorous end to that visit. A taxi drew up with just one passenger, an elderly American lady who had come to 'see the sights'. A ten minute stop: probably, Israel in a day. The priest talked both to the taxi driver and the lady and persuaded them to give us a free lift (it had been a long walk that morning) as far as the lady's next stop – the Mount of Beatitudes. Here we reflected on the stories of the feeding of the thousands – on that very spot perhaps? And again, the silence: 'the silence of eternity interpreted by love'.

The return home was via Haifa for a different kind of swimming. It was here that we suspected that Pam was in the early stages of pregnancy. We missed out on our planned next stop to Athens, and flew straight back to Britain.

But never to return. Why, when there were later invitations to return? To speak at a scientific meeting in Jerusalem and to participate in one of those well organised tourist trips arranged by a local church? Why a place of no return? Because after that 1959 visit another would have been quite impossible to match; it had been so perfect. As the Emperor Joseph said to Mozart after a performance of one of his operas (there is still a debate about which one; maybe after all of them) 'too many notes'. The same might be said of tourists!

There are some places one should never revisit. They would spoil that initial one. And the news of the coming of our first child was like the 'icing on the cake'.

Chapter 15
Scripture Union Nigeria

When we arrived in Nigeria, we already had firm links with Scripture Union (SU) in England. We were using the Bible daily notes produced by them and both of us had taken part as 'workers' at CSSM (Children's Special Service Mission) seaside missions on the Norfolk coast at Sheringham, East Runton and Cromer. CSSM was the outreach part of SU's ministry; one of their two basic aims being that 'the Word of God is presented, especially to children and young people, so that those to whom it is presented may be led to personal faith in the Lord Jesus Christ'.

At East Runton I had met both Nigel Sylvester, who then became the first SU staff worker for the whole of English-speaking West Africa, and John Dean, who in November 1958 became the first SU staff worker for Nigeria. Nigel visited us not long after our arrival in Ibadan; 'a good Runton reunion' he wrote in our visitors book on the 11th October. He encouraged us to become involved in this fledgling SU work. Pam agreed to be responsible for the distribution of bible notes and cards: the second aim of SU was then, and still is, 'to promote thoughtful Bible reading amongst people of all ages.' The cards simply listed the passages of scripture which enabled one to read through the whole bible in a year; they were without explanatory notes. Being cheap, cards had already been in use in the country for a number of years. The circulation of the SU Notes was expected to increase, especially with the appointment of a staff worker.

I was asked to join the very small SU committee responsible for 'overseeing' the work. This was made up almost entirely of expatriates. I can remember just one Nigerian on it – Abraham Akanni who, I think, was the treasurer. I was asked to take this task over from Abraham when he moved away from Ibadan, which is where the committee was based. This turned out not to be a good appointment and I later persuaded the much more suitable Jeff McLachlan (Chief Accountant at the University Teaching

Hospital) to 'sort out the mess the accounts were in' and take over the position. Jeff became, until his death in 2018, a good friend and was both Professor of Tax at Napier University in Edinburgh as well as, for a time, Treasurer for SU Scotland.

John Dean, after a year or so, made our bungalow on the Nigerian College campus his 'home'. The spare bedroom became the SU Nigeria office and bookstore, so much so that John, when not travelling around the country, which was most of his time, usually slept on our veranda – under a mosquito net of course. With no room in the spare bedroom (too many books!) it was in any case much cooler than sleeping indoors.

John Dean in action!

When John left to take up a similar position working for the Fellowship of Christian Students of Northern Nigeria (FCS) in 1961 he was followed by Peter Edwards, then Jane Sutton and in November 1964 by Bill Roberts, who concentrated on the Eastern Region. Bill remained there through most of the Biafran war encouraging the SU groups and becoming involved in refugee work.

The demand for SU Bible notes increased; I see the circulation of notes and cards was about 500 when we arrived and over 3,000 when Pam handed over to the staff at the newly opened SU Office when we left at the end of 1966. However, by that time SU Nigeria had begun to produce their own Notes – an annual one 'volume' pocket size publication called Daily Power. This was written and edited within the country, not without difficulties on the publication side, by 'the 'Daystar Press' in Ibadan. As we shall see, Daily Power now has an enormous Africa-wide circulation and is one of the success stories of SU Nigeria.

Pam enjoyed her task of SU Note distribution in those early days, and in order to meet the individuals reading these notes we sometimes called on them and delivered them by hand if, that is, they lived within a reasonable distance from our home. In Nigeria this informal calling on people without an invitation is termed 'calling to greet'. Usually however distribution involved visits to the Post Office which fortunately was positioned on the campus. When we commenced an Africa prayer meeting in our present home in 2006 a couple, who became strong supporters of the meeting, had worked in the north of the Nigeria in the 1950s and had been among those who had received their Daily Notes from the Post Office at Nigerian College Ibadan.

We also got involved in SU camps – residential but certainly not under canvas, as is sometimes the case in Britain. These were always held in suitable Secondary Schools throughout the Western region; once again most of the staff at these camps were expatriates, usually schoolteachers. These were often also the originators and leaders of the SU group in the school in which they taught. After Independence in 1960 it was said that, because of the rapidly increasing number of new schools, the Government was looking for teachers and 'would go anywhere to find them'. Many opportunities therefore. Before we arrived in the country, many Christian teachers had gone to Nigeria from Britain. It was certainly the presence of SU groups in schools that later contributed to the growth of the Christian Unions in the universities, a situation similar to that in Scotland today.

The last SU camp we attended was as a family. This was at a school (Oyemekun Grammar School, Akure) where we had often previously stayed - since our friend, an Anglican minister, Richard Childerstone, was on the staff. There, one of the camp team, Michael Oye, who later joined the regional SU staff team, talked to our son Stephen, then aged five, and shared with him about trusting Jesus as his Saviour. So, like me, our eldest son first responded to the 'good news' about Jesus from the lips of an African. And, just like his mother at a SU mission, albeit in a very different place – on the beach at Frinton-on-Sea – responded as a child to the love of Christ.

Scripture Union boys camp, Fiditi, Western Region Nigeria, 1960

Nigel Sylvester had pioneered SU work in Ghana (where he was based), Sierra Leone, Nigeria and also Gambia, where later Jim and Muriel McNair, already active in SU in Scotland, made a significant contribution to the fledgling work. Nigel had the foresight to set up SU Councils/committees in each of these countries to oversee the dual activities of evangelism and bible reading. In a large country such as Nigeria the Council was made up of representatives of some of the missionary societies (such as Qua Ibo and the Sudan United Mission) working in different parts of the giant country. Because of the distances involved the Nigerian SU Council met just once a year.

The President was Dr Ishaya Audu, a Hausa from Northern Nigeria. When we first arrived in Ibadan, Ishaya was based at the University Teaching Hospital in Ibadan. Note my summary of his moving life story in Appendix 4.

Because the Council only met once a year a 'Standing Committee' was set up based in Ibadan. I became the last expatriate Chairperson of this before handing over in 1965/66 to Gideon Olajide. Gideon became the Bishop of Ilesha and then of Ibadan. By the time this occurred the majority of the Committee were Nigerian. These included Peter Odumosu, a Principal Private Secretary in the Western Region Civil Service, a brilliant and godly man who sadly died in 1966, Lillian Durodola (the wife of a surgeon at UCH Ibadan) and Isaac George as Prayer Secretary, a gifted mature student who later became Professor of Linguistics at the University of Ibadan. He had studied at the University of Ife, previously the Nigerian College of Science and Technology where I had taught from 1958 to 1961. He later wrote of his experience there, 'My time at Ife was a time of great spiritual blessing, the warm fellowship with more mature Christians and outstanding men of God, and the joy of being used of the Lord to lead the young Christian Union'. I discovered that Isaac was born, as I was, in 1933. It was not uncommon that students were older than the staff that taught them!

The SU General Secretary from 1966 was another outstanding man, Daniel Onwukwe, who we first got to know as an undergraduate (and later a post-graduate student) in Ibadan. Daniel took over as Secretary from Dr John Powell. In his book[1] Emmanuel Oladipo has written particularly of Daniel's influence for Christ in the Eastern Region of Nigeria after the Biafran war ended.

---

[1] Emmanuel Oladipo, *Exemplary Christians in the Nigerian Public Square*, Church of Nigeria Missionary Society, 2018.

The official handing over to Scripture Union Nigeria from SU England. Nigel Sylvester and the Revd Gideon Olajide, May 1966. SU Nigeria becomes 'independent'

So, in a few years what was called 'Nigerianisation' had taken place and SU Nigeria was progressing rapidly to autonomy. This indeed happened before we had left the country just prior to the start of the civil war in December 1966. Two significant changes took place in SU that year. The first was the completion of the SU Headquarters. Clearly, it was now inappropriate for the SU office to be in anyone's spare bedroom, and with Peter Odumosu's help, some Crown land was purchased near to the University on the road into the city and in 1965 building commenced under the supervision of David Calcott. It was completed with a service of dedication the following year.

The other major change, also in 1966, was that SU Nigeria became autonomous, 'independent' from London. This was because the work was now financially viable and not dependent solely on funds sent from England. The young people who had come through SU groups in schools and then the university, had graduated and were working, many in teaching, and were now able and willing to support the work that had been such a help to them in their own Christian walk. The Council and the regional committees were now functioning well, ably led and in the right hands.

Nigel Sylvester, Kayode Adesogan, Dr Ishaya Audu and David Calcott at the SU 'handover', May 1966

It was a moving occasion when Nigel Sylvester, on behalf of SU London, passed over responsibility for SU work in Nigeria to its President (Dr Ishaya Audu) and Chairman (Revd Gideon Olajide) at a ceremony held in the chapel of the Theological College. The hand over was now complete. When a few years later I was a member of the Scottish Scripture Union Council, I was surprised to learn that the very established SU Scotland 'was part of England' and responsible to SU in London. How this changed – and the consequences – is another story. So, in my life I have seen the 'birth pains' of two quite different SU movements becoming indigenous. In my opinion, the long history of SU Scotland also demands to be told.

A few years later I was able to return to Ibadan, visit the SU Office and sit in on a meeting of the Western Regional Committee. For me, sitting there quietly and just listening, this was a time of wonder, praise and thankfulness at what God had accomplished. What an enormous privilege to have seen this happen. John Dean's comment on the early years of SU in Nigeria was spot on – 'one planted, another watered but it was God who gave the increase.'

All the above was very many years ago! I wondered what the situation of SU Nigeria was today, well over fifty years later. For this information I made contact with Niyi Daramola (the Coordinator for the African Region of Worldlink International Ministries UK) and with Emmanuel Oladipo: two key figures within SU, one of whom now resides in Scotland; the other in England!

The word is growth. As a grain of mustard seed, said Jesus of the kingdom of God. The soil of Africa is clearly a good place for the mustard seed of the gospel to flourish. When Bill Roberts was airlifted out of the country he was the last expatriate SU staff worker. 'Blacklisted' by the victorious Nigerian government he relocated to Sierra Leone where he had a remarkable ministry – and found himself in yet another war situation.

Ten years later I note that in Nigeria there were nine staff, all of them Nigerians. Today this has increased to thirty-seven travelling staff, ten regional coordinators and five Heads of Departments for a SU operating landscape of 4,707 secondary schools, over 1000 primary schools and nearly 150 higher institutions. Over 120,000 students are involved (called 'members' in former days) and over 7,000 undergraduates. Camps, a key operation in the 1950s and 60s, are no longer functioning for the very practical reason that registration is difficult; sending the booking forms to schools and asking for returns in time proved impossible. If you plan to run a camp for 20 registrants and 50 turn up, or for 50 and 100 turn up, one can imagine the chaos – and the headaches for the camp organisers – and for the cooks! It proved difficult to keep up the former standards; the camper to leader ratios and the required personal attention for each camper. However, in the last recorded long-vacation camps nearly 70,000 students were reached!

Present activities involve rallies and morning devotions during assemblies in schools, the training of student leaders, workshops for school leavers and, a relic from 'former days', squashes. It is in the publishing and distribution of SU bible notes and other devotional literature that the growth has been most pronounced. Daily Power production has taken off exponentially – now well over a quarter of a million copies. Until the internet took over.

Emmanuel concludes that SU, despite its many deficiencies, has been a powerful instrument in building up the Nigerian church, having produced a wide range of Christian leaders with a good and balanced knowledge of the Scriptures serving in all denominations and in the secular world. From that tiny seed so much fruit. He concludes with praise to God for 'the day of small things' and gives thanks to the Lord, who has been pleased to bless in marvellous ways. 'To God be the glory, great things He has done'!

Chapter 16
Autumn in Germany

One of the benefits of working at the University of Ibadan (note the change in name a couple of years after Independence) was that staff could take a 'sabbatical' every three years or so. So, we might call this an 'advanced sabbatical' – after three years rather than seven. In 1964 I was due such a time away from the University; one term could be taken. I decided to take this from June 1964 until January 1965, the start of the second term. So, one term away from teaching. The question was where to spend this time. My first idea was to spend it at the American University in Beirut in Lebanon, a city we had visited, and liked, in 1959. This was not possible since the research group had been disbanded, but another suggestion was Düsseldorf in Germany, where the Head of the Physiologisches Institut der Medizinischen Akademie was a renowned worker on coronary blood flow regulation, Professor Dr Wilhelm Lochner. He was clearly intrigued by this request to work with him and gladly accepted, partly I think, because he would then have a native English speaker in the department at a time when the scientific community in Europe wanted scientific papers published in my own native language; his previous publications had all been in German. He published his first paper in English with me.

Another advantage of working in Ibadan (there were also many disadvantages!) was that on the journey back to the UK at the end of each university teaching year, it was possible to 'stop off' somewhere in Europe, buy a car and use it for the period of leave. Useful with a family. It could then be taken back to Nigeria by boat. Certainly not overland, although a few adventurous souls tried this, driving across the Sahara. Once back in Nigeria it could then be sold as there would be many would-be buyers in Ibadan for European cars.

To buy a car would enable us to have transport for the whole seven-month period we would be away. We decided to pick up a Renault 4 in Paris, drive it to Düsseldorf, then use it in England over the summer and Christmas periods. On the way we had a few days holiday in Geneva where we toured the Lake in a boat that burst into flames: we had to be rescued by rowing boat. Our elder son Stephen, four and a half at the time, still remembers this incident because in the panic that ensued the passengers moved away from the flames to the other side of the boat, resulting in the imminent danger of the boat capsizing; Lake Geneva is quite deep and we were a long way from the shore.

We then flew to Paris and picked up the car in the centre of the city. Never, if you can help it, drive in Paris. We managed to exit the city but had to return because we had forgotten the insurance certificate – fortunately before we reached the German border. This was long before the EU. It meant a return to the city centre and finding a place to park. Impossible. I had then to park in a forbidden zone and duly received a fine. This we ignored. It is now presumably forgotten by the authorities since we have yet to hear from them. Leaving Paris and France in some haste we drove to Düsseldorf via the Ardennes and so to the Rhine.

Düsseldorf, probably now even more so, was in those days a very affluent city. It proved very difficult to find accommodation especially with a four-year old child. Nothing available in the city itself and all we could find was a very small flat in an old block of flats in a village called Hitdorf-am-Rhine, about twenty kilometres from the hospital where I was due to work. No public transport, so the Renault was really needed. The flat had just one room, doubling as both sitting and dining areas as well as the bedroom, together with a minute kitchen. Shared toilet, no hot water, bath, shower or heating. No one spoke English in the village yet Pam managed wonderfully. One German word that sticks in her memory is that for an electric fuse; the fuses kept blowing due to the demands of heating by a borrowed electric fire. Heating and cooking could not happen at the same time! The sleeping arrangements were such that we put Stephen to bed in the kitchen and then, when we too retired, bring him in across the corridor to the 'main' room.

The whole block was so cold, even in autumn, that soon after we arrived, a knock on the door summoned me to the flat above to check the health of a very elderly man. The room was freezing and the man had died. No NHS in Germany at that time, despite the fact that a defeated Germany was economically recovering from the war much faster than Britain. It seemed to us that little care was taken of the elderly; the unknown man in the flat above was simply left to die in the deep cold of his almost bare room.

We made good friends during those autumn months in Germany. We worshipped at the Anglican Church, set up to cater for the spiritual needs of the local army garrison of which the Minister, Mr Blount was also the Chaplain. Such a wonderfully hospitable family, many meals were taken at the Rectory, whilst Pam and Stephen went there each week for a bath. I had no need because the Department in which I worked had a shower room. We also made good friends with a young couple who lived in Bonn, I think he (Chris) worked at the embassy. The routine was that after the morning service they came to us for lunch and Christian fellowship, as we were on the route to their home in Bonn. I also had the key to the church so that I could play the organ; I remember filling the church with the sound of the slow movement of Bruckner's Symphony number eight well arranged for organ – the orchestra was not missed.

One evening I ventured to the opera house to see an opera for the very first time. Little did I realise what this visit would lead to a lifelong fondness for opera with hundreds of visits to opera houses all over the world from Los Angeles to Vienna and from Sydney to Milan. And many places in between. And to frequent visits to the two opera houses in London over perhaps a period of fifty years. The opera on that eventful evening was Rusalka by Dvořák. This also happened to be the last major opera I saw, a wonderful performance in Prague. Due to the covid shutdown and to age those nights at the opera are now over. Dvořák's Rusalka is special because our good friends from Prague, Boja Ostadal and Frank Kolar once took us to Dvořák's last home and to the lake that was probably the stimulus for this opera which is about a water nymph – and the moon.

I had chosen well. The Düsseldorf department was excellent and we did good work on the possible regulation of coronary blood flow by kinin polypeptides; the prime candidate for this long-searched for mediator was at that time adenosine. However, kinins now seemed a more likely candidate being several hundred times more active at increasing coronary blood flow. Later we followed up this work in Glasgow. However, the Düsseldorf department was very regulated; Lochner was a professor of the old school. For example, there was a certain procedure for going through doors. Lochner first but who would go next? Hans-Jürgen Hirche (the next most senior, equivalent perhaps to a Reader in a British University) or even me? The staff were never too sure about that! Then all the staff had to attend the Professor's lectures, sitting in the front row in their white coats, one of them designated to clean the blackboard (remember this was the 1960's) when 'the Chief' had finished his point and was wanting to move on to the next words or diagram. We all, except if an experiment was in progress, had to go to lunch at the same time led by the 'Chief', the meal eaten very quickly and with me always the slowest. Those thick stodgy German lunches! The conversation always about politics about which I knew nothing.

At least initially. I did wonder what Herr Professor Dr Wilhelm Lochner did in the war but I never asked. Years later, when I revisited the Department from Glasgow, I had a good meal with Lochner and later attended his (Lutheran) funeral. I became friendly with Hirche who became the head of Department in Köln (Cologne). On another later visit, I was taken out by his wife and daughters for a meal, who sadly chose American (McDonalds), all the rage in Germany (of all places) at the time. The evening was better. We went to the Opera! One of the daughters, about ten at the time, was intent on showing me her collection of teas of which she was very proud; it would have taken until she was married to have tasted all of them! I was sad to discover that Hans-Jürgen died quite young. They were always very kind to us during our time in Germany as were our church friends especially the Blount family. We wonder what has happened to them.

This was the first northern autumn for us since the one in Brighton in 1957. And, of course, it was Stephen's first ever. He was intrigued by the fallen dead leaves, crunching them underfoot in his Wellington boots, by a visit to the zoo in Köln and by our weekly shopping there, so different to our experiences in Nigeria. Real Superstores! The one advantage of the flat was that it overlooked the river Rhine which was always very busy. Stephen enjoyed watching from the window the variety of boats of all sizes ploughing their busy ways up and down the river hooting as they went.

At last, the time came to leave and return on the ferry to Harwich from the Hook of Holland to the family in England. Christmas was spent that year (1964) with both sets of parents in their homes on the Essex coast. At that point we also changed our church membership from Gunnersbury to Frinton Free Church (actually a Baptist Church) although we did not remain in membership there for very long. Stephen also saw his first snow! Then, in January it was time for us to return to Nigeria. Or so we thought. But there was an unexpected twist, which takes us to the next part of the story.

Chapter 17
A Time of Separation

In January 1965, when we were due to return to Nigeria after the autumn in Germany and Christmas in England, there was another unexpected event. On January 4th at a visit to our GP we discovered that Pam was pregnant. Because of our concerns that the antimalarial we were due to take before our flight could have been responsible for the early miscarriages, which had occurred several times in the years since the birth of Stephen in 1960, it was decided to delay her and Stephen's journey back to Ibadan. 'As it happened' this turned out to have been a wise decision, so Stephen commenced his primary school education at the local school in Kirby Cross.

This is not the place for a scientific digression about our views on this but later, in the 1980s, concerns were raised, long after we required antimalarial drugs, that pyrimethamine (Daraprim) can be teratogenic and the WHO concluded that it should be avoided in early pregnancy.[1] There had been no studies regarding pyrimethamine and early miscarriages in the late 1950s, a time we were taking the drug. However, we were not the only couple to have had this problem among the expatriate community in Ibadan.

I returned to Ibadan alone on the 11th, leaving just £28-2-0 in our bank account – these were still the days of pounds, shillings and pence! Little did we realise that it would be five months before we saw one another again, the most time spent apart in over sixty years of married life.

The pregnancy proved to be difficult and it was certainly safer for Pam to remain in the UK, living with her parents throughout the whole of the pregnancy. However, that separation for five months was hard, especially for Pam, and the only way to communicate with each other was by way of the often unreliable, Nigerian postal service. Of course, there were frequent letters back and forth over

---

[1] Martindale, *The Complete Drug Reference, 32nd edition,* Pharmaceutical Press, London, 1999.

that period many of which are in safe keeping. They tell a moving story, certainly for us.

There were things about being in Ibadan for those five months that were memorable. Firstly, it underlined the strength of Nigerian hospitality! For me, living alone for the first time, there were invitations, both Nigerian and expatriate, for 'chop' three or four times a week to over a dozen different homes. Christian hospitality especially is heart-warming – when you are on the end of it! But our own house at 1 Ijoma Road was also 'open'; over that time I nearly always had folk living with me. These included Reuben Ariko (for over a month preparing for university entrance), John Dean, Bill Roberts and Richard Earnshaw Smith. Richard was the Chaplain to the Bishop of Lagos. A short time later he was tragically killed in the BOAC VC10 crash. Reuben even tried some of my home cooking. Of a sort! I tried to make rice pudding with rice that had already been cooked. Reuben had never tasted anything quite like that!

I was immediately in the thick of things. The 'squashes' were now held in our garden every fortnight, with over a hundred attending, the first of these just a few days after I arrived with Stephen Smalley (later Dean of Chester) speaking. Beforehand the girls of the CU had taken charge of the kitchen to prepare the refreshments, much to the consternation of the resident 'chef', chairs had been brought in and the lights had been put up. All was ready. And, in our absence in Germany, Isaac George had started similar squashes at the newly founded University of Ife (Ibadan campus), the former Nigerian College where we had first lived.

There always seemed to be much to do. Apart from my duties in the department, there were various committees (UCH, SU), organisation of the distribution of Fact and Faith films and preparations for the next edition of Daily Power SU's one volume, top pocket size, bible reading notes. Then there were attempts by Alan Hay to teach me squash, occasional games of tennis, rehearsals (many required) for the forthcoming performances of Handel's Messiah in the Chapel of the Resurrection, goodbyes to several friends, like the Trews, who were leaving the country, and meetings of the University music circle. There was time for a few days break at Oyemekun Grammar School in Akure with our old friend Richard Childerstone (a long-term missionary and Anglican minister from Norfolk) listening to Mozart and Schubert on long-playing records whilst sitting outside in his garden, the music coming from inside his bungalow.

The Ibadan University Christian Union had been formed and was growing rapidly with bible study groups in each hall of residence and all-night prayer meetings. Several buses were now needed to take students to the Sunday afternoon services at the SIM African Challenge campus at Molete. It seemed to me that a revival was happening. What, I wondered constitutes a spiritual revival? In many ways it reminded me of what happened during the time when we ourselves were students when, in such a small College, many came to Christ, especially in the year below our own.

There were letters from 'home' once or twice a week about the progress of the pregnancy and Pam's need to rest, Stephen's experiences at school and the delights of the coming of Spring, Stephen's first ever and for Pam, the first experience of that season for seven years. Then, on Good Friday, came the so sad and unexpected news from a visit by Pam to her GP, that in his opinion, the foetus was no longer alive. This coincided, earlier that week, with the sudden and unexpected death during Holy Week of a Christian member of the academic staff, the statistician George Hodnett; just a few days earlier, on Passion Sunday, we had been in his home for a bible study thinking around the question – 'does God care'.

Now, burials need to be carried out quickly in the tropics. The day for it coincided with Muslim holidays and so it was Dr Norman Allan and I who needed to collect the coffin in the early morning from the mortuary. We unscrewed the lid and lifted it to ascertain that it was indeed George's body and he was buried an hour later in the University cemetery; the temperature was 90 degrees in the shade.

Then, three days later on Easter Monday, came another letter telling me that the hospital consultant was unsure about things and that he would meet with Pam again a week later. He then discovered that the foetus was small but alive! Pam has always said that our daughter was 'a miracle baby'. And, on that same Easter Monday there was a Thanksgiving Service for George in the packed University Chapel of the Resurrection. Stephen Smalley led the service and George's widow Hazel had asked me to preach; a wonderful opportunity to do so on the day after we had celebrated the resurrection of our Lord Jesus. A few weeks later, after the student examinations, I left Ibadan to re-join the family to await the birth of our second child.

Deborah Joy (how appropriate a name!) was born in Colchester on September 3rd. We remembered that this was the day WW2 had broken out twenty-six years previously. As we had no phone, which was quite usual in those days, the news from the hospital came to me via the local shop and an excited, fast runner! Could have been Africa. But, without the drums!

Chapter 18
Dangerous Times

I have only recently realised how dangerous it was to be in Nigeria during the 1960s – especially for Nigerians. Most of the period we lived there saw considerable political unrest. The declaration in 1962 of a State of Emergency, the rioting and violence that followed the 1965 election and the two military coups that occurred in 1966. Of course, we were sheltered in the University campus (with armed guards at the entrance) but friends and colleagues in the surrounding rural areas such as the teachers in secondary schools and the travelling Scripture Union staff often had difficulties with multiple roadblocks and intimidation.

This is not the place to discuss the complexities of Nigeria's political landscape or the differences between the NCNC, NPC, UPGA, NNDP and NEPU, although you do not have to be a great detective to gather what the initial N stands for. However, some brief outline would help (perhaps!) to explain the background for these dangerous times.

The period from Independence in 1960 to 1962 was fairly peaceful but trouble erupted following the State of Emergency declared that year following the disputed census figures (in 1962 and again in 1963) especially in the Northern region. Stories were told of sheep, or even the legs of sheep, being counted! The Governor of the Western Region dismissed the Premier and Chief Obafemi Awolowo, the leader of the opposition. Awolowo, who was alleged to have conspired to overthrow the Federal Government, was convicted and imprisoned well out of harm's way in Calabar in the far southeast of the country. The emergence of a two-party system followed: but in 1964 the elections were boycotted by the Eastern Region.

It was the build up to the 1965 elections in Western State that was the trigger for considerable unrest. There was political violence, arson, the killing of political opponents, because the ruling party, led by Chief S.A.L. Akintola was alleged to have massively rigged the previous election result and had won by default. This was greeted with general pandemonium and mass revolt, including among students. His initials (adjusted to SLA) became, in Yoruba, Ese-Ole – 'feet of a robber'. The ruling party, sensing the aggressive mood in the country decided to eliminate all opposition. In particular, the dissident academic sector, in their ivory tower, were to be silenced and humiliated.

There is a touch of humour about the 1965 election which reads rather like a combination of a Feydeau farce and a cold war spy story by John Le Carre. This account is well told in Wole Soyinka's book *Ibadan.*[1] Soyinka, a future Nobel Prize winner in literature, the first African to do so, was on the staff of the University as a Research Fellow in the School of Drama, when I too was on the staff: I probably met him when we collected our post. We had already seen some of his plays at the University Theatre, plays such as *The Palm Wine Drinkard* and *The Road*. These were not understandable to us, being in Yoruba, although his wonderful story about his early life (in English!) is, to quote the New York Times 'a classic'.[2]

The Theatre, run by the School of Drama, put on a variety of plays during our time in Ibadan: I remember, for example, an astonishing performance of Ibsen's *Peer Gynt* as well as *Twelfth Night*, *Measure for Measure* and *Arms and the Man*; but especially memorable was the visit in 1959 of the company from the Sheffield Crucible, with a very young Judy Dench, referred to earlier.

The corruption in Nigeria was unbelievable. Traditional rulers who did not comply were chased from their thrones or had salaries reduced to derisory levels (one penny a year for one of them), funds were diverted to government officials, American cars of enormous length with kaleidoscopic fins and wings (the masses declared that 'their wealth had taken off'), parties at which champagne flowed, extravagant mansions, illegal land purchases, overseas 'official'

---

[1] Wole Soyinka, *Ibadan, The Penkelemes Years, A Memoir: 1946-1965*, Methuen London, 1994.

[2] Wole Soyinka, Ake, *The Years of Childhood*, Arrow Books, London, 1981. Just as good is the sequel – *Isara, a Voyage Around 'Essay'*, Methuen London, 1990.

tours (or shopping), children of the elite sent to Eton or Harrow. Public wealth and the great resources of the region (such as cocoa) became the proceeds of outright robbery and placed in the hands of Lebanese and Indian merchants. National political decadence. Opposition outlawed. Police laid siege to villages in the Western Region, they shot up schools and markets, rounded up the wives and children of the 'insurgents' and took them away as hostages, villages were torched and crops destroyed, community leaders spent weeks in prison cells.

Of course, the result of the 1965 election was a forgone conclusion. 'However you vote this Government will remain in power.' 'Who needs the people to vote for us, the angels in heaven have already casted their votes for our party!' Results declared before the votes had been counted.

The Premier (Akintola) had made a recorded message on tape, thanking the people for their support! Soyinka made an alternative taped message which he smuggled into Broadcasting House to be substituted for Akintola's broadcast to the nation. Soyinka entered the deserted Broadcasting House – empty except for radio engineers from the Eastern Region who were responsible for the broadcast and putting in the Premier's tape. Soyinka hid in the Record Room (which, as a frequent broadcaster of his poetry and plays, he knew well) until just before the appointed time for the broadcast when he entered the studio armed with an ancient gun, 'threatened' the radio engineer Mr Oshin (with whom he had a friendly conversation) and substituted his tape for the Premier's. Instead of the Premier's 'official' vote of thanks to the people for voting for him what came over the airwaves was: 'This is the voice of the people, the true people of the nation. And they are telling you Akintola, get out, and take your renegades with you . . .' Having made sure his tape was going out live, Soyinka ran for the get-away car, driven by a young man who had no driving licence; they drove through the night to the safety of Nsukka in the Eastern Region.

Of course, later he was arrested – or rather he gave himself up, and the farcical trial took place. The defence counsel (at the invitation of Amnesty International) was none other than the advocate and writer John Mortimer. In his hilarious autobiography (*Clinging to the Wreckage*) he describes the scene in Court – 'black faces with white wigs and in pinstripes' with their wriggling bare feet sending messages to the judge (toe language). Soyinka was acquitted but, after disappearing for a time, was rearrested and imprisoned.

These events took place whilst we were safely inside the University compound. But, as I think back, and given the hostility of the Government to academia at the time, things might have been very different as they had been in other parts of unpredictable Africa during that period. The situation was not easy for those expatriates who lived in small towns in other parts of the Western Region or even in the larger cities; this was the time I drove outside the campus to 'rescue' our missionary friends from the African Challenge (SIM) compound on the Lagos road. Quite unnerving times.

Chapter 19
Journeying Home

We left Nigeria in December 1966 after spending over eight years there – on and off. Just prior to this I had been invited to my first international conference. This was held in the 'Aula Magna' of Milan University at the beginning of October and organised by the renowned Istituto di Cardiologica Sperimentale under the chairmanship of the doyen of coronary research, Dr Donald Gregg (from the Walter Reed Army Institute of Research in Washington, DC). Surprisingly, he had read a review I had been invited to write for the *American Journal of Cardiology*. In order to take part, I received an air ticket from Lagos to Milan via London. Milan was a good opportunity to meet the key workers in the field including those I had worked with in Düsseldorf two years earlier. Routing through London also gave me the opportunity to purchase warmer clothes for the family's forthcoming initiation to the Scottish winter.

During the weeks prior to leaving Nigeria there were a number of 'farewells' by various friends and organisations including a charity football match against female opposition. This proved to be my last active participation in a game I loved. The 'farewells' included one given by the Nigeria Scripture Union at which we were presented with the ebony carving pictured here. The Reverend (now Bishop) Gideon Olajide, who had taken over from me as Chairman of the SU Council, explained to us the significance of the carving. It shows two disabled men, the smaller one (with crippled feet) was sitting on the shoulders of the taller man who was clearly blind. Apart, they were both 'incomplete'; one could not walk, the other could not see. However, together they could both walk and see. It illustrated the importance of collaboration and togetherness in Christian work. Even a thousand or so miles apart and on different continents, we could continue to support one another in prayer; alone we were incomplete, together we could continue to serve one another in the Lord.

I spoke for the last time at the Hospital and Student services and at the squashes organised by the two universities. At the SIM Challenge student farewell service, which included communion, there was a time of open prayer at which the SU staff worker Mike Oye thanked God that in my teaching and examining I was 'severe'! By this he meant I set high (severe) standards. I think! These farewells were very emotional; we were leaving a country which had come to mean much to us; indeed, a Nigerian member of our church fellowship still regards us as 'Nigerians'. Over the years we had developed many deep friendships, some of which are retained after more than fifty years.

A leaving gift from SU Nigeria. A parable about the church worldwide (see text)

We moved out of the university accommodation and spent the final few days staying with our friends Ken and Phyllis Bennett at the

SIM compound on the Lagos road. University transport took our loads, many wooden crates and a large number of oil drums (good for transporting fragile possessions) down to the docks in Apapa.

Ken, who seemed to know everybody, spoke to the customs officer who then cleared the loads without fuss: I had heard stories of over-enthusiastic officers making travellers unpack their cases for examination before letting them go. Chaos ensued. The reason being that there had been the unlawful 'export' of some of Nigeria's historical treasures (such as the Benin bronzes). There was one officious younger 'officer' who

Farewell Nigeria! A student service at the Africa Challenge Chapel, end of the university session 1966

told us we could not use the passenger lift and there was a scuffle in which his shirt got caught in the lift door and was accidentally torn by an accompanying friend, Dr Graham Thorpe. This incident is recalled, with more additions each time the story is told, each time we meet. Ken's deep friendship with everybody, and his knowledge of the Yoruba language, was so much appreciated.

The plan had been to all travel together on the Elder Dempster SS 'Accra' but three days before we were due to leave our daughter Deborah, then just fifteen months, developed a high temperature. The medical advice was that, as the ship carried no doctor, she should not travel by sea. In the end, as our loads were already at the docks, the decision was made that I should still travel home by sea with Stephen, then aged six and a half, and Pam and Debbie should, after the infection had normalised following antibiotic treatment, return by air. This meant that they arrived home in Britain before Stephen and I did.

The sea journey by Elder Dempster lines had at one time been long used by missionaries coming to work along the coast of West Africa. This means of transport almost certainly ceased many years ago. Why come by boat taking two weeks when you could fly there in a few hours? But this misses the romance of a longish sea journey. Both Stephen and I greatly enjoyed the voyage. We sailed on December 5th, stopped at Takoradi in Ghana on the 7th, where traders came aboard with beautiful wooden furniture – we purchased an 'elephant table' and a table lamp. We were anchored outside Freetown in Sierra Leone on the 10th. Sadly, we were not allowed to disembark. Then sailing north, we stopped at Las Palmas on the 14th, where we had a day on shore and explored part of the island.

The journey through the notorious Bay of Biscay was rough, as one might expect in mid-December, and there were few down to breakfast. Except us! We landed in Liverpool on a dark wet morning on the 19th and were met on the quayside by Pam and Debbie. Together once again and ready (almost) to face life in Scotland, after a Christmas again spent with our parents on the Essex coast.

What does one do during a longish sea journey? Eat good meals, meet friendly passengers and crew and play deck games (table tennis, quoits) at least during the earlier part of the journey before we entered the Atlantic Ocean. Stephen spent a good deal of time in the swimming pool and looking for 'flying fish'. I discovered other Christians were on board, including a couple of missionary doctors, and we decided to meet in my cabin each day for prayer and bible study. I also had to prepare a series of bible reading notes on the book of Acts for the first edition of Daily Power for SU Nigeria.

I was glad to have taken this route home and sorry that Pam and Debbie had not been able to experience a means of travel which was most relaxing after those last few hectic days in Ibadan.

Chapter 20
Later Returns to Nigeria

I did not imagine that, when we left Nigeria after a stay of nearly nine years, I was ever likely to return. This raises in my mind the question as to whether it is ever a good idea to return to a situation that had once been a very special part of one's life, especially if that had been many years before. As an old long-playing vinyl record by the Medical Mission Sisters, once given to me by a Christian friend in Oklahoma says – 'Changing, times are changing . . .' What changes would I find, and would these take away from those intense and meaningful memories we had of our earlier years there? Perhaps sometimes it is best not to return. Just leave the memories and imaginations intact! As an example, we decided never to return to Israel, despite invitations to revisit. Why? Because that one and only visit in the early years of our married life had been so wonderful; so much so, that it could never to be repeated.

So, was it a good idea to return to our old 'hunting ground'? I think probably yes, mainly because it would mean meeting up with so many old friends. How were they doing after all those years?

The first of four invitations came during our initial year in Scotland. 'Jim, would you come back?' This invitation came, from a dear Christian friend, with the offer of a choice of two university chairs! And, it came at a particularly low point in our lives. We were going through the experience of 're-entry', well known to 'real' missionaries, and about which much has been written. This is the trauma of returning, perhaps to retire, after many years working in a different culture and climate. I think of some in that situation as I write.

The next invitation came in 1975 to revisit my former universities; there were now two of them; Nigerian College had become in the early 70s the University of Ife. The invitation came from the British Council, who would cover part of the costs involved. My own university in Glasgow gave permission. It meant that I was able to spend the best part of three months teaching:

perhaps even doing a little research in my old laboratory. It would be interesting to see how things had progressed, or otherwise, in the seven years since I had left. Especially also to see the Christian work in which we had been so much involved, Scripture Union and the student witness in the universities.

There was an additional reason for accepting the invitation. In Scotland we had become involved in the home ministry of two missionary societies working in Nigeria, the Sudan United Mission (SUM) – which later became, as now, Pioneers – and the Sudan Interior Mission (SIM) which had then changed to become 'Serving in Mission', ingeniously the initials remaining the same! Would I be willing, whilst in the country, to take the opportunity of visiting the fields in which these missions were working and encourage, as best I could, those who were working there and to report back to the Home Councils? The answer was yes!

Some things never change, the heat, the smells and the welcome. Another thing that had not changed was the state of the Lagos to Ibadan road. Just as dangerous. Why had I come, putting my life at risk with a family back home? Even worse was the stretch of road between Ibadan and Ife, described in my diary at the time as 'terrible'. And, when I did arrive there was no water and no electricity on the old site, the one at which we had made our first home back in 1958 when both were available! The swimming pool had water but was covered with a green slime. And, no nose pegs provided! My task at Ife was to help plan the syllabus for a new degree and, in Ibadan to teach physiology as my old department was short staffed. A few of the old staff remained, including one or to who had come out with us in 1958. Teaching was supplemented by temporary visiting staff from various UK universities like Bradford and Cardiff. At my 'other university' there were no students in the Medical School. This was just one of the several periods during which the students were on strike, a protest against the military government who were suspicious of activities in places of higher education. Indeed, the conditions in the universities were poor; the Government was no friend of higher education. The universities were grossly underfunded.

I attempted to record my lectures on audio tape (but remember this was over forty years ago). However, there was no tape and by the time it was again available the students, or some of them, had returned. Later water and electricity returned and even the swimming pool was cleaned. It was worth coming back after all!

Best of all, was to meet up with old friends especially former students who were now on the university staff. And, to see that the Christian witness was still progressing; many of the staff had been students at the time of the spiritual 'revival' in Ibadan in the sixties. The CU and the 'squashes' continued and I was able to participate by invitation at a meeting of the SU Western State Committee. Very impressive, SU is in good hands I felt. The right hands! I was able to meet up with Gideon Olajide, my successor as chairman of the SU Council, now Bishop of Ilesha and soon to become the Bishop of Ibadan.

I had meals with, and sometimes stayed with, Nigerian former students and with Alun and Mary Rees on leave from the University of Trent in Canada, who were so influential in the beginnings of Christian witness in the University of Ibadan. Years later I was to stay with them in Canada; we are still in contact with John Powell and with David and Barbara Trew, now into their nineties and also living in Canada. There is something very special about friendships made when young. This is surely because of the similar experiences we all passed through at the time, the unity of working together for Christ and our oneness in Him.

I preached most Sundays. At the University of Ife those who preach are required to sign a book. I found my own name several times in the book back in the 1950s and 60s. It was especially memorable to participate in the Sunday afternoon student services which had moved from the SIM African Challenge compound to the much more convenient (and beautiful) Chapel of Emmanuel Theological College which was situated 'next door' to the University.

I made visits to town in order to buy a Yoruba 'talking drum' (good for a children's talk at church!) but, like much bargaining, this needed a return visit before the price was acceptable to me. There was an attempt to sell me some giant snails, apparently a delicacy. I declined! But I did bargain for some colourful cloth, probably designed in Manchester. Petrol was difficult to obtain, despite Nigeria being a major oil producer, but I was able to visit Ilesha to bring greetings to the very elderly father of a son who lived in Glasgow who had asked me to 'see how my father is': he became very excitable, waving his arms in the air and praising his god (not mine!). I made another visit to Dr Pearson at the Wesley Guild Hospital, famous not only as a Methodist Mission hospital but also the centre for some excellent research in the surrounding villages on child development.

There was also a visit to Lagos, experiencing once again that dangerous road and horrific city traffic, staying with a former Nigerian colleague before catching a flight to Kaduna for a visit to the new medical school at the recently founded Ahmadu Bello University. Here I was met by an old friend Dr Ishaya Audu, the first President of SU Nigeria and a future Nigerian Foreign Minister when a while later the Military briefly handed over authority to civilian authorities. Ishaya's story is in Appendix 4. I just missed another old friend Dr Eldred Parry, Dean of the University Medical Faculty, later knighted for his services to medical education in Africa. There were still more contacts with former students still active in Christian witness.

I was then taken to Jos for a series of meetings with SUM missionaries, some of whom had stayed with us in Bearsden during UK deputation. Among these were David and Bridget Williams (David later taught at the High School of Glasgow – his story is also told elsewhere) and Lucille Rose. Lucille's sister Margaret would come from Edinburgh by bus and train in her eighties to the Bearsden Africa prayer meeting held in our home. That shows some commitment to prayer! Sadly, when Margaret died the service of thanksgiving for her long life could not be held in the church she had attended for the whole of her life because of a church 'split'.

I also made visits to see most of the activities of the Mission; Faith and Farm, the Theological Seminary of Northern Nigeria (TCNN) in Bukuru (where, years before, we had left our first car), Hillcrest, formerly a school for the children of SUM missionaries but now open to all, to Gindiri (where at Christmas 1960 Stephen had taken his first steps) and to the mission hospital at Vom. It was here I witnessed Ifor Thomas perform a Manchester repair, a vaginal fistula and a ureter transplantation all in one day! At the Jos church I heard Emmanuel Oladipo preach powerfully; he was to become the SU leader for the whole of Africa. He now lives with his family in England.

These were the days towards the end of SUM missionary activity in Nigeria, begun over a hundred years previously. We were once present at an SUM annual event in Edinburgh, held at the same room of the church at which, at a meeting in 1904 chaired by Dr Alexander Whyte, the SUM was inaugurated. How moving to view the Minute Book of that event. When we first arrived in Scotland, we got to know Lillian Burt the daughter of one of the first four missionaries sent out in 1904 to that part of Northern Nigeria.

Now, in 2020 the story has come full circle; missionaries from Nigeria are in Britain to share the gospel with a needy people. Only last week on Scottish TV there was the account of two Nigerian Catholic priests who had been told by their bishop in Nigeria to relocate to two vacant churches north of Inverness! And, they were wonderfully welcomed – 'these black priests' - to an area which had not had a minister to care for them for many years. Full circle indeed.

The last part of my return to Nigeria was to Kano, where Pam and I had first landed in 1958 on route to Ibadan. Here I had been invited to visit missionaries of the SIM, to minister in two of their churches and to visit a village that had not been reached with the gospel. This was special; we sat around the village well and I told a simple story (by translation of course) based on another well, to the folk who had gathered out of interest to meet these 'white people from another land'. It must have been like that a hundred years before. So, even in 1975 there were still many in Nigeria who, despite much missionary activity, had never heard the Good News about Jesus. There still are.

Last Visits

One year after the 1975 visits (there were two of them to Nigeria that year) I was asked to return to examine students at the University of Ife. I took the opportunity, at the invitation of the British Council, to revisit Ghana. I had been there just once before, at a PAFES (Pan African Fellowship of Evangelical Students) meeting in 1965 – the occasion when I drove the wrong way up a one-way street in Accra with the permission of the Chief of Police who was sitting in the back seat!

I left for Lagos the day after examining at the University of Edinburgh. What a difference Edinburgh is to Ife! This time the journey from the airport in Ikeja to Ife took all of four hours. The distance is only 130 miles. That Lagos Ibadan road again! I made another visit to Ibadan to see friends and, among many other invitations to homes, was asked by the Professor of Anatomy, Ade Grillo for an evening meal. When I was on the medical faculty we had had our differences; so this was somewhat of a surprise – and an opportunity. I do not remember much about the conversation but he was open to the things of faith and certainly we talked about music. He had both a grand piano and a clavichord – not the usual things you would normally find in a Nigerian home. I played part of Schubert's final great B flat Sonata for him. Strange to hear Schubert, let alone play Schubert, in tropical Africa!

The return journey, back from the Ibadan campus of the University of Ife to the airport in Lagos (Ikeja), took well over four hours. In 1958 it had taken just two. There were problems with the flights to Accra, both flight delays and overbooking. The crowd at the booking desk arguing in Yoruba, offering 'dash' to reserve a seat, was too much. I found a quiet place, sat down and prayed because it was important for me to be on that flight. Then a Nigerian approached me and, seeing that I had little baggage, offered help. He would make sure I was on the flight if I could help him with his baggage – he was clearly overweight. And, not only his baggage! Could we book in together? He explained what he was carrying (not drugs) and I agreed. How he managed to fight his way to the desk and persuade the booking clerk I do not know. Sharp elbows, language perhaps? Anything else? There are times when one feels quite impotent in dealing with problems, especially in a foreign country, and help is needed. On this occasion help was available and I took it. Answered prayer? I think so.

I was met at the airport in Accra by the British Council representative and stayed overnight in a plush colonial style residence before taking the internal flight north to Kumasi where I was met by Alfred Abaitey. Alfred was one of my first PhD students at Strathclyde and the story of how we missed the Nobel prize (?)

is told elsewhere. He and Dorothy were special friends back in Glasgow, as were the children. There was a tour of his Department at the Kumasi University of Science and Technology, just in time for a Departmental party Ghana style, where I also met other old friends from their days in Glasgow and who were instrumental in starting the Bearsden student 'squashes', Daniel and Lucy Gyane. There was a very active Staff Christian Fellowship at Kumasi and I spoke to a group of about thirty. These were very special times. It is still good to continue to keep in touch with these close friends by email; over the years, there has been deep suffering for both these dear families. I was presented with a chief's ceremonial stool, which made it back to Glasgow intact and is still in use. For ceremonial occasions!

Back next day in Accra I met up with some of the SIM missionaries and was invited to the Kolubu Hospital (where a friend from LIFCU days was still active) and to the SU House. Impressive. A fruitful and very pleasant visit. How much more relaxed Ghana is compared to Nigeria. Especially at the airports!

There was one really final visit to Nigeria. In September 1977 I was asked to be the examiner for a PhD student in Ibadan. It is a long way to go for a viva of about an hour and I think it was an opportunity (or excuse) given by the Head of the Pharmacology Department Dinah James for me to make one more visit. Whilst there I was asked to speak at a specially arranged meeting of the University Staff Christian Fellowship which included many of those who met at the Ijoma Road 'Squashes' in the 1960s. Still increasingly active in helping the student witness – and SU. Good also to hear a really impressive sermon on the Sunday at the University Chapel. I felt humbled and thankful for the deepening of the Christian lives of those I met – and re-met.

However, the Lagos road (although now an Expressway) was as bad as ever, with traffic jams at Ikorodu and over two hours to get through immigration and customs. Oh Nigeria!

Appendix 3
University College, Ibadan

The story of the university system in Nigeria, where I taught for several years, really begins very soon after the end of WW2. An enlightened UK Government (as it was in those days) through the Inter-University Council for Higher Education in the Colonies, sent the Vice-Chancellor of the University of Aberdeen, Sir William Hamilton, to Nigeria to investigate the possibility of setting up a university. This would be responsible for higher education in the whole of British West Africa (Ghana, Sierra Leone, Gambia as well as Nigeria), countries separated from one another by various French colonies. Quite a remit.

The original vision was that three universities would be established in the then British Colonies, the West indies, East Africa (Makerere University) and 'somewhere in West Africa'. Ghana was favoured by some but, being larger and more prosperous, Nigeria was chosen. Sir William visited Ibadan and, four miles outside the town and in dense bush, planted his walking stick in the ground and proclaimed 'here shall be the University of Nigeria'.

The first sod was turned on that spot in November 1948, a few months after the first students, 148 in number, had been admitted and housed in temporary accommodation. The first medical students were admitted three years later. This rapid progress was due to the energy of the first Principal and Vice Chancellor Sir Kenneth Mellanby.[1] Nigeria at that time had a population of about thirty million, much higher than its more go-ahead neighbour Ghana, which had 'achieved' independence in 1958: Nigeria had to wait until 1960. This was also the year of the birth of Stephen, our own 'independence baby'.

From the beginning, and at the time I joined the staff in 1961, degrees were awarded by the University of London, by means of a 'special relationship'. The examination papers were drafted in Ibadan and sent to London: the results of the Ibadan

[1] Kenneth Mellanby, *The Birth of Nigeria's University*, London, Methuen 1958.

students were often better than those in London itself. In my own subject (physiology) the external examiners, always from London University, included some eminent scientists such as Sir Henry Barcroft. This link with London continued until 1962 when it was reconstituted as the University of Ibadan and began to award its own degrees. The University Teaching Hospital, where many of the medical students did their clinical studies, was built a short distance away, on the site of the old military hospital and opened in 1957, the year before we arrived in the country.

The preclinical departments were housed on the new compound in 'temporary' accommodation in 1951. To my present knowledge these are still in use. The offices, including mine, and the laboratories were air conditioned, that is when the electricity supply was functioning. Research was well supported by the West African Medical Research Council and we had several scientific papers published in quality journals including the Lancet and Cardiovascular Research.

The University compound, covering an area of almost four square miles, designed by the eminent British architects Maxwell Fry and Jane Drew, was very attractive. I cannot do better than quoting from a former student and friend Kayode (Ezekiel) Adesogan, later a Professor in the Chemistry Department. He came to Ibadan in 1959 from one of the best schools in the country, Government College Keffi in Northern Nigeria. This is what he wrote:

> 'The campus landscape was beautiful to behold, the lawns well mowed, the entire campus was clean, with lush vegetation, it was evident that the authorities had taken great pains to ensure a decent environment, the student halls (of residence) were clean, the facilities and utilities all worked and one could almost eat in the toilets!' Kayode was also impressed with the hall meals – 'very good, enticing, three course lunches and dinners with 'a quarter of a chicken for Sunday lunch' and no washing up. Wednesday evening dinners were 'High Table' when the meals were even more sumptuous. Each student could submit ten clothes each week for washing and ironing and they would be returned at the end of the week neatly ironed. For me, I found the kingly treatment most fascinating and flattering'.

However, Kayode, when he retired in 2005, spoke of university education in Nigeria as 'bleak', with a downturn in Nigeria's economy, and the successive military governments playing scant regard for education. With universities 'sprouting up' everywhere, there were too few suitable academic staff. No wonder then for the 'brain drain' of many of the best qualified to positions in other countries. Nevertheless, as a Christian, Kayode felt he had left the university a more committed and mature believer. As we will see, this was in part due to the influence of the rapidly developing Christian Union and the deep friendships made there.

'Nigerianisation' began in the university soon after Independence in 1960. Soon after I arrived there in 1961 Sir Abubakar Tafewa Balewa, Prime Minister of the Federal Republic of Nigeria, became the first Chancellor and Dr K.O. Dike the Vice-Chancellor; the first three Vice Chancellors had been from Britain. In the University Calendar for 1964-65, I see that there were very few Nigerians on Senate, although they did comprise most of the governing body, the University Court. Most of the academic staff were still from the UK. Those of us on the staff realised that our presence in Nigeria was temporary, since indigenous staff were returning from the UK and USA after having completed their post-graduate training.

Appendix 4
Ishaya Audu

We first met Ishaya Audu soon after we arrived in Ibadan in 1958. He was a doctor specialising in paediatrics at the University College Teaching Hospital where we went for our Sunday worship, then taking place in the Nurses Home. It was reported on good authority that an attractive and vivacious nurse, one Victoria Ohiorhenuan had 'set her cap' on Ishaya as a very suitable husband. The 'couple' came to see us a fortnight before their wedding, to which we were invited on Christmas Day 1958. A wonderful way to celebrate our first Christmas in Nigeria and being a little homesick. I am unsure whether the purpose of their visit to us was seeking advice about marriage from a more experienced couple – by all of fifteen months.

This Christian marriage raised a few eyebrows because, very unusual at that time, it was intertribal; Ishaya was Hausa (and from Northern Nigeria) and Victoria Yoruba (from the Western Region). It seems that, unlike Ishaya, Victoria's Christianity was only nominal; indeed, it was only much later in life that she had a charismatic experience that revolutionised her life – and that of the family.

Later, in 1962, in Lagos (where Ishaya had a senior appointment at the main Hospital) their home was the first Nigerian home to which we were invited to stay; the first of many. This invitation was on the condition that I preached at the Chapel on the Sunday. When later Ishaya was in London for post-graduate studies, including at our own alma mater University College, he was invited by my mother-in-law to stay with them and to preach at a missionary weekend at their church, Caterham Methodist. As we were home on leave at the time, we were able to attend. Fine preaching!

The Audus then moved north where he became the first Vice Chancellor of the new Ahmadu Bello University (ABU) in Zaria, named after the Premier of the Northern Region the Sardauna of Sokoto. He remained there for nine years. ABU at the time was described[1] as an 'international, happy and peaceful community' attracting high quality staff from around the world including Professor (later Sir) Eldred Parry, once also in Ibadan, as Dean of Medicine. I remember whilst entrenched in Glasgow in 1967 receiving a letter from Ishaya offering me the choice of two 'chairs' at ABU; I could take my pick! Sadly, not the right choice for me.

After a sabbatical in London (well earned) Ishaya was appointed the first Minister for External Affairs and later Nigeria's Permanent Representative at the United Nations in New York. Once there he refused to stay in the most prestigious hotel opting for a self-catering flat. Unlike others, he was not corrupted by stealing public funds and he refused 'gifts' of foreign currency. 'He played a very clean politics'.

Dr Audu was the first President of Scripture Union Nigeria. It was said of him, living remember in the Muslim north, that anybody and everybody who met him knew he was a Christian – like 'the proverbial city set on a hill, whose light cannot be hid', a life characterised by integrity (rare in Nigeria even among professing Christians), humility and the quality of his relationships – indeed 'an exemplary Christian in Nigeria's Public Square'.[2]

I last met Ishaya at the SU Council meeting in May 1966 (see photo) and then on one of my returns to Nigeria, when I paid him a courtesy visit at ABU. It was good to have known him and be challenged by the quality of his life in Christ in a country that has been well described as a 'land of disorder' and corruption.

Then it happened. Ishaya was ordered back from New York because the UN Secretary General was visiting Nigeria. He said goodbye to his family for what he thought was for a few days. However, on his flight from New York there was yet another coup and, on General Buhari's orders, he was arrested at the airport and imprisoned in the infamous Kirikiri maximum security prison. He spent the next twenty months there, praying, studying the bible, preaching and teaching other prisoners Hausa. He was stripped of his salary and pension leaving his family in New York without

---

[1] Emmanuel Oladipo, *Exemplary Christians in the Nigerian Public Arena*, Church of Nigeria Missionary Society, 2018.

[2] See footnote 1.

income. It was during this period that Victoria came to a living faith in Jesus.

After his release, the remainder of their lives were spent in setting up a self-sustaining hospital near Zaria; to pay for operations the Fulani herdsmen paid in goats or sheep. The Audus opened schools and hostels for Fulani villagers, and their home to 'children from the bush', certainly not house trained. For me, the saddest part of the story came when, dying of cancer and bound for the US where one of his doctor sons had arranged for an operation, and leaving his homeland for the final time, he was denied the use of a wheelchair by the airport authorities because he did not have a first-class ticket. Such an insult to a man now regarded as one of only fifty people given special recognition for their services to Nigeria. Ishaya died less than a month later in August 2005; the cancer had spread too far. Truly, Ishaya Audu is one of whom it could well be said 'this world is not worthy'.[3]

[3] Hebrews 11:38.

Appendix 5
Student Witness

This is a good place to write about the beginnings of the Ibadan University Christian Union. At the time we arrived in Ibadan in 1958 there were already Christians on the staff of both Nigerian College and the University. The key figures there were Alan and Mary Rees (very Welsh!) who as early as 1957 had begun to open their home to students for food, games, friendship, discussion and a Christian message; just like the 'squashes' to be held later when we arrived at Nigerian College.

There is a good record of the subsequent events in the 'history' of the Ibadan Varsity Christian Union (IVCU) written by Simeon Ifere.[1] He records that it started in January 1961 at a meeting in the flat of Dr John Powell, a member of the Chemistry Department. A group of eight evangelical Christian students including Ezekiel Adesogan, Reuben Ariko and Deborah Ajakaiye met to formulate a draft constitution for a Christian Union. This was accepted a month later, on February 2nd with Ezekiel (Kayode) Adesogan as President. One of the students Deborah, then requested permission of the authorities (not without some opposition) to start a Christian Union on the campus. The CU developed quickly, as witnessed by the numbers at the 'squashes' at the home of Alan and Mary and later, after they had left for Canada, in the garden of our conveniently situated home, behind the Chemistry department, in Ijoma Road. Those attending the Sunday afternoon student services at the SIM African Challenge compound at Molete also increased greatly.

I think that the early enormous growth of the CU can only be ascribed to the remarkable work of the Holy Spirit. Growth came through friendship evangelism and a strong emphasis on prayer and bible study. Moreover, it was indigenous, Nigerian student led with perhaps some help, especially in the early stages, from the presence

[1] Simeon E. Ifere, *God's Response to Nigeria, The Story of NIFES*, NIFES Press, Jos, Nigeria 1995.

of sympathetic academic staff. Many of the then students (such as Daniel Onwukwe, Edet Utuk, Mike Oye and Ebong Mbipom) subsequently had great influence nationally, on the wider Nigerian Church and, throughout Africa, on the Pan African Fellowship of Evangelical Students (PAFES) and on movements like SU and the Fellowship of Christian Students of Northern Nigeria (FCS). This is all well recorded in Simeon's history.

I was interested to learn of the situation today. In 2020 NIFES (Nigerian Fellowship of Evangelical Students) became the third largest IFES movement in the world (based on the number of students) after those in Kenya and Ethiopia. There were in the country 400 CU groups including nine in Ibadan alone. All mushrooming from that small meeting of eight students at the University of Ibadan in 1961. It was an immense privilege to witness those beginnings and the amazing early growth. Updated news can be obtained from the NIFES website or from their email (info@nifes.org.ng).

It is of interest I think to look back on those early so small beginnings. What can be learnt? What was responsible for the enormous growth that followed? Were there 'beginnings before the beginning?' My conclusions are:

- One major contributary factor was that many of the students arriving in Ibadan had come into contact with Scripture Union in their schools. The influence in these schools was often the presence of a sympathetic staff member, mainly those with experience of such SU groups in the schools back home in the UK. A good number of Christian teachers felt this as a 'call' to Africa – and not only in West Africa; similar things were happening in East Africa. The emphasis of SU has always been on the corporate and individual study of the bible and on evangelism – simply telling friends about Jesus. Then another major influence became SU camps and (especially) leadership courses. All this had received a huge stimulus by the appointment of Nigel Sylvester as staff worker for West Africa, followed in Nigeria by John Dean. The continuation of this was the 'Nigerianisation' of staff, committees and councils, completed by the time we left the country, and the handing over of responsibility for the work. The work was now autonomous.

- The presence in the early (pre-CU days) of Christian academic staff such as Ralph and Enid Schram at UCH, Alan and Mary Rees, John and Margaret Powell and others at the University and at Nigerian College. For me this emphasised the importance of the open home for bible study and for informal, and then somewhat more 'formal' organised home meetings ('squashes'). In many cases these were based on experience from their own student days, such as, in our own case, those in the London home of Professor and Mrs Fairbairn.

- A willingness to hand over responsibility to Nigerians themselves. This was clearly seen both in the student work in the universities and in the phenomenal growth of SU. We became just interested observers!

It was for all of us 'observers' a most wonderful privilege to witness, in the limited time we spent in the country, such a vivid movement of the Spirit. A continuation of the account of the young church in the book of Acts!

'To God be the glory great things He has done!

These are our three children, born in different places, at the beginning (1960), end (1969) and middle (1965) of the 1960s. They are placed here to emphasise that during all my adventures in Africa, Scotland, Eastern Europe and further afield, my family – these three and their 'mum' – were for me always the essential place of stability, welcome, love and blessing. To them I owe so much. Taken in 1971

Part 3 SCOTLAND

Chapter 21

Welcome to Scotland!

That loudspeaker announcement at Glasgow airport for incoming passengers always gives me a lump in my throat, especially if Pam and I have been out of the country for several months staying in our daughter's home in Australia or coming home from our frequent visits to Hungary. This is simply because we are home! Or, for me as so often, flying in alone from some other destination, and when looking out of the window as the plane flew over Bearsden, I could see our home in Russell Drive, checking the car had already left to meet me at the airport, if the washing was hanging on the line and if the grass had been cut in my absence!

But why is Scotland home for me, one born within the sound of Bow bells in the east end of London?

This raises the issue of 'Scottishness'. Am I still a Londoner and English? I was once given a form to fill in to become a member of a Glasgow library on which you were asked to state your 'nationality'. Among the alternatives were 'British' and 'Scottish'. I put 'Scottish' to the obvious pleasure of the young lady at the desk – and despite my lack of a relevant accent. A few weeks back in church I was asked the same question and I replied that I could best be described as an 'Anglo-Scot'. The response was more Scot than Anglo! At the same church service the visiting preacher asked me which part of Scotland I came from, as he could not place the accent! I simply replied, 'from the East End'!

I suppose that if you have lived in the country for well over fifty years, have a degree from a Scottish university, have taught in one for over thirty years and as a long-term Fellow of the country's highest institution 'for the advancement of knowledge and useful learning' one could make some claim to 'citizenship'. I like Will Storrar's comment[1] that he felt at the same time Scottish, British and European! That describes me quite well. Scottish because Scotland has been my home for nearly fifty-five years, British because of where I was born and brought up and European because of my close links with Hungary, the old Czechoslovakia, France and Germany. And, in football, if Scotland are playing England, I support Scotland in the first half and England in the second! Or the other way round.

However, the question of Scottish identity remains an issue for debate. My wife could certainly make the claim to be Scottish as her maternal grandfather was from Buchan and a member of one of Scotland's most historic clans. We, as 'incomers', have seldom found antagonism just because we were born somewhere else. We have found a welcome 'in the glen' and in the great city of Glasgow. One Church of Scotland minister wrote to me: 'How many have great cause to thank God that you did come to Scotland all those years ago'. The statement that it was 'God who brought you here' I believe is true. But how did it happen? From Nigeria to Scotland. Well, here is the story.

Most expatriates living in Ibadan and working in the University knew they were only in their positions for a limited time. Nigerians were being trained outside the country, mainly in the UK or the USA, ready to return home and replace us in Nigeria's premier university. In addition, those like us with children were thinking about their education; opportunities for such were limited if you remained. As a picture taken in 1965 shows, when our eldest child Stephen started school, non-Nigerians even in the University primary school were very few. So, we had to think about returning to the UK – or elsewhere; some of our friends found jobs and homes in Canada. We started to look for ways to leave.

Returning home was not easy. If you applied for a position in the UK then you would need to be there for interviews. That was 3,000 miles away and telephone contact was difficult; I once

[1] William Storrar, *Scottish Identity, a Christian Vision*, Handsel Press, 1990. (For me an ideal introduction to the subject – and from a Christian viewpoint.)

had to wait all day to get a line to make our only phone call from Nigeria to Britain, and that was to tell our parents that they were now grandparents. And there was strong home competition for university positions. If you had been out of the UK for eight years who would remember you, even if you had been home and present at scientific meetings over the summer periods? It is true that the British Council gave limited financial assistance to return home for interviews but only once every two years. And, there were restrictions. The place (the Square) to which I might have returned if there were still departmental vacancies and if staff remembered me or knew of me, would have been one possibility. Indeed, before I had left for Nigeria, there had been an offer to remain there. 'If you go to Nigeria' my PhD supervisor had warned, 'you will be committing intellectual suicide and it might mean it would be impossible for you to return to the UK.'

In fact, my old department had fallen apart after the retiral of Gladwin Buttle; the new departmental head was anxious for a 'clean sweep'. Now it frequently happens, in France and Germany for example, that when an academic departmental head retires and someone outside that department is appointed, there is often a 'clear out' of existing staff who are often forced to look for other positions; or find remaining difficult. This is what happened to the staff in the Department of Pharmacology at the 'Square'; almost all the staff, those who once remembered me, had either left or retired.

Hence, to return to the UK was not easy. It was then, facing possible difficulties, that I received a letter 'out of the blue'. Bill Bowman was one who had left the 'Square' after Professor Buttle had retired and had taken up a position in a newly formed department at the University of Strathclyde in Glasgow. This new department had resulted from the expansion of the small School of Pharmacy. Where pharmacology had been taught previously at the University of Glasgow, it was now to be taught in a new Department of Physiology and Pharmacology at Strathclyde. Bill remembered me as an undergraduate and knew that I was still active in research. The 'blue' airmail letter offered me the possibility of joining him in Glasgow, but as he said, 'I do not expect you to remain' – however 'it would give you a foothold in the country from which you could more easily move to another university.' Very kind. In fact, I remained at Strathclyde for the rest of my academic life! The only time I was tempted to move elsewhere was when I received a letter from the Nobel prize winner Sir John Vane inviting me to move to London as a Professor of Pharmacology. Quite easy to decline the invitation as I was happy in Glasgow, as were my family.

I accepted the invitation to join the newly formed department at Strathclyde and duly received a letter of appointment from September 1966. And without an interview! There was one other incident that I think perhaps contributed to this offer. A few years before, we had invited to dinner the external examiners at the Nigerian School of Pharmacy, two of whom had taught us as undergraduates ten years before. Now, the other invited examiner, who I had never met was Professor John Stenlake who happened to be the Head of the School of Pharmacy at Strathclyde. Perhaps, it was that special meal that helped to make contact with the Head of the School which I was now being invited to join. And, maybe there had been an 'interview' over the dinner table. Just as well the cook was in good form on that occasion!

I was reluctant to leave the Ibadan Department to take up the appointment in Glasgow in 1966 immediately as the chairman John Grayson, was to be away for most of the opening term of the 1966-67 session. So, accepting the position in Glasgow I asked if the appointment could be held over until January 1967, already one term into the Strathclyde academic year. This was granted and meant, for the first time, remaining in Ibadan over the long summer vacation when almost all of the other university staff were away. Quite a lot of research was achieved over that quiet period. However, not so quietly, politically things were 'hotting up'. Over that period almost all the Ibo staff members left the campus for their homes in the Eastern Region. Going one day for my post I saw this huge convoy, cars and lorries overladen, getting ready to depart. Never to return.

When one is three thousand miles away from a place we had called 'home' for several years, about to return to a very different country (Britain) which we had last lived in ten years before, there were a number of things to consider. Among these was where to live, especially never having been to Glasgow, or indeed anywhere else in the West of Scotland. At this point we come to another of those strange 'happenings' which seemed to have been part of our lives. 'It so happened' that we discovered that a visiting academic, a geographer, from the University of Glasgow was staying in Ibadan. We invited him to our home and questioned him about where to live in or near Glasgow. He lived north of the Clyde, a very divisive river, and therefore suggested a number of possible locations north of the river like Kirkintilloch, Lenzie, Milngavie and Bearsden. Fortunately, we were therefore not tempted to live south of the Clyde where we seldom go even now.

Our new acquaintance also 'happened' to know of a builder (Taylor) constructing new houses in the Boclair area of Bearsden. Further, he could give me an address. So, another 'blue airmail' letter to Scotland requesting details was followed by a response with plans of these new houses. We chose one of these, asking for a few modifications, and requesting that he put our name down to reserve one, which we promised to visit when we arrived in Scotland. So, a day after I arrived in Liverpool by boat from Nigeria in December 1966, I took an overnight train to Glasgow and, after sitting on the steps of his workplace in the centre of Glasgow in the early morning, met up with the agent.

I was impressed both by the Victorian architecture of the city and the surroundings of the 'garden suburb' of Bearsden itself. He took me by car to see the houses under construction. I chose one which was due to be completed in the February, found a solicitor in the city, signed the relevant forms and flew back to London the same evening. A place to live, found in less than twelve hours and all without my wife seeing it! This home turned out to be the ideal place to live, with delightful neighbours (called Maisie on one side and Muriel and Eric on the other) and since on the estate nearly everyone had moved in recently, we got to know people quickly.

There was one problem. Because the house would not be ready until February and I was to start at Strathclyde on January 3rd (1967) where was I to live in the meantime? Meanwhile Pam and the two children were to stay with her parents in Holland-on-Sea, Essex, to which they had retired, until our house was ready.

Now for yet another 'happening'! As I have recorded each Sunday afternoon we bussed the university students to the African Challenge (SIM) compound on the Lagos Road for the special worship services. Helping at the Challenge at the time were two young men, one of whom came from Glasgow. When he asked me where I would be staying for the six weeks or so before our home was ready to move into, I said I knew no-one in Glasgow. He said he would get in touch with friends, Dr and Mrs Jack Kelly (Jack was a consultant at the Victoria Infirmary) who lived on the southside of Glasgow in a big house and that they would gladly put me up. I was rather reluctant to get in touch; such hospitality was quite usual in Nigeria but in Scotland? However, on returning to Britain, I was persuaded to phone them. I was told that they were expecting me and that the room was ready! Typical Glaswegian hospitality! It turned out that their home was a house church, probably one of the first in Scotland, meeting for worship every Sunday afternoon. A wonderfully friendly place to stay until our first home at number 47 Durness Avenue, Bearsden was completed and we were ready to move in.

There was another problem. What to do with our many loads which had arrived with us on the boat? The Royal College Building, in which the pharmacology department was situated, had very wide corridors – tiled rather like a Victorian toilet – and the crates and oil drums were parked there until I had time to unpack and slowly take our possessions to our new home. Or to wait for my laboratory to be constructed.

For folk who have lived and served in another country for many years, 're-entry' is a big issue. What happens to Christian missionaries for example when, after maybe years of service on the mission field, they eventually return home? Many of them would have years in front of them before it was time for a real retiral. There is the transition from one environment, in which they had been happy and fulfilled, to another, their 'home' country, which had changed beyond recognition during their absence from it. Of course, after nearly nine years in Africa, we too were to suffer from re-entry.

For missionaries these difficulties are threefold. First, how would they manage financially? Pensions for former missionaries are not large and personal support tends to diminish once they have left the field. Some supporters had given to the 'work' rather than to the individuals who do that work. Perhaps former missionaries would not be eligible for a State Pension or, even if they were, the cost of living would have increased so much in their absence abroad that they might find it hard to cope.

Second, where should they live? They might not, even as a married couple, have had children or, if they had, such children might not be living in their home country.

Third, they might not have wanted to leave a country in which they had lived for so long but by then others, native to that country, had been trained to take over the work in which they had been so much involved. Anyway, even if they would have liked to remain this was impossible because they would not be allowed to buy property. I remember one missionary wanted to purchase a small property in order to retire in Nigeria; it had been his home for so many years. This was not allowed. He was heart-broken; he knew the local language, indeed it had become his own, and all his many Nigerian friends were there. In contrast, if these same Nigerian friends wished to live in the UK it would have been possible! And still is.

But perhaps the most difficult things to cope with on returning are the changes in society and in the church. The church the missionary had left years before to serve the Lord, and indeed who had been supporting him (or her) would no longer be the same. The minister will have changed, maybe several times, as will the membership. The returnees could feel like 'incomers', not belonging. Of course, many missionary societies do want to 'look after' those who had faithfully served them – and their Lord – but these societies too will have changed. Perhaps, they no longer even exist or have become amalgamated into a larger and less personal organisation. My own difficulties of transition, as outlined above, were nothing compared with theirs. However, God looks after

His own and works things out for them in sometimes quite remarkable ways.

It took about a year for us to feel 'at home'. This I would put down to a welcoming church, involvement in those Christian activities which had meant a great deal to us in the past, including during our time in Nigeria, and friendly, helpful colleagues and neighbours. We were beginning to settle, albeit hopefully not 'on the lees'.[2]

[2] Jeremiah 48:11; Zephaniah 1:12.

Chapter 22
Settling In

We settled quickly into our new home, our first permanent abode since our marriage nearly ten years previously, and we soon made friends. We were helped by those living around us. There was a sense of community; some had moved from other parts (although not as far as us); some, like me, were new additions to Glasgow's two universities. Some had moved out of the city of Glasgow itself to the suburbs north and west of the city. Bearsden was one of these, a large and attractive commuter village with a number of new housing developments. Incidentally, one of these, built not much later, is our present home, St Germains which was built (in the 1980s) in the grounds of an old 'manor house'. However, in 1967, despite our new home being in one of the most attractive of these new developments at the top of Boclair hill, we sometimes still felt like 'strangers in a strange land'. And, were there other Christians living in the neighbourhood?

Not long after our arrival Pam read an article in the magazine of the Billy Graham organisation called 'Crusade' about home fellowship groups; folk meeting in homes for prayer and bible study, usually ladies because the men would be out working. Pam decided to investigate and started by obtaining, from the General Secretary at the Glasgow Scripture Union headquarters the Revd John Butler, a list of SU supporters living in the area. One wonders that with the strict security measures now in force this would be allowed today. Almost certainly not!

There were several such local SU supporters and Pam visited each of these, with daughter Debbie in the pushchair, knocked on doors and introduced herself. Much surprise that this young mother with an English accent had taken the initiative and made contact. Pam suggested a meeting together over coffee for the sharing of experiences, as newcomers to the area, and for prayer and bible study along the lines of the Crusade article. This happened, with deepening relationships between the families concerned and this led to further contacts and friendships around the local area.

There were five families involved and each worshipped in a different church (not in the immediate area) and denomination. Less than a year later, in 1968, outreach coffee meetings among neighbours started in one or other of the homes with one of the ladies looking after the young children in another room. These gatherings ended with someone invited to share about faith in Jesus. Even over fifty years later some of those invited still remember those gatherings.

The meetings continued for several years before the dynamics of the group changed, with children beginning school and with changes in family circumstances. This meant that most of those involved took employment or moved away from the area. However, it was the initiative of the outreach coffee mornings, perhaps among the first in Scotland, which was a stimulus for a deepening of faith among Christians in the immediate area and, for a few, the beginning of new life in Jesus. Later, in the early 70s, evening bible studies commenced, again not linked with any particular church. I found recently a record of what was studied and who led them, the leadership being shared around the group. This group included the then Principal of the Bible Training Institute in Glasgow, the Revd Andrew McBeath.

These home bible study groups were one key factor in attempts to start a new Christian church in the area and, because some of those involved were from Baptist Churches in the city centre but resident in Bearsden, this ultimately (after considerable discussion!) became in 1974, Bearsden Baptist Church and part of the Baptist Union of Scotland. The story of the present building in Roman Road, the home of the church, together with what happened in the early days (growth within a few years to a membership of well over a hundred) has been documented; one version (on line) is available from me. Sunday services were commenced in 1973; my own records show that I was first invited to preach there in July 1974. Within a year of the church starting an outreach began in another part of Bearsden – in Castlehill which still meets in the local Primary School and with which we were associated for many years.

For us as a family a major early (1967) consideration after moving to a new area, which for us was Bearsden, was to find a church. I am unsure why we did not investigate the local churches; at that time there were at least four local Church of Scotland places of worship within walking distance, as well as an Episcopal Church at Bearsden Cross. In January I spoke to Christians who knew the Glasgow church scene well, about a possible spiritual home. During this period, when I was alone and waiting for entry into our new home (which happened the following month) I participated in the Kelly's 'home church', a charismatic gathering and began to search for a more permanent place of worship.

After a number of 'trials' in the city centre, none of which I found 'family suitable', it was suggested that we might try St David's Church of Scotland in Knightswood, about a twenty-minute drive from our new home. I had previously discovered that the minister, Dr J.G.S.S. Thomson had contributed to the 'New Bible Dictionary' (published in 1962 by the Intervarsity Press) which I had in my possession. This for us, was a good sign! So, one Sunday morning in February 1967 we turned up at the church with our two young children in tow. We will always remember the welcome we received at the door from one of the elders; this man had that rare gift of welcome, essential for any church community. We could here digress on the gifts required for such an office as 'welcomer', but I will refrain! Except to say that every church needs folk to welcome people at the front door and help prevent them leaving by the back one.

When I returned for the evening service on that first Sunday at St David's, Dr Thomson knew who I was and arranged to call on us. His teaching ministry was of a very high level but so often the 'highlight' of the services was when he led the opening prayer of worship. You were transported into the very presence of God. I have never heard such prayers of worship. That was surely because of his personal piety; his own practice of prayer shone through. This is also clearly shown in his book *The Praying Christ* – first published in 1959[1] and then reprinted many years later. John Dean had given us a copy as a present for Christmas in Nigeria that year.

---

[1] James G.S.S. Thomson, *The Praying Christ, Jesus' Doctrine and Practice of Prayer*, Tyndale Press, London 1959 (and reprinted about forty years later!).

Little did we know that nine years later Dr JGSST would be our much-loved minister in Glasgow!

'The doctor' as he was always called, had an unusual career. Born in Prestonpans, East Lothian he responded to God's call and, after training at the Faith Mission College in Edinburgh, set off to Algeria in 1935 and worked, with his wife, as missionaries among the Arab community. They were still in Algeria when, in the Second World War, they were trapped and detained by the Axis forces until, in 1943 after the German defeat, they were repatriated back to Scotland arriving with little more than the clothes they were wearing. A gifted linguist, and with four degrees from the Universities of Edinburgh and Oxford, he taught at New College Edinburgh in the Department of Hebrew and Semitic Languages for five years and then became Professor of Old Testament at the Columbia Theological Seminary in Atlanta, Georgia. He returned to Scotland in 1960 as Minister of St David's Knightswood in Glasgow's West End.

St David's was a church that became our home for several years. In many ways it was unique, for example in the way that, during 'the doctor's' ministry so many young men felt called into the Church of Scotland ministry: I think about thirty or so, some of whom we still remain in contact with as friends. Those years sitting under his ministry were for both of us just what was needed after those years in Nigeria. We had active roles in the congregation and I was ordained an elder and, together with Norman Cruickshank, later to become the minister at Overton, West Kilbride, had responsibilities for the district of Bearsden attempting, not very successfully, to move families from their present membership in Knightswood to one of the Bearsden churches.

Two of the families that were on my 'list' became very special friends. One was Eileen Clarke, a long-term and much-loved Scripture Union staff worker. The others were Roy and Elizabeth Hart and their family of boys; Roy later became Session Clerk. I valued this ministry, one of the strengths of the Scottish Church, of having a pastoral role within the church community and I learnt much from those I was responsible for. Helped too by Dr Thomson's group teaching on pastoral visitation as well as the excellent manual written by David Short and David Searle.[2] Other denominations have seen, or are beginning to see, lay pastoral work as essential to the life of a congregation and we too have benefited from this. As they wrote, 'It is impossible to imagine a greater privilege within a church community.' However, many so involved are self-taught in a ministry for which much needs to be learned. And surely pastoral work remains a prime responsibility of the minister; he is not simply to be an intermediary, the 'middle man' passing this ministry on to others.

Whilst in our first Scottish home a different ministry opened up. Like so many opportunities for serving Christ, this commenced 'by chance' or as we could say, providentially – 'it just happened that'; the guidance coming by a seeming accident. I had been asked by a missionary society in Nigeria, with which I became much involved, the Sudan United Mission, to look out for and befriend one of their former students. He had gone to school at the Mission's main educational complex at Gindiri near Jos, a place we had visited a couple of times whilst living in Nigeria. This former student was now studying for a PhD in chemistry at Strathclyde and this department was housed in the Royal College building where I also now worked. So, I began a search for him. It did not prove too difficult because, asking around, I was told there was a 'black African' working in the basement. Sure enough, I discovered someone answering to that description and introduced myself. However, this African was not the person I was looking for. A case of mistaken identity.

So this was how I met Daniel Gyane, a Ghanaian from Kumasi, a fine Christian who was studying at Strathclyde; his wife (Lucy) was a nurse in one of the Glasgow teaching hospitals. They were concerned about the spiritual welfare of African fellow students living in the city and we discussed how a Christian fellowship group could be set up in a place where they could relax and meet other believers. So it was that the Overseas Student Squashes began in our home, based loosely on those we had hosted in Ibadan and before that, when we ourselves had been students, at the home of Professor and Mrs Fairbairn in London.

[2] David Short and David Searle, *Pastoral Visitation, a Pocket Manual*, Christian Focus, Tain 2004.

These 'Squashes' were held monthly. Our Bearsden home had a large L-shaped living area suitable for the 30 to 40 students who came each time. Bearsden, being some distance from the halls of residence, the students were transported in cars belonging to some of the Strathclyde Christian staff. A few members of the Christian Union also attended. The evenings included much appreciated food, games and some specifically Christian content from a carefully chosen speaker. When the weather permitted, there were also excursions to nearby beauty spots such as the University Conference Centre based at Ross Priory on the banks of Loch Lomond. Pam and I believe these meetings, that continued for the seven years we lived in Durness Avenue, met a real need at the time. Almost a thousand students attended over that seven-year period and years later we sometimes received overseas phone calls from former attendees asking if the fellowship meetings still continued since one of their children was coming to study in Glasgow. When we moved to what became the family home in Russell Drive in the centre of Bearsden, there was no large living area suitable for entertaining so many students. However, by that time both the African and the Chinese Christian students had founded their own city centre churches, which continue to thrive years later.

Later, in the 1970s, there was a city-wide initiative to link overseas students with members of the city churches. This was called GIFT (Glasgow International Friendship Team) and was initiated by Dr John Twidell, also on the Strathclyde staff, who had had experience of a similar venture in Oxford. Perhaps GIFT was a for-runner of Friends International in Glasgow, with which another member of the Strathclyde University staff later became much involved. There are still many opportunities to welcome, in a home environment, the many overseas students studying in Glasgow.

Chapter 23
Settled – but Not Too Much

At the end of my first year at Strathclyde I had managed to obtain funding to continue research and to order the necessary equipment to supplement that which I already brought from Ibadan. There was, and still is, much competition for such funding so I was fortunate to receive this so early. This came from the Medical Research Council and the Wellcome Trust. And my laboratory was almost ready. This was situated on the roof of the oldest building in the University, the Royal College Building – seven floors up.

There were three such laboratories belonging to the Department on the roof; one of them, because of the number of Australian visitors working there, was known as 'kangaroo valley'. The roof space between these laboratories could be very hazardous in winter: one of the cleaners took the route between them and slipped on the ice; she finished up with one of her legs through the railings with a seven story drop on the other side. As one might expect, the laboratory was cold in winter and often very hot in summer; this was during the decades when Scottish summers often included sunshine. I decided to make use of the sun by growing tomatoes on the windowsills. Good if I was around at the time but when on holiday my research students had other things on their minds, rightly more important than watering the professor's tomatoes. When we moved as a department to a new building the rooftop labs were closed. Health and safety. But for over twenty years the roof of the Royal College was a hive of fruitful activity and, over that period, nearly forty postgraduate students and post-doctoral fellows worked there with me.

One of my first research students came from Australia, from Brisbane. So, I was beginning to 'make a name' for myself even as far away as the Gold Coast. Her name was Glynne Moore. I promised to meet her from the plane – a very long and time-consuming flight especially in those days. But, how would I recognise her at the airport? She would be carrying a koala! Not a real one of course.

Glynne took a little while to settle in and there were a few upsets between her and the other, somewhat quieter, Scottish students in the laboratory. But settle in she did and on graduation with a well-earned PhD, she married a student from another department and 'moved south'. I think she never returned to her homeland. At that time, she was working on a new drug from a small company in Germany who had asked me to be a consultant for them. When the drug was available clinically as an antianginal, I was asked to be a member of a team of cardiologists to 'promote' the drug in various countries such as Pakistan, Egypt and Russia. More about the adventures on these trips later. Even more special for my 'story' was that the first scientific meeting on this drug (called oxyfedrine) was in Vienna and it was there that I again met Laszlo Szekeres. This particular meeting and the introduction to this particular German drug firm was made through Dr Ralph Kohn, a quite remarkable man, one of my 'heroes' and about whom I add a short account in chapter 25.

The early 1960s in drug research were dominated by beta-adrenoceptor blocking drugs which were then in clinical trials to slow, and thus protect the heart. It was anticipated that they would be useful in conditions such as angina pectoris. Later, a Christian friend in London, Professor Brian Pritchard showed they could also lower blood pressure in patients with hypertension. The story of the development of these drugs is a fascinating one but is outwith the scope of this memoir, except that I was asked to help in evaluating these drugs by a number of drug firms worldwide.

Later we became interested in the disorders of cardiac rhythm that often result when the (coronary) blood flow to the heart is reduced, such as happens when someone has a heart attack. These rhythm disturbances are quite often fatal. Could they be prevented? This led to a long period of consultation with a company in Holland and the discovery of a drug which was highly active in suppressing, or preventing, these life-threatening ventricular dysrhythmias. A good drug albeit with limited marketing potential. Better, and more profitable, to market yet another and safer anti-inflammatory drug! If there was competition between the design, production and marketing of say, a potential anti-malarial drug (with fewer side effects than the existing ones) or yet another beta-blocker, the latter would win every time. How different, and so welcome, is the present attitude of drug companies such as Pfizer, Astra-Zeneka and Janssen to the development and production of vaccines against the covid virus. Produced at cost and made available worldwide. It makes me proud of such drug companies, most of which I had worked for as a consultant at one time or another.

Over this productive period in that roof top laboratory the interest then was in the evaluation of 'useful' drugs for serious clinical disorders. There was some success.

Most of this research was directly linked with my original interest, which began in Nigeria, in coronary blood flow and how this is regulated. The basic question that concerned many at that time was how does blood flow increase to match the demands of the heart when these too are increased, for example during exercise? And how is this 'match' between demand and supply so precise? When, for example the heart beats more forcefully and quickly during exercise how does the message ('more blood please!') get back to the coronary vessels 'telling' them to dilate and hence increase flow accordingly? Are there substances released from the cardiac muscle that dilate these coronary vessels? Or is there a neural feedback? Or is it an inherent quality of the vessels themselves? And what happens when the vessels can no longer cope with the increase in demand of the heart for more oxygen, for example, when the vessels are narrowed? And clinically, how can we improve the availability of oxygen to the ischaemic (oxygen deficient) myocardium? It was these questions that concerned me on my arrival in Glasgow.

It was at this juncture that an unusual meeting occurred. I would describe this as providential. Now, the use of this word raises questions for a Christian believer, as it certainly does for an unbeliever who would put it down to chance. Can all events in life, even in science, be described in this way? Just today I received an email from a good friend, the same age as I am, who also happens to be writing his memoirs and was writing about this same meeting. This is what he says – 'one's career seems to be the result of careful planning but was in reality a string of luck.' Was the event I am about to describe providence or luck? I believe the former; God is interested in my life in science just as he is in my spiritual life. I am one of those Christians who has rejected the sacred-secular divide. All my life, not just a particular part of it, is in God's hands. He is concerned with the 'all of me'.

The particular significance of this event was this. Just a year after I arrived in Glasgow a meeting was arranged to celebrate the life, and retiral, of Dr Bill Fulton, a cardiologist at Stobhill Hospital in Glasgow, whom I had met a few months earlier. Bill's interest, indeed his lifework, was on the coronary collateral circulation. His book on this had been published in the United States three years earlier.[1] For the uninitiated, collateral coronary vessels are those (new) blood vessels that develop in life by, almost always, growing out of existing smaller vessels. They can grow to such an extent that they can 'replace' existing larger vessels that have been narrowed (or closed) as a result of structural changes, such as the result of atherosclerosis. The collaterals are, as Bill had shown, a normal response, a defensive mechanism, when there is potential damage to existing vessels. Clearly such vessels are important for organ survival especially in the heart. My friends Wolfgang and Jutta Schaper later showed[2] how these vessels develop. How they grow – and why.

This celebratory meeting for Bill was concerned with all aspects of the circulation to the heart, my own main research interest. Although, as a recent and largely unknown resident in Glasgow, I am unsure how I was invited. There were two strange things about this meeting. First, there was almost no coronary vascular research in the UK at the time; only one other group, in the 'deep south', were working in this area and that not too productively. So, a scientific meeting in the UK specifically on the 'blood supply to the heart' was very unusual.

Second, it 'happened' to take place in Glasgow just a year after my arrival in the city. Then the meeting took place at the Science Park of Glasgow's two universities which 'happens' to be in Bearsden, where I lived. I could have walked there.

[1] William F M Fulton, *The Coronary Arteries*, Charles C Thomas, Springfield Illinois, 1965.

[2] Wolfgang Schaper and Jutta Schaper, *Collateral Circulation. Heart, Brain, Kidney, Limbs*, Kluwer Academic, Dordrecht, Holland 1993.

It was a significant meeting because at it I met two individuals who, one way or another, have greatly influenced my research career. The first was Wolfgang Schaper, one of the most brilliant scientists I have known and who, well over fifty years later and with his wife Jutta, is among my best friends.

The other individual was someone I 'happened' to be sitting next to during one of the meeting sessions. lain Ledingham worked in the Department of Surgery at the Western Infirmary, one of Glasgow's main teaching hospitals, chaired by the formidable Sir Andrew Watt Kay. lain shared with me that his research group had begun to be interested in coronary blood flow regulation and invited me to join them. Later I was appointed an Honorary Research Fellow in the department and remained there, together with one or other of my own research students (successively Dick Marshall, Susan Coker and Cherry Wainwright) for almost ten years. The clinical members of the group included cardiologists, anaesthetists and surgeons, most of whom were studying for a higher degree or for publications which would help towards promotion within the NHS. The progress was rapid; within six months of joining the group we had our first published results.

One very unusual feature of the Department of Surgery was the presence of a hyperbaric chamber; indeed, I seem to remember that at one time there were two of these. There were two reasons for the presence of these chambers. One was to study the physiological effects and dangers of deep-sea diving; these were the early days for the exploitation of the oil and gas reserves in the North Sea; appropriately there was another hyperbaric chamber in Aberdeen. The second reason was to treat miners with coal gas poisoning; there was a helicopter pad on the roof of the building to bring miners so affected into the department and, in the chamber, use oxygen at pressure to 'drive' the carbon monoxide out of their lungs. Soon however the last coal mine in Scotland was to close and the chamber became redundant, except for experimental purposes.

We discussed the rather crazy idea of bringing patients with acute myocardial infarction into the chamber, taking them (carefully) up to two atmospheres pressure (2ATA) and giving them oxygen to breath. At 2ATA this would greatly increase the oxygen pressure in the blood, so 'driving' more oxygen into the area of potential cardiac damage resulting from oxygen lack. Sadly, in experimental studies to examine this clinical possibility, we found that this did not increase oxygen availability because oxygen itself (especially at 2ATA) was powerfully coronary vasoconstrictor and it was not possible to overcome this with coronary vasodilator drugs. Working at 2 (on a few occasions 3) ATA has interesting effects; cerebral effects equivalent to drinking a small glass of whisky, a little light-headed and much laughter, heard of course by the safety engineers below. One also had to make sure that one's bladder had been emptied before the long procedure of slowly and safely increasing the pressure in the chamber. Or not to forget one's lunch; it takes a long time to descend to normal atmospheric (room) pressure.

I discovered recently a list of my scientific publications and was surprised how productive those early Glasgow years had been both at the Western Infirmary and in the roof top laboratory at Strathclyde. A good number of students received their PhD degrees and many had productive careers, mainly in the drug industry.

However, for me perhaps the most important 'happening' at the Western was concerned with the care of patients who had developed septic shock. In those days, before the existence of intensive care units, such dangerously ill patients were treated, at least in Glasgow, in Departments of Surgery. lain Ledingham was the physician responsible for the care of these patients: the mortality in these was about 90%. This led to lain setting up a 'shock group' to explore how to reduce this high mortality. I was again invited to participate, a new venture for me. This was to become a major interest in the following years. A little about this when we think about sepsis and septic shock.

Chapter 24
Sepsis, Shock and Organ Failure

It was the usual procedure in the 1960s, before the formation of separate departments of Intensive (Emergency) Care Medicine, that patients requiring help following severe infection, and the resultant sepsis, were treated in surgery departments, because one of the main causes of sepsis in those days followed surgery on the gastrointestinal tract. This was because there are millions of bacteria living happily, if bacteria can be happy, in our guts; indeed, they are greatly beneficial to us. However, if they migrate into the general circulation this can lead to the dangerous development of sepsis. At that time, in the 1970s, mortality in such patients, once sepsis had developed, was high; perhaps as much as 80 to 90%.

Iain Ledingham, working in the surgery department at the Western Infirmary in Glasgow, where abdominal surgery was a speciality, put together a multi-disciplinary team to study what the early consequences of the escape of bacteria into the circulation following surgery might be. Because of my long interest in the effects of bacterial endotoxin, which is released when bacteria are broken down and is one cause of sepsis, I was invited to be one of this team. The Strathclyde group had long investigated the effects of endotoxin, not only on circulatory dynamics but also on lung function and metabolism.

Of course, septic shock was not only a UK problem. This occurred worldwide and groups from Europe and the United States were attempting to solve this problem. How can we prevent the high mortality of such patients? There were meetings each year in Brussels and in Vienna during the 1990s to discuss these issues and to which I often contributed. In Vienna these were known as the Wiggers - Bernard Conferences, named after two great physiologists of previous generations. The chairman was Gunther Schlag from the Institute of Experimental and Clinical Traumatology in Vienna. I notice that I was the opening speaker, talking about cardiovascular dysfunction in sepsis, at the last such meeting held in the charming castle of Krumbach on the Rhine in 1994. Last, because Gunther died the following year. However, such was the interest of surgeons, anaesthetists and physiologists in shock, that an International Shock Society was inaugurated. I became Vice-President of the European Shock Society and an editor of its journal.

One basic cardiovascular problem in sepsis is the fall in blood pressure and the difficulty of elevating it to acceptable levels. The usual approach was to infuse the body's natural pressor substances, the catecholamines adrenaline and noradrenaline. How often during TV soaps, like Casualty or Holby City, has the command been heard – usually shouted – more adrenaline! The difficulty in sepsis is that catecholamines fail to elevate blood pressure; the vessels have become refractory both to exogenous catecholamines and to the sympathetic nerves, which normally control blood vessel tone.

Now comes another instance of Providence. I received a letter, this was the pre-email dynasty, 'out of the blue' from a Professor Jean-Claude Stoclet, who worked at the University of Strasbourg. Would I accept one of his PhD students who was interested in spending a year in another laboratory to learn techniques not available in Strasbourg. As I did not know the Strasbourg department Professor Stoclet invited me to give a lecture to his department. At that time our main research interest was attempting to solve the question of how preconditioning protected the heart - yet another scientific adventure. However, I decided at the Strasbourg lecture to talk about sepsis and endotoxaemia. Why I decided to do this I am unsure but that decision led both to a fruitful and most enjoyable scientific collaboration and to a deep friendship with Jean-Claude and his wife Janik. Indeed, our final overseas holiday was spent with them in their delightful 'chateau' home in Bretagne.

We decided that the problem of this loss of reactivity was one we could solve by working together and, to achieve this, we applied to the European Commission for financial assistance. This was successful and paid for both a post-doctoral fellow and for a PhD student, both from the UK but to work in Strasburg. Within the first six months the problem had been solved; the vascular derangements in sepsis were due to an overproduction of nitric oxide (NO) within the walls of the blood vessels. We showed this using a drug that prevented the effects of nitric oxide by suppressing its synthesis. This restored vascular reactivity. The results were presented at a meeting of the Physiological Society in Oxford and published in 1989 and had clinical repercussions. A short time later I was watching the BBC TV evening news when the final item was a report from a London hospital intensive care department that blocking the synthesis of nitric oxide 'improved survival in patients with septic shock'. There were just two patients who had been given the drug – one died and one survived, a mortality, not of 80% but of 50%!

Of course, there is much more to this story than I have outlined above! This is partly because there are at least two enzymes responsible for NO production. Could one of these enzymes be selectively suppressed? Could we say no to NO? Is survival really improved when more patients are treated with such drugs? Clearly two patients are not enough! This was the beginning of a long story which is still evolving.

But what this continuing research emphasises is that the problem of patients who die with sepsis is still unsolved. Apparently, world-wide at least 250,000 people still get sepsis (or septicaemia) every year – and of these at very least one in five will die. That is over 50,000 each year – or 140 every day. Shock developing from sepsis is still a major clinical problem.

Chapter 25
Two Remarkable Men

One of my favourite books by John Stott is the one written in his eightieth year entitled *People my Teachers* or 'around the world in eighty years'.[1] In it he introduces his readers to seventeen outstanding people, most of whom he had a personal link with. Many of those included were Christians such as Richard Wurmbrand (whom we once invited to speak to the university staff at Strathclyde), Dr Paul (Jungle doctor) White and Festo Kivengere. But he also included Charles Darwin, Mohandas Gandhi and John Franklin (who sought a way through the North West Passage).

I have been greatly privileged in my relatively long life to have known personally a number of quite remarkable people; scientists including some of the greatest of my generation, and many Christian friends who have taught me by word and life much about Jesus and faith in him. Like 'Uncle John', to write about seventeen of these would not be a problem but I have settled on just two, John Stott himself and the Jewish scientist, multilingual polyglot, musician and business man, Ralph Kohn.

Dr Ralph Kohn

Ralph was one of the most remarkable men I ever met. He made contact with me just two years after I arrived in Glasgow and arranged to come up and visit me. I am not sure how he knew about me, perhaps through publications or through one or other of his contacts in the British Pharmacological Society. I remember he said he had heard that 'I was the best cardiovascular pharmacologist in Europe'! Flattery will get you somewhere. Perhaps! He had strong links with pharmaceutical (drug) companies all over the continent and, when developing new drugs, these companies believed it would help them to get their drug into clinical trials, and hence on to the market, if some of the basic pharmacology had been performed in a UK laboratory. Ralph was very persuasive. Over time I agreed to

[1] John Stott, *People My Teachers*, Candle Books, 2002.

look at many such drugs. The first of these came from Germany and seemed to have potential as an anti-anginal medicine. We did an extensive investigation resulting in participation at a meeting on the drug held in Vienna in 1970. It also resulted in a request from the company to 'consult' for them, which I did over a long period of time.

Over the next twenty years or so Ralph introduced me to a number of people working in the pharmaceutical industry who were interested in developing new drugs for the treatment of cardiovascular disease. These included almost all of the UK pharmaceutical companies and others in France, Italy, Russia, Switzerland, Hungary and especially Japan. Links with an American company came rather later, not I think through Ralph. All these contacts involved extensive travelling over more than a twenty-year period. This meant that when talking about family affairs, my wife Pam has often reminded me that I was 'never there'. Here I am reminded of the story of a famous Professor of Cardiology at Oxford who, it was said, was also never there. His colleagues put a sticker on his car that read 'caution, driver is a visitor to Britain'. And, in the annual departmental Christmas musical pantomime wrote – 'What is the difference between God and Peter Sleight? God is everywhere but Peter is never in Oxford'. That could have been said of me over quite a long period. Never in Glasgow. Always elsewhere! Incidentally, this same Peter Sleight was a great encourager to me; after a disastrous lecture to the British Cardiac Society, in which the projectionist had mixed up my slides, he commented, arm around my shoulder, 'Jim, that was the best lecture I have ever heard you give!'

To return to Ralph Kohn. His story is fascinating. Born into a Hasidic Jewish family in Leipzig in 1927 (the family home was close to where Bach had lived) they fled Germany in 1933 and made their home in Amsterdam (where Ralph learnt Dutch) before having to flee again on the last free boat to leave occupied Holland in May 1940, an hour before the Dutch Government capitulated. Ralph later wrote that this escape was due to a combination of luck, courage, decisive action, well-placed contacts and the heroic efforts of the Kindertransport organisation. After five days afloat they arrived in Manchester where later Ralph studied pharmacy and pharmacology (as I was also to do) before a post-doctoral fellowship took him to Rome to work with two Nobel Prize winners. It was in Rome that he discovered his fine baritone voice. However, it was in science and not music that his career lay. He joined the Philadelphia-based company Smith-Kline-French (SKF), which gave him contacts all over Europe and eventually he bought a small Swiss drug company marketing one of their products with some financial benefit. His main interest was in double-blind clinical trials, evaluating independently drugs (mainly from smaller drug firms) and seeing them through to marketing. He set up a company (Advisory Services Clinical and General) to do this, won the Queen's Award for export Achievement in 1990, set up many scientific conferences (mainly at the Royal Society in London) and made his company an international concern. After it was sold, Ralph set up the Kohn Foundation 'for charitable purposes' and became a philanthropist.

His interest in music remained strong. He gave the first of several recitals at the Wigmore Hall in London in 1968 and later made a number of recordings accompanied by a number of famous pianists including the Schubert specialist Graham Johnson.

At one time there was talk that, if invited to Glasgow for the European ISHR meeting in June 1990, we could give a recital together, although this would have involved a good deal of practice on my part. Fortunately for me this failed to happen as Ralph would be out of the country on those dates! Music played a major part in his philanthropy; examples were his financial support of the Monteverdi Orchestra, the Wigmore Hall-Foundation International Song Competition for young singers and an annual Bach Prize at the Royal Academy of Music in London. He was also a great supporter of the Royal Society in London, where one of the refurbished lecture rooms bears his name. Ralph was an honorary Fellow of a number of scientific and musical establishments including the Academy of Medical Sciences, the Royal Society and the Royal Academy of Music. Other honours included the award by the Federal German Government of the Cross of the Order of Merit and the freedom of the City of Leipzig; his Honorary degrees, were for both science and music. He was knighted in 2010 for 'services to science, music and charity'.

We last met in Edinburgh in 2014. I had received a message from him to say he and his wife would be in Edinburgh for the Festival on August 27th because a close friend, the pianist Andras Schiff, was to play. Could we meet for lunch? It was so good to see him for one last time, a three-hour lunch in which we discussed Leipzig (a special city for both of us although for different reasons), music, Hungary, the work our daughter was doing among 'native Australians', the bible, writing, how exercise protects the heart and old memories of previous meetings about which, as Ralph wrote afterwards, of 'my hectic activities when we worked together'.

One of his family friends said of him – 'Ralph had the right degree of gregariousness and the largest circle of friends of anyone I have ever met'. 'A conversation with him in person made you feel life was worth living'. That too was my experience; a very warm-hearted man 'who evoked a corresponding warmth in professional colleagues and friends alike'.

At the Edinburgh lunch I also met his wife Zahava Kohn (Rosy Kanarek) whose own story is as fascinating as her husband's. Her family also escaped from Germany in the 1930s, travelled via Amsterdam to Palestine (where she was born) and then returned to Amsterdam because of her mother's illness. Here they were trapped by the German invasion and rounded up, held at the camp at Westerbork and then to Bergen-Belsen. Her story, movingly told both on TV and in book form,[2] is a journey from the depths of despair to hope – and survival. I treasure my own copy of her book. And, as we discussed, would I have survived if my brother and I had been born, in 1933 and 1938 respectively, not in Britain but in Germany or Holland?

My last letter from Ralph talked about our lunch together. He wrote 'We had a marvellous time in Edinburgh – you and Andras Schiff were the highlights . . .' Flattery to the end!

Revd Dr John Stott

I first met John Stott in the Chapel of King's College during a mission to London University. I can date that meeting – the evening of Tuesday November 17th 1953 when I shook his hand after he had preached from John 3:14 – 'As Moses lifted up the serpent in the

[2] Zahava Kohn, *Fragments of a Lost Childhood*, The Holocaust Centre, 2009.

wilderness, so MUST the Son of Man be lifted up, that whoever believes in him may have eternal life'. This is followed by the most famous verse in the bible (v 16) – 'God so loved the world that . . .' That evening I made my commitment to follow Christ. Can there be a more significant day in one's life than that? John gave me a small booklet (*Becoming a Christian*) and another booklet introducing me to bible reading. John was just 34 at the time, the age two of our seven grandchildren are now. Forty years later he wrote to say he still remembered that university mission (only his second) and the exposition of those verses from John's Gospel.

My last meeting with 'Uncle John' (as he became) was when he stayed with us in our Bearsden home during his farewell 'tour' of Scotland at the age of 80. I write these words about John on April 27th 2021 exactly one hundred years to the day after his birth; and whilst listening to Mozart's 'Haydn Quartets'.

Much of John Stott's life has been covered many times, for example in Timothy Dudley Smith's fine two volume biography.[3] There is little for me to add except a comment or two about the few times we met together over the nearly fifty years between our first and last meetings.

After that life-changing event in November 1953 I spent a year as a member of All Souls Church Langham Place, where John was Rector. Wonderful teaching from him; a model for all would be preachers, including me. Why then did I move from All Souls less than two years later? The reason was that my parents and younger brother, who like me had no church background, also began to attend All Souls. However, this was a long journey each Sunday morning from our home in Chiswick with my mother anxious to get back to cook the important Sunday lunch! So, after discussions with folk at the IVF in Bedford Place, my brother John and I took up their suggestion to try Gunnersbury Baptist Church, which was a mile or so from our home and which we later joined. Strangely, I had heard their minister John Caiger preach at All Souls during an exchange of pulpits in January 1955. I can still remember what he preached on!

My next significant meeting with 'Uncle John' was in Nigeria when he came to take a mission in April 1962 at the University

---

[3] Timothy Dudley-Smith, John Stott: *The Making of a Leader*, Inter-Varsity Press, 1999 and John Stott: *A Global Ministry*, Inter-Varsity Press, 2001.

College, part of an African wide university mission tour. Of this occasion I remember three things. Firstly, he came to lunch, where we introduced him to some of our young African friends. Among these was Solomon Gwei, who was at that time training at the SIM Bible College in Igbaja. Solomon came from the British part of Cameroun and had often preached back home in pidgin English. John asked him to preach the gospel in pidgin at the lunch table and this he did. Solomon was, like so many African preachers, an enthusiastic, powerful and lively preacher. That lunchtime 'pidgin preaching' had a strong effect on all of us!

The second recollection was his request (more like a command!) that I did the 'follow up' for those students who had come to faith. This I did. The third thing I remembered, and which had a long-lasting effect on me, was the knowledge, unobtrusively leaked out, that nearly ten years after the 1953 London mission I was still on John's prayer list – which already must have been enormous.

Our last meeting with John was during his farewell tour of Scotland in 2001. There was a formal dinner at which he spoke about his vision for the Langham International Partnership, his desire to train would be church leaders overseas, to put into their hands good Christian books and, for some, to provide scholarships for post-graduate studies in selected theological departments of British universities, such as, in Scotland, Aberdeen and St Andrews. Two of our old friends from their student days, Liz and Malcolm McGregor, are now involved in the pastoral care of some of these Langham scholars. This, just one of John's many legacies.

It was a privilege to host John for just two nights during which, over meals, we introduced him to our son Stephen and his wife Fiona, our young pastor Mark and his Greek wife, and also Paul Watson, a young, episcopalian minister and at one time a missionary in Sri Lanka. Of course, John was very much at home with these young people. We took John to Ross Priory on the banks of Loch Lomond for birdwatching – his great hobby – and for soup and a sandwich. Then, the following morning (June 14th) we shook his hand for the final time, as he was collected, for the journey to Edinburgh for his last meeting in Scotland by Greer Johnson and another old friend Nigel Sylvester (yet another Runton reunion).

A few days later he wrote from London thanking us for our hospitality and sending us the revised edition of the first of his many books, 'Men with a Message'. The original, published in 1954[4] is still on our bookshelves. In his last letter to us he expressed heartfelt thanks for our friendship over many years. But how much more his friendship has meant to us! I thank my God for every remembrance of 'Uncle John'.

Looking back, what for my own life have I learnt from his? Of course, there is the example of his preaching both heard and written about,[5] there is his kindness and courtesy (those thankyou letters) but two things in particular. The first is about prayer. To discover I was on his prayer list so many years after we had first met was one of the prompts to start my own daily prayer list.

I have shared some of this previously; a reader in Holland wrote to me after reading my first book and said that, although she appreciated the book, the thing that helped her most was my sharing in it about prayer lists. Why, as Christians, do we not usually share about such things? Is it a false modesty – 'it is between me and the Lord'. Do we ever tell people that we pray for them? After all Paul himself often did this. Would it encourage people to know I prayed for them? And, how long should I keep them on the list!

The other thing I learnt from John may seem surprising. That was vulnerability with age. Not, I hasten to explain any mental or spiritual vulnerability (although, knowing him, he would have questioned the latter!) but his physical vulnerability at the age of eighty. Even our heroes are more vulnerable with age. In his last annual letter before he moved to his retiral home, John wrote of the rather treacherous steep stairs in his Bridford Mews flat being a trigger for his move to his retirement home. Our stairs at home where he stayed with us were likewise steep and treacherous. In the dark he could so easily have fallen. I was not seventy at that time but it was a warning of our own vulnerability with age. Not long after John's visit we left the family home. Pam had found a flat for us, our present and hopefully final earthly home. No stairs inside!

---

[4] John Stott, *Men with a Message*, Longmans, Green and Co., 1954. John Stott revised by Stephen Motyer, Candle Books, 1997.

[5] John RW Stott, *I Believe in Preaching*, Hodder and Stoughton, 1982.

Our favourite tree – many happy memories of reading under it.
Painted by Daniel Hough when aged nine

View from our Window of St Germains Loch, Bearsden

Mount Gambier – the Valley Lake

The 'Residence', Mount Gambier. Our 'home' for the Scottish winters.

The Vasalóház (iron) House is the 'tilting' building on the left. This is not an optical illusion – it was designed like this! We lived in a flat in this building in the first few years of 2000.

Dr Juhász Judit, our oldest and dearest Szeged friend with her Trabant car. Some say the fastest of all cars made of cardboard – especially driven by Judit!

A view from the Colonsay manse

A favourite Colonsay beach

View from the road to Ibadan about ten miles outside Lagos.
Original painting by H. Moukoko purchased in 1959

A Nigerian market view

Aunt Phoebe's house (on the left).
The Royal Oak is on the right

Welcome to Eydon

Aerial view of Eydon

This card, written in pencil with the picture painted by a M. Bouret, was sent by my father from 'somewhere in France' on 14th April 1940 not long before the evacuation from Dunkirk.

It reads:

My dear wife,

2 more letters arrived today Apr 6th & 11th, gradually getting them all. So glad you are all OK now. Myself well. Pleased all settled about Bognor. Writing long letter tomorrow with all news. Fondest love to you & the boys. God bless you.

Your affectionate husband Jimmy XXX

Cpl J Parratt 1984399 14 Section 4 Coy. RE BEF

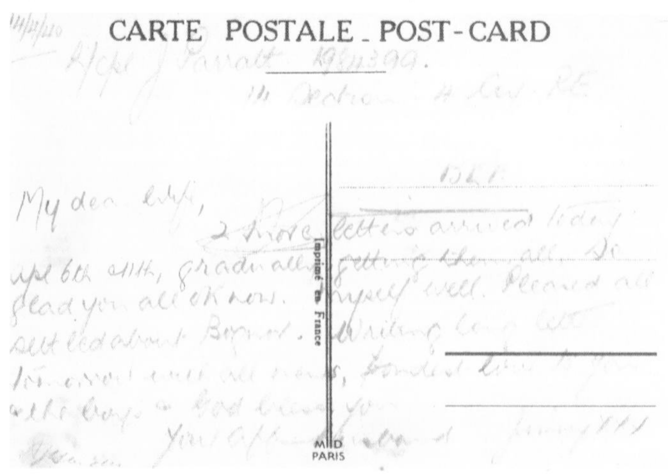
CARTE POSTALE _ POST-CARD

Imprimé en France

MD
PARIS

Chapter 26
Life as an Academic

All my official working life (and beyond!) I have worked in the university sector, firstly as a postgraduate student in London, then on the university staff in Nigeria and then, for over thirty years in Glasgow; and in the same university. I was also, and perhaps still am, an honorary Professor in the Szeged Medical University in Hungary. From when I entered university as an undergraduate student in 1952 to my final retiral from Szeged in 2006, that means well over fifty years as an academic in three quite different countries. What then is involved in being an academic and particularly one with faith in Christ – a 'Christian academic'?

I have written earlier of what it was like to work in two African universities. I now turn to my many years at Strathclyde University in Glasgow, to which I was appointed from a distance and without a formal interview. Then, as now, unusual – indeed unprecedented. First, some words about Strathclyde as a place of learning and research: this story too is rather unusual.

The roots lie back in 1796, which means that I was on the staff in 1996 when it celebrated the 200 years anniversary. The account of the early years has been well told by John Butt. It was published, in that bicentenary year, as *John Anderson's Legacy*.[1]

I was due to commence my new university career in this ancient 'centre of useful learning' on January 1st 1967. Of course, when I turned up on that day at the oldest building in the university, the Royal College building on George Street, I found the doors locked against me. Had they retracted the appointment and had second thoughts, realising their mistake? No, I had failed to realise that in Scotland New Year's Day is a public holiday. At that time Christmas Day was not. I was in Scotland! As with others in a similar situation I found the transition from Africa to Scotland a difficult and frustrating one. This experience taught me something about the phenomenon of 're-entry' that I wrote about earlier. In

---

[1] John Butt, *John Anderson's Legacy*, Tuckwell Press, 1996.

this newly formed department, and as a newly appointed member of staff, I had no office and no laboratory.

I was given a desk situated in the preparatory area between the two student laboratories and began the onerous task of applying for research grants, aimed at organisations who might conceivably be interested in supporting research in cardiac pharmacology in general and on the regulation of coronary blood flow in particular. I was fortunate to find interest in supporting this research from the Medical Research Council, the British Heart Foundation and later, the Wellcome Trust and the Scottish Hospitals Endowment Trust. Within a year I was given laboratory space on the roof of the building, and a temporary office situated in one of the corridors. But that first year, as one might expect, made me query whether I had made the right move. Indeed Bill Bowman, my very supportive Head of Department, did not expect me to remain: Strathclyde was to be a temporary situation allowing me to look within the UK for a more suitable position. Indeed, during that year I received two invitations to return to Nigeria to head up departments (I was given the choice of two!) in a new medical school situated in the north of the country. I also ventured as far east as Edinburgh to investigate a position there. In the end I decided to stay at Strathclyde. And a very good decision it turned out to be. When I retired in 1998 I was still there!

During this settling in period, I was greatly helped by the welcome I received from my departmental colleagues Graham Waton and Jessie Duncan – we had lunch together each day in the Staff Club – and from a good number of Christian colleagues in other departments. The news had got around on the Christian grapevine that I had arrived! This led to two things; deep friendships, and the decision to meet together regularly for prayer. This Staff Christian Fellowship continues; at the last count there were over thirty staff and former staff on the email list to receive news of the University Christian Union. The staff continue to meet each Monday lunchtime for prayer. The key mover in all this was Dr Alex Macintosh and I write more about him later. Alex also inaugurated a meeting at the beginning of each session at which Christian Union members, and interested freshers, were invited to make contact with the Christian staff. We introduced ourselves, told them where to find us and invited them to come and see us if they needed any help during their time at university. Over the years some did just that, especially those from overseas who had found the transition to Scotland and university studies difficult. This became later a university-wide means of helping students to cope with the marked transition from school to higher education.

What is involved in being a member of staff at a university? Am I 'an academic'? This my dictionary defines as being scholarly, unpractical and purely theoretical! I was once even asked how often I went into the place where I was supposed to work; as though all I did was to give a lecture or two and then spend the rest of my time at home! Most people would answer that question by saying that you teach undergraduates and, sometimes post-graduates too. If asked what else, they might talk about administration, design of courses, setting and marking examination papers. Few would say anything about research, which can be defined as 'the advancement of knowledge in a particular field' and with any practical applications of such new knowledge. My own experience of university life is that most, perhaps two-thirds, of my time was taken up in research. This is because my own subject of pharmacology is a very practical one, well defined as 'useful learning'. I would also say that such research is cooperative, it usually involves several people, often in different parts of the world. Necessary if an answer to a particular scientific problem is to be both solved and applied. So, to simplify, the staff member of a university spends his or her time in teaching, administration and research; people are better at one or other of these; few are experts in all three. I think my teaching was reasonably good, my research commitment was predominant and my administrative skills, if any, were heavily dependent upon an efficient secretary or secretaries, of which the department was superbly equipped. Essential, especially when I became Head of a Department, which at that time consisted of about sixty staff and post-graduates – apart from well over a hundred undergraduates. All this took up about 110% of my time. As my wife can testify.

University departments are complex structures; apart from the teaching staff there are secretaries, technicians and administrators. The staff themselves are stratified, meaning that there are variations in seniority under (usually) one Head of Department. The most senior staff are the Professors, next the Readers and Senior Lecturers with Lecturers and Assistant Lecturers further down the scale – or up the scale if you count profitability and usefulness. When I was appointed to the University of Strathclyde, I became a 'Lecturer in the Department of Physiology and Pharmacology' despite having come from a more senior position (Senior Lecturer in Physiology) in another university. Promotion to more senior levels, certainly in the 1970s, depended almost entirely on research and was based mainly on the number of publications in scientific journals; the more highly prized journals the better. I was fortunate that I had already published a good number of papers in 'good journals' and, as my research developed in Glasgow so these increased and I began to be 'known' outside Glasgow and to be regarded as something of an 'expert', especially in cardiovascular pharmacology – defined as 'the effect and mechanism of action of pharmacological agents (drugs) on the heart and blood vessels'. I have written just a little of this in *Highways of the Heart*.

My promotion within the Department was quite rapid; I was appointed Reader in 1970 (three years after joining the University) and a Professor (in a personal capacity) at the age of forty, in 1974. Later, in 1983 the University created for me a 'named chair' (Cardiovascular Pharmacology) which still exists – unfilled! The first of such named Strathclyde University Chairs was in Natural Philosophy/Physics created in 1796 (when it was known as 'Anderson's University' – see Appendix 6 about the remarkable John Anderson).

It is interesting that although teaching is the prime task of an university academic, there was not, at least in those days, any kind of assessment of the ability (or otherwise) to teach. This is now remedied in many universities, at least for newly appointed members of staff, and this includes feedback from the students themselves. This sometimes results in quite salutary reading!

I had little interest in university administration, although one of my closest friends, Derek Nonhebel (who like me had spent time working in a university overseas, in Chile) became an important administrator within the Science Faculty. It was Derek who, as Secretary of Helensburgh Baptist Church, first invited me to preach at that church; I had an annual summer visit booked for many years and it was in fact, the last church I was ever to preach in.

In 1986 I became not only Head of a vigorous active department (Physiology and Pharmacology) which was preparing to move to new premises in Cathedral Street, but also Head of the School of Pharmacy. This was at a time of crucial meetings with the Royal Pharmaceutical Society with regard to the acceptability of our pharmacy degrees as an entry into the practice of pharmacy in the UK. It was during this period too that an Institute for Drug Research was set up within the department.

There was little time to be involved in wider aspects of university administration. However, at this time and for some time after, the Department certainly contributed greatly to administrative affairs within the University as a whole. During this period two staff members became Deans of the Science Faculty and Bill Bowman was at one time University Vice-Principal. However, moving that far up the university hierarchy was not for me. Neither was I interested in sitting on outside committees such as the Greater Glasgow Health Board or the Committee on the Safety of Medicines. The main reason for these decisions was that I was frequently away from Glasgow. My daily diary for the 1980s and 90s reveal I was overseas almost every month and in London almost every other week. For example, in 1997 I was out of the country 17 times visiting 11 different countries worldwide. As someone quite seriously once said to me, 'Jim do you still pop into Strathclyde occasionally?'

After I competed my term as Head of Department I did rather little teaching. The main reason was that I was then given leave of absence (a Sabbatical) so I was away from the university for most of a year which was spent, by invitation, in Szeged, Hungary. A productive year. There was another reason however. This was that during my tenure as Head of Department, the University Senior Officers were persuaded that we needed more, younger staff. Two or three staff were appointed and, as they wanted to teach, when I returned my previous teaching commitments had been taken over by these newly appointed staff. They were reluctant to return them to me. Of course, I was disappointed!

The other main reasons for my lack of involvement in university politics were my responsibilities in Europe as a Council member for the International Society of Heart Research. These included being a local (!) member of the Organising Committee for the International meeting in Prague, the first in a former communist country. This led to delightful regular meetings with the Czech-Slovak group leading up to the meeting itself in 1995, and then as a regular external assessor for physiology research in the Academy of Sciences of the Czech Republic.

Receiving the Purkinye Gold Medal of the Academy of Sciences of the Czech Republic May 1995 with our old friends Professors Jutta and Wolfgang Schaper

However, much of my time in the 1990s was spent chairing a Europe wide group, supported by the European Commission, primarily concerned with ischaemic heart disease. This gave me the greatest satisfaction of my life in science. The original aim, with the fall of communism, was to attempt to link scientists in the former 'eastern bloc' with laboratories in the west. It linked university laboratories in Poland, the Czech Republic, Slovakia, Hungary and the former DDR with those in Germany, France, Holland and Spain. And Scotland. Not an entirely successful venture but it did forge deep friendships and individual research collaborations through meetings in Glasgow, London, Krakow, Bad Nauheim, Bratislava, Budapest, Szeged and Strasbourg. Certainly, twenty-five years later many of these friendships continue.

Old friends: Boya Ostadal and Dvořák!
Near the composer's final residence at Karlovy Vary

Aerial view of Ross Priory, Gartocharn, Loch Lomond – the scene of many European Union conferences during the 1990s.

The time spent in Hungary was increasing, with quite fascinating research findings, as were meetings of the European Community funded investigation into the causes of the vascular derangements that occurred in the early stages of septic shock. This was in collaboration with a delightful group in Strasbourg led by Jean-Claude Stoclet. Most of my last years at Strathclyde were thus almost entirely 'research years' in other European countries. As my wife has often told me about family happenings during that period – 'Jim, you were seldom there'. There was also a deeper involvement in preaching (most Sundays when I was back in Scotland) and in the affairs of the Glasgow Bible College which was, at the time, passing through a critical phase.

Chapter 27
A Christian in Science

What difference did it make that I was a 'Christian academic'? What bearing did my faith have on my working life in a university environment? We are to be, as are Christians in other places of work, an admixture of salt, light and leaven; we are to be the wheat among the tares of this world. As my former minister Dr Thomson wrote in *The Praying Christ*, referring to the prayer of Jesus in John's gospel chapter 17, 'For the Christian to be of the world is unthinkable, but he must be in the world, to give his witness to the world. He is kept from conformity to the world but not from concern for the world'. Part of that concern is to share the life-changing gospel. That is surely part of what it means to be a 'Christian academic'.

How many of my immediate colleagues knew I was a Christian? At the rather few official dinners I was always asked to say 'grace' as a thankyou before the meal but I was somewhat taken aback years later when perhaps my closest colleague in the department expressed surprise that I was religious at all. A Jewish agnostic, he had had continuing conversations with one of our Christian post-graduate students (now Professor of Pharmacology at the University of Oxford) and had discovered from her that I was a 'believer'. This started with me a continuing, email dialogue. So, not much salt during my time at Strathclyde!

A relevant question I think is how far should one go in what has been called 'proselytizing' in a university environment? At one time one of my post-doctoral Fellows, from Ghana, told me that one of the PhD students working in my laboratory had recently (through his witness) become a Christian and that as there are now three of us, shouldn't we 'do something about it?' Quite a challenge for me! After thought (and prayer!) we decided to issue an invitation to others in the School of Pharmacy to join with us to think through and explore the Christian faith. About eight 'signed up'. These included two post-graduate students from China. The original idea was to hold this outwith the university premises (in our home) but the Chinese students pointed out that, because they had taken part in a demonstration outside the Chinese Embassy in London and would be 'on camera', they would be on the 'to be watched' list. It would be dangerous for them, if they were to return to China, to have been regularly to a home of a staff member. We therefore decided to meet in my office (safe for them) in the early evening. This we continued to do for two years; the first year was spent on the person and work of Christ, leading to possible commitment; the second on how to continue the Christian walk.

In the event this couple did not return to China but, after completing their doctorates, obtained jobs in Perth, Australia. Years later I visited them there; they had some links with the local Chinese Church.

One more example of being a 'Christian in Science': official, formal dinners can give opportunities for quiet witness. At one such – and seated at the top table! – I sat next to a very eminent lady scientist, Professor Jutta Schaper, the General Secretary of the European Section of the International Society for Heart Research, ISHR. I could see she was somewhat 'down' and asked her if I could help. She confided that she had just learnt that her sister in Germany was seriously ill. I said we would pray for her.

This led to something quite remarkable, not only a deep friendship with her and her husband who was just as eminent a scientist – Professor Wolfgang Schaper, but it also led to an unusual invitation. Some years later Jutta and Wolfgang organised a scientific meeting in their home town of Bad Nauheim. This took place over a weekend and Jutta asked me if on the Sunday morning I would 'preach' in her home to some of those friends who had attended the meeting. I knew some were from communist countries, and some were certainly Party members, so I accepted, not to preach but to speak about my own Christian faith. But only on the condition that those invited were agreeable 'to Jim sharing about his faith'. It seemed all agreed; after all we had known each of them for many years. So, on that Sunday (and after a good lunch!) they listened as I spoke about my coming to faith from John's gospel (3:14 and 15), the passage that had brought me to Christ so many years before. Afterwards I suggested that if anyone wished to follow up on what I had said they would find reading John's gospel helpful. I had a pile of these with me. Jutta immediately gave each one present a copy – whether they wished to have one or not! I am unsure about the repercussions of this unusual gathering but whenever I meet one who was present that Sunday, he always reminds me of 'that home meeting' that had taken place so many years earlier and at which I had spoken.

One final example. I first visited Hungary many times during communist times and indeed was there on a sabbatical from Glasgow at the time when the Berlin wall fell. I remember many discussions in the laboratory, after our work for the day was completed, about the Christian faith, usually whilst drinking the remains of the day's coffee. Indeed, my closest Szeged colleague Dr (now Professor) Ágnes Végh had several questions about the resurrection of Christ. This story has a number of repercussions which I will leave until we come to an account of our time in Hungary but I mention it here because of the changing atmosphere to speaking about Christianity that took place immediately after the fall of communism: as one friend was fond of saying 'communists out, Christians in'. It should be remembered that no one could hold a senior office in a Hungarian university unless they were a Communist Party member. Things were about to change at least in the initial few years of freedom.

The point about these examples of being a 'Christian in science' is that they could not have occurred if I had not remained in science and certainly not if I had moved into the Christian pastoral ministry in Scotland. God was continuing to work out his purpose in my life.

The question remains: how to be salt for Christ in the university environment? Or indeed in any 'working environment'.

First, we are told[1] 'always to be ready to give an answer to every man that asks you a reason for the hope that is within you'. Note the 'always' and the 'every'! What does 'being ready' imply? Are we well enough prepared for living as Christians in the workplace by our churches? Sadly, in my experience, not always. Or, not at all.

One thing I am still slowly learning is that the Holy Spirit is great at initiating such situations (usually unexpected!) and providing the words for speaking about Jesus if we are willing to pray that the Spirit will provide such opportunities. The difficulty,

[1] 1 Peter 3:15.

certainly for me, is that we are often unwilling to 'give each day back to the Lord' and ask for opportunities for witness. Elsewhere I give examples from my own life. Sadly, these were rather few and far between.

This 'memoir' is a good opportunity to write about some of my colleagues at Strathclyde and especially those who had a big influence on my own Christian life. The most significant of these friends was Dr Alex Mcintosh (see Appendix 7).

My academic life at Strathclyde ended in 1998 at which time I had reached the statutory age of 65. It was celebrated in London as a better centre for visitors from overseas and which included nearly all of the European colleagues involved in the 'Network'. The celebration included a recital at the Wigmore Hall, by a young string quartet flown in from Hungary (as a thank you to me) and a sumptuous dinner hosted by the Ciba Foundation.

SUGÁR STRING QUARTET

Liszt Ferenc Music Academy of Szeged
Director: Richard Weninger

BENCE ÁBRAHÁM – violin
MARIANN BUDAI – violin
KRISZTINA MEGYES – viola
TIMEA PÉTER – cello

The quartet was formed from student musicians of the Ferenc Liszt Music Academy of Szeged in 1995. Its name was taken from Rezső Sugár (1919-1982), a hungarian composer.
Despite of the short existence, the Sugár Quartet had performed several successful concerts both in Hungary and abroad. In 1996 and in 1997 they were invited for concert tours in Finland. 1996 was particulary successful year in the life of the quartet; it was the first prizewinner at the Hungarian Chamber Music festival in Budapest and the Hungarian Radio recorded with them Rezső Sugár 2nd String Quartet. In 1998 the quartet attended a one month international music course in Germany.

SPONSORS:

HUNGARIAN CULTURAL FOUNDATION
"FRIENDS of GLASGOW"
EXP UK

Concert poster at the Wigmore Hall, London,
during the celebration of my retirement in 1998

For a time, I was given an office in the new building in Cathedral Street that the Department had moved into the year before. Here, I continued to write. Laboratory accommodation to continue to do research was not provided; retired academic staff were not allowed to continue to stay in the department in which they once worked, rightly so I believe. Later my office was required for a new member of staff and I was moved to share space with two others in the basement of what was at one time the animal house. On one side of the space was a sign reading 'electricity – danger of death'; on the other side was the abattoir! So, I moved to new office and laboratory space in Szeged and several wonderful years working in Hungary followed. But that is another story.

There is an organisation, of which I am a long-term member, called 'Christians in Science' (CiS) which organises conferences and local groups in most of the leading university cities in the United Kingdom, although, at the moment, sadly not Glasgow. The ones in Scotland are in Edinburgh, Dundee and St Andrews. Anyone with an interest in the interface between science and the Christian faith is welcome at these local meetings. You can find more information at secretary@cis.org.uk or from the Executive Officer Mary Browett at maryb.cis@outlook.com. There is an excellent journal published jointly with The Victoria Institute entitled *Science and Christian Belief*. This was first published in 1989 and is now produced four times a year. Here is a flavour of the articles published. They include almost every aspect of the relation between science and faith, including 'a philosophy of science for Christians', the limits of science and faith, human enhancement, determinism, brain function and free will, miracles in medicine, chance or providence, neuroscience and human freedom, the creation/evolution debate and discussions on the early chapters of Genesis. And much, much else! In each issue there is a particularly interesting book review section.

A perhaps more dynamic organisation, based in Scotland, is 'Grasping the Nettle' set up in 2014 and stimulated by the TV showing of 'The God Question. Science, God and the search for truth'. This is a unique interdenominational initiative of the Scottish churches to better equip Christians to understand issues of science and faith. Check the website – www.graspthenettle.org or email office@graspthenettle.org. There are quarterly newsletters.

If any readers have an interest in these issues, both Grasp the Nettle and the CiS, would be good places to start. Perhaps especially for those who have been programmed, often by unbelievers (in the biblical sense) to the idea that there is a fundamental and conflicting difference between scientific evidence and Christian faith. For me, there is no conflict: all truth is God's truth, whether it is scientific or biblical.

Some books I have found helpful are:

(1) John Cottingham, *How to Believe*, Bloomsbury, 2015. One of my favourite books, by a leading philosopher.

(2) Timothy Keller, *The Reason for God*, Hodder and Stoughton, London, 2008. A popular introduction, to give to your friends!

(3) Arthur Peacocke, *God and Science. A Quest for Christian Credibility*, SCM Press, 1996.

Peacocke is both an Anglican priest and a renowned biochemist. For 'wistful agnostics'.

(4) Colin Russell, *Cross-currents. Interactions Between Science and Faith*, Christian Impact, London, 1995.

(5) Malcolm Jeeves and R.J. Berry, *Science, Life and Christian Belief. A survey and Assessment*, Apollos, Leicester, 1998. Both authors are 'working' scientists. 'Science is the true friend of Christian Faith'. An indispensable guide.

There are many, many others. Several feet of my bookshelves! Certainly, no need for me to add to them.

Chapter 28
Ninety-nine Not Out!

This is not the age of the author. Rather it is yet another diversion. On preaching, which surprisingly has played a major part in my life'

Soon after arriving in Bearsden, we had a neighbour who was involved with a Glasgow free church, not to be confused with The Free Church (of Scotland). By 'free' I mean non-denominational. This was in Maryhill and was the home church of Grace Archibald (a pioneer missionary in Nigeria) and Jim McRoberts, the founder, in the early 1930s, of the Gospel Male Voice Choirs, to which reference has already been made. The invitation was to speak at one of their Sunday services. Since no-one in Scotland had ever heard me speak this was not without risk. On both sides. However, a number of invitations to other churches followed. These included the Seamans Bethel on Glasgow's Clydeside, which on closing became a night-club (unconnected with the invitations) and a church in the Darnley district of Glasgow which met in a room designed by Rennie McIntosh.

Lay preachers are seldom well trained and sadly this shows! Fortunately, I had the experience of being in a church where the minister took a class in preaching and I had also heard many really gifted preachers such as John Stott, John Caiger, Martyn Lloyd-Jones, J.G.S.S. Thomson and Professor James Stewart, whose book on preaching in the 'Teach yourself' series was for me most challenging; alongside those by James Black, Haddon Robinson and John Stott.

As a member of the Church of Scotland I also received invitations to take services from as far away as Kilmarnock, Airth, various Glasgow churches and the two very different churches in Calder near Edinburgh. A gown was required for one; the other was much less formal. This became a regular summer commitment. A move to the newly established and 'open' Baptist Church in Roman Road, Bearsden opened doors to speak in many other Baptist churches from Edinburgh to the Inner Hebrides and from Perth to Ayr and Peebles. There were two consequences. First, I was invited to become a member of the Scottish Baptist Lay Preachers Association (SBLPA). This involved a trial 'preach' before the committee and then, quite an ordeal, to speak to the rest of the association at their annual lunch in Edinburgh (on Noah – a preacher . . .'). Later I became the President of this illustrious body.

The second result, a few years later, was a request, which I declined, to allow my name to go forward to become President of the Baptist Union (of Scotland) and then, somewhat later, to consider becoming a Baptist minister. This latter I took seriously. The first step was to train, not full-time (I was chairing my university department at the time) but through three years of part-time study at the Bible Training Institute Glasgow (BTI) for the Cambridge University Diploma in Religious Studies, which Cambridge believes to be the equivalent of a BD degree. What happened after that was completed has already been described.

As a layman with a more than full-time job, preaching most Sundays somewhere in Scotland and, as was often the case, when I was out of the country during the preceding week, challenging. Preparation in hotel rooms or on the plane. Not really satisfactory. Some sermons were preached more than once but, as one of my favourite Christian writers Professor E.M. Blaiklock said of the Beatitudes, 'perhaps like all good sermons this famous discourse was given more than once'. In good company then.

Is what you preached ever remembered? A word of caution! At one church I was spoken to on arrival by a lady who said she remembered what I had last preached on at that church several years previously. She then proceeded to give me the three points (this was a Baptist church where the 'tradition' is that sermons must have 'three points'!). Encouraging then until, on reaching home, I discovered from my records that I had never preached there on that passage; the message was remembered (important) but was not preached by me!

Perhaps it is helpful to take notes of sermons. At one of my favourite churches, Lambhill Evangelical Church in the north-west of Glasgow (a church where I have preached ninety-nine times over fifty or so years) the gifted organist Robert Glen regularly takes notes, which are available the following week; or sent to the housebound by post. At one service Robert turned what I had said into a 'hymn'.

Not quite up to those by Timothy Dudley-Smith perhaps but, for me, a real encouragement. The words and music are below.

On two occasions I was asked by churches to be their Moderator, which meant helping them to find a pastor and chairing the vacancy committee. Successful, I think. One such church was on the beautiful island of Tiree, stuck out in the Atlantic and staying with old friends. They, for me too soon, found a pastor so visits were rather few. The journey by air is spectacular, flying over other Hebridean islands and Scotland's glorious west coast.

I think in fifty years I must have taken services about eight hundred times over most of the south of Scotland and elsewhere; in India, Australia and Hungary. Even England! Most of all in my own former church (170 times in all). The last time was in another favourite church, in Helensburgh, a month short of my eighty-sixth birthday. Just as well one seldom knows when you will preach for the last time! I wonder will that ninety-nine ever become one hundred? Even at this late stage?

Chapter 29
Summer Holidays

On 'thought for the day' on BBC radio 4 recently, the writer and broadcaster Ann Atkins spoke about her family always returning to the same place for their summer holidays, in her case the beaches of Norfolk – known also to us. We had, in the early years of our children and grandchildren growing up, the same experience going, not to Norfolk but to the Essex coast at Frinton-on-Sea. Situated between two very different seaside resorts (Clacton-on-Sea and Walton-on-the-Naze) Frinton had the reputation of being 'up market', even 'posh', certainly wealthy, the home of commuting 'men of means' or, as my mother described them, 'city gents'. Frinton was also the home of an early Dr Who, who had sadly left his Tardis back at the BBC TV centre. There were no supermarkets, cinema, 'pubs', or fish and chip shops. Until that is a 'revolution' took place against the Frinton 'no change' diehards, who were eventually outwitted. The chippie now does a roaring trade.

The barrier that was an attempt to keep the town 'as it once was', and to exclude day trippers from London, was the hand operated 'gates' at the railway level crossing. When closed, which was quite often, the long queues of cars attempting entrance to the town could (should) have put people off coming to Frinton but never did. Residents knew another secret way into their home town avoiding those dreaded 'gates'.

You may be thinking, as we were neither 'city gents' nor wealthy with mansions in the town, why we were there at all. The answer is that my wife's family had been going to Frinton for the best part of a century; her grandparents had spent their summer holidays there from the early 1910s, and, on retiral, had built a house there called 'White Gables'. So Frinton became the favourite holiday venue for their own children (six girls) and many grandchildren – including Pam. Each year in August there was a seaside mission for children run by the Children's Special Service Mission (or CSSM), a branch of Scripture Union and run by students from the universities of

Oxford and Cambridge (of course) resplendent in their college blazers. It was at one of these that Pam, at an early age, asked Jesus into her life. We have in Frinton then much to thank God for and with fine sandy beaches and good churches it became a very special family holiday venue for over forty years.

Summer holidays. My parents at the seafront 'hut', the centre for many holidays at Frinton during the 1960s through to 2005

Frinton had a tennis club, frequented most years by famous, and not so famous, players from Wimbledon, a lovely golf club overlooking the sea, a theatre and a 'Bible Depot' run by a Frinton legend called Earnest Luff, an elderly (in our time) white-haired gentleman, once a missionary to village children, often observed riding about town on his equally ancient bicycle. The depot was a good place for meeting like-minded folk exploring the selection of bibles and Christian books. There was a medical clinic run by three ex-missionaries of whom the brothers Davies became special friends. John and Dorothy Davies, former missionaries with Interserve (then BMMF) in India became very special to our family. We thank God for them! Later they left Frinton and moved to, of all places, Bethnal Green now populated by members of the

Bangladeshi immigrant community. Another mission field for their 'retirement'.

Separating the beach from the town was a well-kept area of grass known as the 'Greensward'. It was here, in 1955, that I asked Pam to be my wife. There is no plaque to celebrate this event but there is a seat near the spot put by the family to celebrate lifetimes of wonderful holidays spent in the town. Along the shoreline were many colourful beach huts one of which we purchased. The first one we bought was carried out to sea in a winter storm but the replacement became for many years the place where the family spent many sunny summer days (this was England remember) swimming, reading, lunching and helping in various ways the work of the SU mission.

Although we were in the early 1960s resident in Nigeria, we managed to purchase a bungalow a mile outside the 'gates' in the village of Kirby Cross, with views over the railway line across wheat fields down to the sea. This was at the suggestion of my father-in-law, known to the family as 'Gramp', a wonderful man who also happened to be our bank manager and who set up the loan. Not easy in those days because we were non-resident in the UK. The bungalow served as a base to which we returned each summer 'on leave' from Ibadan. Perhaps this was one reason why Pam's parents bought a retirement bungalow at Holland-on-Sea, a few miles along the coast. My own parents bought the Kirby bungalow from us when we moved to Scotland at the end of 1966. This meant that we still had a base for making Frinton our usual holiday destination until all our parents had died by the early 1990s. So, over forty years of annual visits for us; and a place our children will always remember because of their frequent annual contacts with their grandparents.

One of the most moving events of these Frinton days for me, was when my father was dying of cancer. I never found it easy to talk to my father about spiritual matters although, as already mentioned, they had begun attending church after my own conversion in London. One Sunday in August 1977 I was preaching at the church they often attended at 'Homelands' (a church plant 'outside the gates') and on my return after the evening service I went in to see him, ill in bed, to say goodnight. He asked what I had preached on and how sorry he was not to have been present. It was on Stephen's martyrdom – Stephen 'saw heaven opened', 'Jesus standing' and the 'glory of God'. When I spoke of heaven, he gripped my hand and said 'Jim, that is where I'm going because I love Jesus'. He died a few days later.

My mother died in 1990 just short of her 90th birthday after catching a foot in a string bag and breaking her hip.

I give God thanks for such good parents.

Pam's parents lived to a good age. Her mother, blind and a braille reader, died shortly after they had moved into a residential home, with Pam present at her bedside and Gramp praising God for her 'homecoming' and for a good life. The many, very heavy volumes of her braille New Testament were sent, very appropriately, to Nigeria (by sea!) for the SUM Blind School at Vom. We often participated in evening prayers with Gramp; his prayer lists written on the back of old used envelopes. He died at the age of 91.

Now it happened that the leader of the SU Frinton beach mission in the early 1960s was Bill Roberts and we remember speaking to him about working for SU in Nigeria. This indeed he did in 1965, a year or so before we left Ibadan. The Frinton SU mission was not only for children (bible studies, a daily service on the beach with a sand pulpit) but was also for parents; about fifty or so, were also catered for with times of prayer and a 'bible reading' each day which, over the years, I gave on three occasions.

We left Frinton for the final time in September 1997, after celebrating our fortieth wedding anniversary there with all our family present. A suitable end to over forty years of family holidays, with four generations present.

Chapter 30
Scottish Islands

I have much enjoyed visiting the islands off the west coast of Scotland and, since such visits almost always involved preaching in them, the islands of the Inner Hebrides. Perhaps here we have the 'real' heart of Scotland.

Islay

The first of these visits came many years ago – indeed in the 1960s through the lady secretary of the two Baptist Churches on Islay at Bowmore (at the centre of the island) and Port Ellen. It is a strange shaped island with 'more whisky distilleries than people' and, apart from the beaches at Port Charlotte and the main 'centres' of Bridgend and Bowmore quite isolated. We drove on one occasion along the narrow single-track road to Portnahaven which, at the south-western extremity of the island, sticks out into the Atlantic facing the lighthouse on the island of Orsay. For us, on that one visit, the place seemed quite lost in time. It was, at one time the home of the sadly missed Scottish politician John Smith. Indeed, we slept in what was once the schoolroom where he was taught.

Like some islands Islay is neither easy to get to nor, even if one wanted, to leave. And there is a particular problem for laymen taking church services there because, if one uses the ferries, to either Oban or Tarbert, it is midday on Monday before it is possible to get back to Glasgow. This eliminates most lay preachers (from the Baptist Lay Preachers Association – SBLPA) on whom the churches, until recently, depended. It was relatively easy for me to rearrange my timetable but for others it was much more difficult.

However, someone gave me a contact at Loganair who had a Sunday evening flight from Islay at that time; less than an hour on one of the most beautiful of flights on a clear day that is! I made contact with the airline pointing out that this was a service to an island community and that there was benefit for the islanders to have their churches supported in this way. Very generously the airline gave to all who 'served the island churches' a special flight discount and I and others, made use of this on a number of occasions. Interestingly, another member became so enamoured with the island that he and his wife moved there to live and he became the Pastor of the two churches. He only recently retired.

It became a tradition that each Wednesday members of the Islay churches would go to Colonsay on the ferry, have picnic lunch there (at the church) and encourage the much smaller church membership. Wednesday was the only day in the week that it was possible to catch a ferry on route from Islay to Oban with a stop off at Colonsay; the ferry returned from Oban the same evening to enable the Islay folk to return home. Many took their bicycles in order to do a round tour of the island.

Colonsay

Of all the islands of the Inner Hebrides we visited Colonsay[1] was by far our favourite and just over two hours by the Calmac ferry from Oban: a wonderful journey that takes you past the 'bridge over the Atlantic' to the top end of Jura (and that treacherous whirlpool, Corryvreckan where George Orwell nearly drowned) to the pier at Scalasaig.

Many years earlier I had been in contact with the secretary of the Baptist Church, Ena Williams, to see if help was needed by that church over the summer months. That visit was the first of many over the years, indeed until 2010. The advantage was that accommodation (basic at that time) was available at the Baptist Manse which was conveniently situated a couple of hundred yards from the church itself. Indeed, even if one did not possess a car one could live there and take the services provided someone gave you a lift there in the first place since the distance from the ferry point at Scalasaig to the manse at Kilchattan is about four miles. The manse then could be rather lonely.

On our first visit we arrived after dark and it took a complete circular tour of the island before we could determine which of the isolated buildings was the manse. A young friend of mine and

[1] Kevin Byrne, *Lonely Colonsay – Island on the Edge*, House of Lochar, Isle of Colonsay, Argyll 2010.

his new wife staying there once had a scare late in the evening by something being pushed through the letter box. They had gone to bed early being tired from the journey only to be rudely awoken by the noise of clatter from the box downstairs; friends had discovered where to send the congratulatory cards! One story told us, true of course, was about a recorded delivery parcel arriving in the early morning hours. The process was that the postman received the mail off the ferry and, having sorted it, drove around the island delivering it. If the ferry was late, as quite frequently happened, then so was the postal delivery. When one parcel was delivered and required a signature the occupants were awoken in the hour after midnight by the arrival of the island postman. The record book showed the exact time of delivery. What did those at Post Office Headquarters make of that time I wonder? Probably nowhere in the UK was the time of delivery so early in the morning of the following day. What efficiency! World record. First class post!

Sometimes there was a delivery for the occupants of the neighbouring island of Oronsay. This was probably for the folk of the bird sanctuary. To reach Oronsay one has to drive, or walk, over a stretch of sand known as the Strand. It is only possible to reach the island if the tide is right; the two islands are separated by the sea except at low tide. Oronsay is a place of pilgrimage; but only for the three hours that access via the Strand is possible. Otherwise, an overnight stay.

Why was Colonsay so special for us? It is certainly beautiful with marvellous beaches, especially the wide expanse of sand at Kiloran Bay, said by some Colonsay inhabitants to be the best in the Inner Hebrides, at Ardkenish (good for seals and otters) and, our favourite the beach at Balnahard near the northern tip of the island. This requires a stiffish walk, especially at the beginning with the climb around the highest point on the island at Carnan and Beinn Beag, keeping a lookout for choughs. The path then passes Balnahard Farm, where on one occasion we had to wade through sheep awaiting shearing and frightened a corncrake out of a ditch, go through a herd of cattle (viewing us with suspicion) and cross the machair to reach the sea. This is a good place to see wild goats, said by some to be descendants of those that swam ashore from a wreck of the Armada. One of our friends Pam Carter the artist painted the Bay for us; there is a photo reproduced in the colour section in the middle of the book.

Colonsay is a wonderful place for wildlife. Herons sometimes breed there (the young ones are surely among the ugliest of all birds), we were often welcomed in the morning by young rabbits (and buzzards on the watch out for them) and on several occasions from the garden of the Manse we saw eagles. Is there, we often wondered, a more delightful spot to spend a holiday. With some work of course!

We had several consecutive years taking the August or September church services on Colonsay. When we first went these were held at both churches each Sunday but later the two church memberships decided to combine them. This meant that on one Sunday the combined service was held at the Church of Scotland, in the delightful church near the hotel and landing pier at Scalasaig (doors and gate kept shut to prevent an incursion by sheep) and the next Sunday the worship was held at the Baptist Church at Kilchattan. A notice at the gates indicated where the next service would be held. Initially some at the Baptist Union in Glasgow was not too happy about this but the view of the (five) church members prevailed. It was a good idea; if it was the turn of the Baptist Church to hold the service, the visiting preacher for the C of S (usually a minister from the mainland) was always asked to share in the service in some way. And, vice-versa. In a small island with few members in either church this was a good situation and usually the congregation consisted of members from both churches, with the exception of the disabled members who could not manage the steps into the Scalasaig church. There was always a good number of visitors in the summer from all over Britain. Even some folk from England had heard of Colonsay and became regular visitors. On occasions there were up to fifty or so attending services including children, so some provision needed to be made for these too.

Pam and I always visited each of the members and these were good friendly and spiritual times and much appreciated. The problem with many such isolated communities is that the few members are often elderly and/or disabled. One physical advantage of the situation of the Baptist Church was its proximity to the island primary school and at one time the idea came to hold a weekly children's meeting known as the 'Colonsay After School Club'. The school bus driver (then Kevin Byrne, one of his many tasks; islanders are good at multi-tasking) was happy to come for the children on Thursday afternoons (an hour later than the usual closing time) for games, bible stories and, of course, refreshments. At one time we provided teaching material from the Scripture Union. These meetings started but after a few years fell away because of the age and infirmity of those willing to help and fewer children on the island. They were last held in 2005.

The church on Colonsay

Among the house visits we made was to Ena Williams, the now invalided church secretary who had made the initial invitation to come to the island many years previously. We happened to be on the island just after she died. The tradition on the island, perhaps for other islands too, was that the coffin is brought into the church the day prior to the burial and is 'received' into the church by the minister (me on this occasion) and elders (if there are any). It is a moving experience to gather around the coffin in the otherwise empty church and give thanks to the Lord for the life of the departed believer. The church lights are then left on until the thanksgiving service. The church was packed for that with people standing outside - in the rain. The coffin was then carried to the cemetery, set in a lovely situation about half a mile away. Almost all the island population was in attendance including the Laird.

The new secretary (Eleanor) and her husband became good friends. Alastair had been born on the island and, because his home at Machrins was just (and only just) short of a mile from the school, he was not eligible for a lift on the school bus. This meant walking. In winter this must have been hazardous at times. The school population was always on the border of survival with fewer than ten pupils. And remains so. Once pupils reach secondary school age they go to Oban and, depending on the reliability of the ferries (and the weather), it might be some time before they see their families again.

Our last visit was in June 2010 and we left in rather dramatic circumstances. We were booked to take an early ferry back to Oban, which meant an early rise in order to pack up after our two weeks stay and to clean the house. On route to the ferry we also called on Eleanor to say goodbye. Pam felt unwell and remained in the car. At the ferry point we said goodbye to various friends; most of the island go to the ferry point to say goodbye to those travelling or to welcome new arrivals, but again Pam remained in the car. She was ill when we boarded and slept for much of the two-hour sea journey. Clearly, something was 'not quite right'. We decided to drive the two-hour car journey back home and go directly to our GP surgery. The locum on duty told us not to go home and unpack but to drive straight to the Western Infirmary and report to the Stroke Unit. Pam remained there for six days. The scan showed areas of cerebral damage; there was complete loss of the sense of smell and problems with balance. Looking back, we should have foreseen this; there had been quite severe problems with her balance earlier. The point of relating this story is the response of our friends on Colonsay when they heard the news. Phone calls, cards, letters, flowers sent through the post. Even eggs from Walter Williams (the best in the world he always claimed) arrived intact in the post. One of the cards simply said 'you are one of us'. From the Gaelic- speaking church secretary on the island this was, for us, quite moving. A few years later we were invited back to the island to stay for a week at the C of S manse situated centrally in Scalasaig.

Good to meet up with friends again, although by that time Eleanor and another member had died. In 2012 Eleanor wrote a short history of the Baptist Church on Colonsay to celebrate the bi-centenary. This was published on the island at the House of Lochar in 2013 and printed just before her death[2].

Mull

Unlike Colonsay, Mull although a big island, is easy to reach from the Scottish mainland; less than an hour on the frequent ferries from Oban. Mull is shaped rather like a clenched fist with the thumb stuck out, this being the Ross of Mull with the single-track road, which is very busy in the summer months, because at the far end of it is the ferry port (Fionnphort) to the island of Iona. A brief word about this, for me, somewhat over-rated, over busy place of pilgrimage. The best places are the beaches on the side furthest from the Abbey, always until quite recently a building site.

Mull has good beaches at the 'top end' like Calgary (we spent a lovely afternoon there once watching a family of blue tits flying in and out of a hole in a metal post), the highest mountain on the islands Ben More (966m) and one of the scariest single track B roads in the islands coursing along the cliffs from Killiechronan to Calgary.

There has been a Baptist Church in Bunessan on the Ross for many years. After steady decline there was a resurgence of activity and growth with the arrival several years ago of a couple from the mainland. The later arrival of Bill and Jan Roberts (the story is told later) was another stimulus for growth until they moved to Tobermory. The manse is a caravan situated adjacent to the church, well equipped; heating, running water and a TV. A characteristic of Sunday services was that afterwards all are invited to lunch in the church 'dining room', the few members supplying soup and sandwiches. As some have travelled a fair distance to reach the church this was always much appreciated. Sadly, Mull Baptist Church has since closed.

---

[2] Eleanor and John McNeill, *The Baptist Church in Colonsay 1812-2012*, House of Lochar, Colonsay 2013.

One can draw certain conclusions from our experience of small island churches. For their survival input from 'outside' is essential but better would be a real 'calling' from God that here is a neglected spiritual harvest field which badly needs local leadership. Folk sensing this call would need to live on the island all year round and become part of the community. Second dwellings for people from the mainland is not enough for church stability. Church numbers are few, they are usually elderly and jobs (secure employment) are scarce. Scottish islands have in the past been places of spiritual revival. Another is badly needed. 'Pray ye therefore . . .'

Tiree

This elongated far-out island, famous for surfing, sticks out into the Atlantic and has nearly one thousand inhabitants. It is a long way by ferry from Oban. We were invited to holiday there by old Bearsden friends, Ian and Eileen Tainsh in a delightful surround-sound cottage with separate holiday accommodation; which we did not have to use! After I had preached (part of the deal) I was somewhat surprised to be invited to be the Moderator of the Baptist Church which was 'vacant' – that is the church was looking for a pastor. The members met for services in the community hall rather than in either of the two Baptist buildings, then out of use although one of them has now been 'reconstructed' by the members. The Tiree church has a good-sized fellowship with a number of children; the chosen place for meeting is ideal being quite central.

To be asked to help was delightful and I wish sometimes the vacancy could have been prolonged! It so happened that a retired couple, the husband a former minister in England, had bought a retirement property on the island and it did not take long for them to be called to the pastorate. Before that I had a few meetings with the vacancy committee, sometimes flying back to Glasgow. This, on a clear evening is a spectacular fifty-minute flight over Colonsay (in the distance), part of Mull and Jura and the wonderful Scottish west coast. Tiree, was a good church fellowship to be associated with, albeit for only a short time! And, a wonderful place to stay!

We also spent a few days on the neighbouring island of Coll. Very few inhabitants, great unspoilt beaches and a great hotel. We only intended to stay one night but because the ferry back to Oban could not dock because of the weather we had a three day stay. Great food, free tour of the island. A good place to be stranded!

All about this and other islands can be found in standard guide books. For us they are some of our favourite places anywhere in the world.

Of course, there are other Scottish islands, over eight hundred of them. We have not visited all of them. Has anyone we wonder. We have been on Skye a couple of times, Arran (where once we were fortunate to sail all around the island on the Waverley), Staffa and Fingal's Cave (by boat from Iona) and Orkney, where the purpose was to attend the St Magnus Festival, to meet up with old friends from Bearsden, who took us on a tour of the amazing Neolithic village at Skara Brae, and to check out the relatives of a future grandson-in-law. These met with our unqualified approval!

Appendix 6
John Anderson

Born a son of the manse in 1726 (both his father and grandfather were ministers of the Church of Scotland) John Anderson graduated (at the age of nineteen) from the University of Glasgow, before becoming a tutor to the son of the Earl of Moray. This involved a time spent in France where he became interested in road construction, soldiers pay and the pressure on the Huguenots to convert to Catholicism. After a short time in London, he was appointed Professor of Oriental Languages (Hebrew) at the 'Glasgow College', as the University of Glasgow was then known. Just two years later, in 1757, supported by Adam Smith, he was appointed to the Chair of Natural Philosophy. Although classically trained (Latin and Greek) his greatest interests were in mechanics and in 'mathematical and experimental physics' (in contrast to what was later to be known as 'theoretical physics'). As he wrote – 'we must despise every theory that does not rest upon decisive experiments', a lesson even today for the so called 'armchair scientist'.

His interests were wide; the classical languages, literature, music and experimental physics. His well-attended public lectures (the lecture hall had to be extended twice because of increasing numbers) on subjects such as mechanics, electricity, climatology and even the 'science' of games such as tennis, golf and billiards. The emphasis was always on 'useful learning', for example the application of physics to such things as lightning conductors and ballistics; his cannon (the 'Anderson gun') was used by both the French and American military. His commitment to practical science and his concern for a wider access to education, especially for women, was allied to his devout Presbyterianism.

Beginning in the 1760s there were attacks on the teaching curriculum of Glasgow University with a demand for reforms like those being proposed for the two colleges in Aberdeen, Kings and Marischal. Too much time was being spent in the older

Glasgow University on 'logic and metaphysics' rather than on more 'useful' and relevant subjects such as 'practical mathematics', commerce and natural history. Another demand for change was on the governance of the university – everything was in the hands of the professors with no outside 'interference' from the laity. A new academy in Glasgow was the best means of remedying these deficiencies.

It seems that the Glasgow professors of the eighteenth century were a quarrelsome and litigious lot! Thirty years later The Glasgow Chronicle wrote about Anderson (who was nicknamed 'Jolly Jack Phosphorus' because of his interests in all things combustible) that he was 'a great enemy of lucre-loving professors' – presumably those in his own university! Anderson wanted reform, and argued strongly for it, harvesting help from outside the university: such a strongly held view set him at odds with the majority of the College.

Anderson died in 1796, just five years after Mozart, and in his will left much of his property 'to the Public for the good of Mankind and the Improvement of Science' and for the foundation of 'Anderson's University'. He set out the subjects to be taught. These included 'Systematic Divinity according to the Church of Scotland' and 'Critical explanations of the Scriptures'. He even suggested the names of suitable 'professors'. Clearly, Anderson's populist brand of evangelical Presbyterianism was well represented! He wished the courses studied to be open to women as well as men with the idea of 'making the women of Glasgow the most accomplished in Europe'. The governance was to be by an effective laity recruited locally. This was to become the model for the later reform of all Scottish universities including the 'ancient' ones, St Andrews, Edinburgh, Glasgow and Aberdeen.

Included among the courses to be taught, at what was to be called 'Anderson's University', was medicine. This included 'Materia Medica' – a forerunner of pharmacology. Indeed, 'Materia Medica' was one of the first university chairs to be established in Anderson's Medical School (in 1797): until quite recently Chairs in Pharmacology in the ancient Scottish universities were named 'Materia Media'. The Medical College, founded in 1799, was an original and integral part of the original 'Andersonian Institution' (later 'Anderson's University') until it was absorbed into the Faculty of Medicine of the University of Glasgow as late as 1947. David Livingstone, the African explorer, was a graduate of Anderson's Medical School, then situated in George Street opposite the present Strathclyde Royal College Building.

In the nineteenth century there was a rapid development of the 'University'. In 1912 it became the Royal Technical College with University College status affiliated with the University of Glasgow – one wonders what John Anderson would have made of that! – and the title was again changed in 1956 to the Royal College of Science and Technology, Glasgow and, once again, to the University of Strathclyde in 1964. Always however the emphasis, as Anderson proposed, was on 'useful learning', for 'the good of mankind and the improvement of science' – a good motto for an international university.

Appendix 7
Dr Alex McIntosh

Alex was a lecturer in the department of bacteriology and had been a staff member for several years before I joined Strathclyde University in 1967. He was one of the first to make contact with me because he had an interest in the work of the Sudan United Mission, although it was years later that he was able to make a visit to Nigeria to observe the work for himself. It was during that visit that he took a number of photographs which are now in my possession. Somewhere!

Alex came from Falkirk and was greatly involved with one of the Brethren Assemblies. Early on in our friendship he invited me to preach there, I think in 1967. I was invited back but only in 2012 so that first message must have had a profound and memorable impact on that fellowship! Alex was much involved in the running of several seaside children's missions in Scotland and in the Sudan United Mission (SUM) camp held under canvas in Keswick during the Convention. This took a lot of preparation each year and, in fact, Alex was the prime mover in the setting up of this camp. In the early days of the Mission there had been a strong Scottish input into the work; indeed, it was Dr Alexander Whyte from his church in Edinburgh who proposed the name Sudan United Mission. We got to know the daughter of one of the four original SUM missionaries (J.B. Burt who went to Nigeria in 1904) who was then resident in Glasgow. She was introduced to us by Alex.

Alex was a gifted speaker. He had a unique style that made him very popular. Certainly, if he was preaching in the locality I made sure I was there to hear him. The annual letters he wrote for his friends at Christmas were masterpieces of wisdom and humour. Worth collecting, keeping and publishing. Somewhere I still have a file of them and if I can find them before this writing is finished there will be some quotes.

There were two incidents involving Alex in the university that were, for me unforgettable. The first was a lunchtime meeting in his office to which he had invited someone else on the staff who had shown an interest in the Christian faith. I too was invited. The gracious way by which he led this person to a commitment to Christ was an object lesson in clarity, patience and love. The other incident was after I had completed the Cambridge University Diploma at the Bible Training Institute in preparation for a possible call to the Christian ministry. Alex telephoned me to ask if he could come and have lunch with me during which he told me, in no uncertain terms, 'Jim, you should not enter the ministry'. As clear and definite as that. He explained that, although he thought I might make a reasonable job as a pastor of a small church (doubtful I think) I should continue to bear witness in a much-needed area for witness – the university sector.

He was right. I think the Lord wanted to test me as to my willingness to change direction and enter the so called 'full time' ministry. Indeed I was. However, that was not the Lord's plan for me. Certainly the teaching and preparation involved (the diploma took three years of study by evening classes) were good for my 'theological education', including for my preaching ministry, but God, through Alex, closed that possible door. Interesting that soon after that conversation in my office, the strong links with Hungary began to open up. Again, more about this later.

There was one other aspect of Alex's Christian life that had a great influence on me. Alex was on many Scottish Christian committees of one sort or another and he was always on the lookout for somewhat younger people to replace him. These included me! So, through his suggestions I was invited onto the Board of the Bible Training Institute (later renamed Glasgow Bible College and, later still, The International Christian College), the Scottish Council of the Universities and Colleges Christian Fellowship (UCCF), which I was to chair for ten years from 1986 and, soon after I arrived in Glasgow, the Scottish Committee of SUM, which I was also to chair. The last two meant participation in the regular meetings of the relevant UK Councils in England. Alex made it a rule, a good one I think and which I followed, that having found a replacement for himself on a committee he promptly left! Particularly important if you had chaired that committee.

After Alex had retired he gave to three of his Strathclyde friends (Derek Nonhebel, Alwyn Tooth and myself) a book, *The New Lion Encyclopaedia of the Bible*[1] in which he thanked us for one of the most enriching friendships of my whole life. He wrote, 'I cannot think of Christian fellowship being bettered for warmth, consistency and rapport. Your spiritual input has had a formative influence on my Christian service. If our successors find the same warmth, uplift and pleasure that we have found in each other's company, they will do well'.

I reproduce this to illustrate what significant Christian friendship can be like. Lord, make it true for me.

Alex died in his late seventies and together with two other Strathclyde staff (Derek Nonhebel and the then Vice-Principal John Spence) I attended his funeral in Falkirk, sadly sparsely attended. Alex McIntosh had perhaps the most profound influence on me, as a Christian academic, of any of my many Scottish friends. I thank God for him.

---

[1] John Drane (Editor), *The New Lion Encyclopaedia of the Bible*, Lion Publishing, Oxford 1998.

Arial view of the St Mátyás church complex, Szeged

Professor Lásló Szekeres making a point

Part 4 Behind the Iron Curtain

Chapter 31
A Letter from Behind the Curtain

It all started with the receipt of a letter, with attractive stamps, 'out of the blue'; or perhaps one could say, out of the 'grey gloom' of eastern Europe, which was in the late 1960s still in the firm grip of communism. The letter came from Hungary, from the chairman of the Department of Pharmacology in Szeged (at that time the number three city of Hungary) Professor László Szekeres. I could quite easily not have responded but he said that he had read some of my published work on the coronary circulation and that this was a deep interest of his colleagues. Would I be willing to collaborate in some way? I knew nothing of Szekeres nor, for that matter, of Hungary apart from the reports of the uprising in 1956. Why I responded at all is, from this distance of time, unclear. The fact that I did so was to have profound repercussions not only for me but for my whole family.

I accepted the invitation to collaborate and flew to Budapest in May 1969 to be met at the airport by Professor Szekeres whom I shall now describe by his 'shortened' name of Laci, the Hungarian equivalent perhaps of Jim rather than James. Accompanying him was his deputy Julius Papp whom I had met briefly at a scientific meeting a year or two earlier in Oxford. Julius, like Laci, had worked there in cardiac electrophysiology with Miles Vaughan Williams, a key figure in research on how drugs modify cardiac rhythm. The particular interest at that time was on newly synthetized beta-adrenoceptor blocking drugs. It was most likely this meeting with Julius that triggered the letter of invitation to visit and discuss how we could, as research groups, perhaps work together.

We drove first, not to Szeged but to the old Roman city of Pécs, a visit that was also to have significant implications for my family; much later two of my granddaughters were to be born there. Laci wanted to show me the city from which he had graduated in medicine and where, before coming to Szeged, he had himself worked. Both here and then in Szeged I was provided with accommodation in the teaching hospital. This too was to have consequences! Later Laci (and his various successive wives!) became firm friends.

How could it be that a Christian and a signed-up member of the Hungarian Communist Party became so close? This became a question asked by members of my family and my colleagues at university. Of course, no one could be a senior member of any university in Hungary, or elsewhere in the communist block, without becoming a party member. This was difficult to discuss; my surmise is that being of Jewish descent he was, in the final stages of WW2 (when so many Jews in Hungary were sent to concentration camps) grateful for the Russian occupation, at least initially.

How dedicated to communism Laci was I am uncertain but he knew about my own Christian faith and, as we will see, perhaps later he became open to it. Just a little! This reminds me of a story I read in my early adulthood about the friendship between a Catholic priest and a communist mayor in a fictional Italian town. Something about 'Don Camillo'?

What were the results of this initial visit 'behind the iron curtain'? This was my first experience of conditions in a part of the world I never believed I would visit. However, in all I was to do so over fifty times. Indeed, we were to live there for a period, even before the fall of communism in 1989. I agreed to collaborate by receiving some of his staff to work in Glasgow and that we would work on projects of mutual interest.

There was another result of interest. Back in Szeged and knowing of my Christian commitment he made an arrangement for me to visit one of the oldest churches in the city, one of significant historic importance; indeed one that held relics of the patron saint of Hungary, King Stephen. To take me there I would need someone to translate and he chose his librarian, who although she was a graduate in Italian, had a good grasp of English. The priest was most kind and at the end of the visit I asked a few questions about the life of the church under communist rule. As we took our departure, I asked my translator to tell him how much I had appreciated the visit and that, although I was not a Catholic, I did love the Lord Jesus. A very firm grip of the hand and bright eyes were the responses!

When we had left the church, she allowed the driver (of the huge black Russian car) to go on ahead so as not to overhear the conversation. She then asked what I meant and how was it that I could be both a Christian and a Professor in a British university! This, she said, could never happen here! As we talked, I asked if she had a copy of the bible. No. Bibles were not available in Hungary. She was going to tell her husband about the conversation and I promised that when I returned home I would get hold of a Hungarian New Testament and send it to her. But how!

The first task was to get hold of one, so the Bible Society of Scotland was contacted. No problem. Except the first one that was sent was in Turkish! Later, one in Hungarian arrived so the next task was how to get it to her. Prayer! Now, it so happened that I was to meet Laci in Amsterdam the following week so I took it with me and, tongue in cheek, asked him if he would take it to her. Declined with a smile. 'You see Jim, if my bags were opened at the airport and a bible was found inside, I could be, as a party member, in some trouble!' 'Of course, Laci I quite understand'. In the end we simply posted it to her addressed to 'The Librarian, Department of Pharmacology . . .' After all, librarians are used to receiving books and journals from all over the world. Ten days later we received a postcard to say it had arrived. Was it read? Did it have an impact? Only God knows.

A bigger problem was how to return to Scotland. Láci had left me at the airport with the words – 'You are ok now Jim, safe flight'. Not that simple. I was a wanted man. You have to stay in Hungary! Interrogation at immigration. 'Where have you been? Why have you not reported to the police when you moved from one place to another?'. This was because, in those days one had to report to the police either in person, or through the hotel you stayed at, in order for your passport to be stamped. An eye was kept on you. Neither I nor, surprisingly, Professor Szekeres knew of this regulation. And, as I had not stayed in any hotel, because my accommodation was arranged privately through the department, my passport showed no evidence of where I had been. This turned out to be a difficult conversation in a third language (German, helped a little because of my stay in Düsseldorf in 1964) since no one spoke English and I had no Hungarian. I was told to return to Budapest and report to the British Embassy for help. The authorities seemed to like me so much they did not want me to leave!

In the end I discovered my letter of invitation, sensibly written both in English and Hungarian and I was let through to the departure lounge after reclaiming my baggage. Too late. The departure time for the flight to London had long gone and there was no other flight to the UK that day. More prayer! However, when I entered the departure lounge the passengers were still there; there had been a tremendous thunderstorm and the BA pilot had refused to take off. But, all quite stressful. I said to myself on the plane home, that was my first – and last – visit to Hungary. Never again! Little did I know! As we shall see God had other ideas. My dear wife for some time also refused 'to go there', behind that curtain. With today's ease of travel to eastern Europe, at least until Brexit and the Covid epidemic, it is difficult to appreciate the severe restrictions there were for travel during the communist era.

That initial visit to Hungary was not however, the first 'behind the curtain'. A year or so earlier I had been invited by a young Czech pharmacologist (Jan Drimal) to speak at a small meeting held in Smolenice Castle outside Bratislava, now capital of Slovakia but then part of Czechoslovakia. This must also have been through someone reading the scientific literature. The details of that visit are somewhat hazy. My young host picked me up, took me to my hotel, then to a café and then into a taxi. He wanted to talk. The hotel and café would not be safe to talk in (bugged) and he made sure the taxi driver did not understand English. So we drove round and round Bratislava in the back of a taxi discussing the political situation and what it was like living there for him and his delightful young wife. The meeting itself was dominated by an American pharmacologist called Aviado, the only other person there from 'the west', who clearly thought I was trying to 'steal' his prodigy. How did he get permission to be there I wondered? I have many American friends but Dr Aviado is certainly not one of them. Some time later I received in the post from my new young friend a long letter and the long playing records of one of my favourite operas, Janacek's *Cunning Little Vixen*. Years later again in Bratislava I tried to contact Jan but nobody, even those who lived and worked in the city, seemed to know who he was. I wonder why.

Somehow, I do not remember how but probably by train, I made my way to the capital Prague, which has come to be my favourite European capital city apart perhaps from Budapest. From the city centre I made my way by tram to my small hotel with no idea (and no Czech language) where to dismount! Now, one of the characteristics about all communist cities was the darkness; very few, if any, street lights. However, when the other standing passengers discovered I was British they were so friendly and enthusiastic to help; they made sure I got off at the correct stop. I checked in at the hotel and discovered there was an opera that evening at the National Theatre. I left my case with the receptionist, not even checking the room, and took the tram back into the centre to discover the performance was about to start. At the box office I was given by a very kind lady the last seat, behind the double bases in the orchestra pit just in time, for an opera I did not know – Smetana's *Dalibor*, to begin. Of course, I understood little of the complicated story (complicated plots are not unusual in opera) and with the wonderful Czech Philharmonic in the pit, the performance was an unforgettable experience. And, could that possibly have been the great Vaclav Talich conducting? My first introduction to the glories of Czech opera. Then back to the hotel in the dark, still with no street lighting. This was the beginning of a deep love for all things Czech, deep friendships with scientists and that wonderful Czech music!

The next morning, I had a contact, through a former General Secretary of the Baptist Union of Scotland, with a pastor in the city centre. I had his phone number and rang him from a public telephone. I introduced myself and he asked, I think to determine if I was genuine, about the family of my Scottish contact about which I knew rather little. Despite this he believed it was safe to talk to me and invited me to a prayer meeting that evening in his church. I have never been in such a prayer meeting and sadly, never will be again. Crowded (standing room only), prayers with no gaps between and in at least three languages, an overwhelming sense of the presence of the Holy Spirit.

Although the congregation was allowed to meet, the pressure on the pastor was heavy; his children were allocated to different schools distant from the church and involving considerable public travel. They would never be allowed to attend university because they were the children of an 'unproductive' member of society. Pressure on Christians during those times was intense. How many of us could have coped? My introduction to being a Christian behind the iron curtain.

Chapter 32
East Germany – Dangerous Times

East Germany (or the DDR – the Deutsche Demokratische Republik) was for me, the most repressive and authoritarian of the communist regimes apart perhaps from Russia itself. The secret police, the Stasi, were everywhere.

There is a very good Oscar winning film ('magnificent and unmissable' said the Daily Telegraph) called 'The Lives of Others' which gives an excellent idea of what went on behind the scenes in the DDR during the period from the end of WW2 to the collapse of the Berlin wall. It is the story of an author and his actress girlfriend who were under 24 hour, 7 days a week surveillance, from an apartment above their own; even their shower area was bugged. The reason why they were being watched was that information about the suicide rate in the DDR, the highest in the world at that time apart from Hungary, was getting through to the West and published in the free German press. Where was the leak coming from? What typewriter was being used? (The State had information about every typewriter in the country and who owned them). The typewriter being used had been smuggled across the border from West Berlin and hidden underneath the floorboards.

The story is well told and illustrates the fact that almost everyone, everywhere was under surveillance. But the DDR was a real, not fictional, police state and one had to be very careful. Perhaps especially those who entered the country from the West. I think if I had seen this film prior to venturing east I would not have gone!

In fact, I made several visits to the DDR, visa in hand, usually by crossing the border through the U-Bahn in Berlin or, in later visits, by flying to Templehof Airport in East Berlin from where you could reach other parts of the DDR by train. Berlin at that time was divided into four 'zones' or sectors (American, French, British and Russian). The U-Bahn (underground rail) route involved leaving West Berlin and entering the darkness of the first station in the DDR, where the immigration and customs officials were based. I always found this an unsettling and daunting experience as the two stations, on either side of the border, were so strikingly different; the one bright and busy, the other dark, gloomy and almost empty. I will always associate darkness with communism. On the DDR side of the border your luggage would be scrutinised, your passport and visa checked and rechecked and the letter of invitation to enter the country carefully scrutinised and stamped. Of course, you always required an invitation authorised by a Party official. In my case this invitation came from Professor Werner Förster from the Department of Pharmacology at the University of Halle-Wittenberg, a good friend of László Szekeres. Halle was the birthplace of Handel. No trouble for him to leave his homeland and live most of his life in England; no wall in those days! And, it was on the door of the main church of Wittenberg that Martin Luther nailed his famous 'articles'.

But, why did I go at all? Well, I was assured it was safe to do so and I had met Förster previously in Hungary. His interest, like my own at that time, was in the mechanism of action of aspirin and what dose should be given as a prophylactic to patients for the prevention of a heart attack or subsequent to having a stroke. We had found that the enzyme inhibited by aspirin (cyclooxygenase) produced substances that were helpful (prostacyclin) and harmful (thromboxane) to the body. A low dose would inhibit the harmful cyclooxygenase product but not the helpful one. A normal dose of aspirin (300mg) would inhibit both; a lower dose (75mg now prescribed as low-dose aspirin) would be better and we had published this data in *Nature*. Förster and I believed that even this 'low dose' was too high! It was for work in this area that Professor John Vane, of whom a little more later, won the Nobel Prize for Physiology and Medicine.

I found, on more than one occasion, a marked difference in the attitude of people on the two sides of the border. Let me illustrate. On one visit I had to travel from West Berlin to the DDR on a Sunday. The U-Bahn ticket office nearest to my hotel was closed and I did not have the correct coinage to buy a ticket from the machine. This meant I had to board the train without a ticket. When the train drew into the last station before the border the platform was lined with ticket inspectors. Never have I seen so many of them in one place at one time. All passengers were ordered to show their tickets and those without one (like me) were taken for 'interrogation'. I attempted to explain (in German) the reason but, as this was not getting me any where I resorted to English. They did not believe I was English, which I suppose says something for my seeming prowess in the German language at the time; maybe they thought I was trying to get out of paying a fine by pretending to be a tourist. So, I was fined. But these inspectors were so officious and unpleasant I thought I had wandered by mistake over to the other side of the border! The considerable fine was paid.

After I re-entered the train and proceeded into the DDR through immigration control and customs, I found that I had to find my way to the railway station in order to get to Halle. The folk I asked could not have been more courteous and helpful. What a difference to those inspectors I had talked to earlier.

On one visit to Halle to speak at a conference organised by Förster I arrived a day early. This is not good for conference organisers at one of their busiest times; they had more important things on their hands than to have to look after a 'guest from the west'. Knowing of my deep interest in music I was introduced to one of the youngest and more junior members of staff, Dr Erich Blass. I got to know him and his delightful wife and their four-year old daughter really well and they invited me to their tiny flat in the nearby city of Leipzig. Although both were musicians (violin and flute) they knew nothing of the compositions of English composers like Elgar, Vaughan Williams and Delius so on subsequent visits to Halle I took them long playing records of works by these, and other, English composers. They gave me bound inscribed copies of the complete piano sonatas of Beethoven which I still possess. Frau Blass also queued up for tickets to attend concerts in the St Thomas Church (where Johannes Bach was at one time organist and musical director) and in the famous home of the Leipzig Gewandhaus Orchestra, then still occupying the 'old' original building.

This particular concert was interesting! In the first half was a performance of the Beethoven 'Triple' concerto. A popular concert because of the Beethoven. Our cheaper, affordable seats (junior university lecturers were low paid) were high up in the balcony. These gave good, if rather distant, views not only of the orchestra but of the expensive seats in the stalls occupied by the Leipzig bigwigs. In the second half a Shostakovich symphony was programmed and the seats in the stalls emptied. Was this an anti-Shostakovich demonstration or an anti-Russian one? Anyway, we moved down! The plan on my next visit was that the three of us would attempt to play one of Bach's trio sonatas. Sadly, this was never to happen.

One evening in their flat listening to music I almost missed the last tram to the railway station for the train back to Halle. In the same railway carriage there was a young couple also returning to Halle. This particular train (unlike the double-decker commuter train we had taken earlier to Leipzig which stopped often) turned out to be an inter-city so took much less time to reach Halle where the station was in darkness. Neither I nor my companions realised we had reached Halle until the train drew out of the very dark Halle station. The next stop was the border and I had left my passport in my hotel room and my ticket, anyway not valid on 'express' trains, was from Leipzig to Halle and we were now travelling away from Halle! This would take some explaining! Fortunately for us, after about twenty minutes (and with no sign yet of a ticket inspector) the train made an unscheduled stop at a small station just in time for us to take a train in the opposite direction. Difficult to explain to the inspector that we were travelling to Halle on a train going to, and not from, Leipzig! When I told this story to my hosts they were horrified. Not only had I missed the official dinner but I could have been anywhere in East Germany that night and stuck at the border without my passport! I could have finished up in jail.

I never discovered what happened to Werner Förster although I did manage to get him and his wife to a Glasgow meeting in 1990. After the fall of communism those who were formerly in positions of authority not only lost their positions but were also in disgrace. And, their accommodation had been provided by the state.

There was a tragic ending to my friendship with the delightful family Blass. A month or so after I returned to Scotland, I received an envelope postmarked in Leipzig and framed by a black border. It was from the brother of Frau Blass to tell me that Erich had been drowned in a swimming pool accident whilst in Moscow at another scientific conference. Strangely, on the day he died he had written a postcard to me from Moscow which I received some days later and which I still have. The question in my mind then was this? Was this really an accident or murder by the secret police either of Russia or of the DDR. If the latter did our friendship play a part in his death?

The last time we met was on the concourse of Halle railway station to which Erich had come with a plastic bag containing many long-playing gramophone records. He wanted me to have his favourite recordings of the Beethoven symphonies conducted by his favourite conductor Franz Konwitschny. Of course I refused, but after some debate I did accept a recording of the Schubert song cycle 'Die Schöne Müllerin' sung by the famous east German tenor Fritz Wunderlich. With cameras everywhere this exchange from one plastic bag to another might have looked suspicious. Was Erich a marked man? Did his contact with me and our actions observed on the station concourse contribute to his death? On balance I think this unlikely. An accident? But why in Moscow of all places?

I did return again to Leipzig a year or so later to try to discover from other staff members in Förster's department what had happened on that fateful day at the pool and about the circumstances of Erich's death. No one was willing, or able, to talk. The whole incident was shrouded in secrecy. But I never view the 'The Lives of Others' without thinking if my brief friendship with Erich had anything to do with his death. Those readers who know the tragic ending to the story of that Schubert song cycle, the records of which were given to me on that East German railway platform, will perhaps understand why I seldom now listen to that particular recording.

There is a horrifying postscript to this story. Not long after receiving the news of Erich's death I received another envelope from the same family member in Leipzig with that same black border. It was to tell me that Erich's wife and four-year old daughter had committed suicide. I learnt later that the brother, who had given me this tragic news, had himself also committed suicide.

A very tragic incident in my life 'behind the iron curtain'.

Chapter 33
Russia

This was my third excursion behind the 'iron curtain'; my first two being to Hungary and Czechoslovakia. The purpose of this visit in 1975 as part of a group, was to give an overview of recent advances in the drug treatment of angina pectoris and to promote a drug called oxyfedrine produced by Chemiewerk Homburg in Germany. The initial meeting about this drug, its pharmacological actions and clinical effectiveness, had been in Vienna in 1971 and it had been on the market in western Europe since that time. I had been asked to be involved in determining its mode of action several years previous to this.

We arrived, most of the group feeling somewhat apprehensive about the visit, since very few had been outside Western Germany, on a flight from Vienna, fortunately not by Aeroflot which did not have a very good reputation. The Tourist Agency met us and took us by tour bus to the Hotel Leningradska where we had to leave our passports. Mine was a biggish room (bugged of course), the ends of the corridor being guarded by two huge women. No doubt former wrestlers or weight lifters. No getting past these 'ladies'! Their tasks included noting the comings and goings of each room inhabitant and of any guests. No soap or hot water in the room and a terrible evening meal at the nearby Hotel Metropole.

The next day, a Wednesday, we were taken by another tour bus to the village of Zagorsk, about fifty miles from the capital. Here there were several churches and a cathedral on the same campus together with a Seminary, apparently one of only two in the whole of Russia. Only one of the churches was in use where very elderly and devout women were queueing up with lighted candles in order to kiss one of the ikons and then queueing to take water from one of the holy fountains. It was like a scene from Mussorgsky's opera Boris Godunov. The other churches were museums with hundreds of ikons. The toilets in the area were what in Nigeria would be called 'bush'. This visit was a good indication of the lives of Christians in Soviet

Russia. That evening there was a dinner in yet another Moscow hotel with recordings of the Red Army Choir in the background.

The scientific meeting next day was at the State University Institute of Cardiology, at which I was to speak, but before that, whilst eating an apple (my breakfast) I had a dental problem. However, there was no way I was going to see a Moscow dentist! Despite this mishap the meeting went well and my communication led to a number of questions, always a good indication that it had been heard (translated of course) and understood.

I had expressed an interest whilst in Moscow in meeting up with Professor Natalia Kaverina, whose interesting book on the coronary circulation published in 1962 I had read in Ibadan. It was in those days very unusual to have a book translated from Russian into English. This meeting was not easy to arrange especially as Natalia (the Head of the Laboratory for Cardiovascular Pharmacology at the Academy of Medical Sciences of the USSR) was 'not in favour' and thus not 'on seat'. We visited her department, met her deputy and managed to obtain her home address. Again, not easy! As my Hungarian friend László Szekeres was at the conference and had studied in Moscow (at that very Institute) and was fluent in Russian we managed by public transport, the excellent and very ornate underground system, to find and walk to her home and have lunch with her. Mission accomplished and (perhaps) unobserved. The next task was to take a taxi to GUM, a huge department store built like a railway station in order for László to buy a Russian TV, better he said than a Hungarian one. There was then a city tour: Moscow is (in part) a beautiful city especially the Red Square area, familiar from TV programmes. Then a visit to the Kremlin. No audience with the President (perhaps not 'on seat') but for once we did have an English-speaking guide.

The final evening was taken up with a dinner, in yet another hotel and at which we were 'presented' with a record of the Red Army Choir (again!) before being taken to the wonderful Bolshoi Theatre for a performance of Prokofiev's opera *The Gambler*; much use of flash lighting and the revolving stage.

Next day we retrieved our passports and flew back to Vienna. One could almost feel the relief of my German colleagues as we landed safely in 'the West'!

Chapter 34
Poland

My last visit to Poland during communist times was just before the dramatic changes that took place there in June 1989. I visited in order to accept an invitation to become an honorary member of the Polish Physiological Society, which required me to give an invited lecture in Warsaw. However, because of my involvement with the European Section of the International Society for Heart Research, I already had scientific friends there. Indeed, the first meeting with colleagues from the Soviet Bloc was in Milan in 1966 whilst I was still working in Nigeria. Among the participants were two attractive, enthusiastic 'girls' from Poland; how they managed to escape from such a deeply communist state to the West during a particularly cold part of the 'cold war' was a mystery. Twenty years later I was to meet one of them in Sydney: I was embarrassed not to recognise her; she had married an Australian and her contours had changed somewhat since that first meeting in 1966. Good Aussie food! Later, another Polish friend told me her story. Her parents were communist intellectuals whose views did not fit with those of the strict authoritarian Polish State. Under some pretence, they were invited, with their young daughter, to Moscow, where they were both shot and their daughter placed in a Russian orphanage for twelve years. Even as I write I am still moved, not only by this story, but by those of others who became close colleagues, about their experiences of living as children and young people under communist rule. I remember I am the same age.

This visit proved to be one of the most emotional of all my excursions behind the 'iron curtain'. My Polish friends and colleagues were, like me, children during the Second World War and had witnessed the almost complete demolition by the Nazi troops of their capital city at the end of the war. The Russian army, on the other side of the Vistula River on which Poland's capital stands, did nothing whilst the Nazi army first firebombed the dwellings in the Old City of Warsaw and then dynamited the whole area, including the Royal Palace. There is a memorial to those who were killed during that period with a wall of plaques for members of the Resistance, including a statue of a small boy with a helmet on his head, much too big for him, taken from a Nazi soldier and symbolising the role children had played during the uprising against Nazi occupation by acting as messengers and scouts for the Resistance. One of the most moving sights, I was told, was among the rubble a broken statue of Christ on the Cross, the one surviving arm outstretched as though in condemnation or accusation.

My friend Krisztina told me that at the age of five she and her parents were taken out of the train going to the death camps by a German soldier because 'you remind me of my daughter at home'. She remembers still the straw in the carriages trod down and turned into a sea of mud by thousands of feet; and the smell. The only things they salvaged from their dynamited, burnt out home were old photographs of her parents wedding, one of herself as a small girl and one of her grandmother who was murdered in Auschwitz.

Krisztina told me too of the community spirit when the people set about rebuilding what was once a beautiful city. Each week there was a day off from school and work to enable help in the reconstruction. Her own present home in Konstanew, about twenty km from Warsaw, had once been occupied by the Nazis; I stayed for a couple of nights there.

Next morning Leschek, her husband (Professor of Cardiology in Warsaw's Central Hospital) took me on the 140 mile journey to the 14th century Jasna Gora monastery in Czestochowd, the most popular shrine in Poland. This was in order to see the Black Madonna, a much venerated wooden ikon brought to Poland from Hungary in 1382. This Catholic shrine has eight services a day with special guards (church members) responsible for marshalling the huge crowds. I was taken to the front of the queue to have a good view of the ikon. Not too impressed by that but much more by the devotion to the Lord of so many people. On this particular day the crowds included hundreds of deaf pilgrims from many European countries all 'signing' one another, and with so much joy and laughter – an incredible sight!

On the long journey home, the road lined with men and women selling the mushrooms they had picked in the forest nearby, Leschek talked about the political situation and shared his insights on the activity of Solidarity; more than a trade union but a political force to be reckoned with. Indeed, there was a huge banner above the church which said 'Solidarity lives because you died'. Did that refer to Christ I wondered? Leschek explained that Solidarity could not exist without the church and that it was just as much a movement for independence as a trade union for shipyard workers.

Solidarity started in Gdansk and was the first independent trade union in the whole of the Soviet bloc. Starting in the late 70's it was forcibly suppressed by the government, under pressure from the Soviet Union, with much persecution of its leaders. It re-emerged in 1989 and had been legalised and allowed to participate in free elections the very month I was in Poland. Nearly all the non-party candidates were elected in the June elections. My friend Krisztina, who had earlier narrowly escaped imprisonment, was next day to be made a professor in her university department and would wear her Solidarity badge at the ceremony!

Next day (busy schedule!) Leschek took me to Chopin's birthplace and on the return journey we called in at the Franciscan monastery at Niepokalanow. This monastery was founded by the priest Maximillian Kolbe, after he had returned from a long and effective ministry in Nagasaki Japan. During the war he had sheltered and hid over 2000 Jews and other refugees from other parts of Poland. Because of this he was arrested and taken to Auschwitz (Oswiecim) where he led prayers each day. After a prisoner had escaped nine other prisoners were 'selected' and sentenced to death by starvation. One of the nine, a Polish army sergeant, was heard to say that he had a family and two children. Kolbe stepped out of line (an offence the punishment for which was normally to be shot) and asked to take his place – 'I wish to die in place of this man. I am old and he has a wife and children'. He was the last of the nine to remain alive and the guards then injected him with a fatal dose of carbonic acid. The monastery at Niepokalanow has a museum dedicated to Kolbe's memory. He was canonized by Pope John Paul II in 1982; the man he saved was present at the ceremony.

The monastery is now a hospice and Leschek is their doctor. Apparently, he joked, it is a good place to collect 'control urine samples'. The residents do as they are told!

I made several visits to Poland after the fall of communism, all to the Jagiellonian University in Cracow at the invitation of Professor Richard Gryglewski. Years before, Richard had introduced me for the award of the medal of the Polish Physiological Society. Richard and his wife Teresa were great hosts. I remember that on his desk at home was a photo of a meeting he had had with the Pope. But what I remember most about Richard was his absentmindedness! Especially where he had put his spectacles. Once, on a visit we made together to the Tatras mountains, we spent an hour retracing our steps covering the area where he thought he must have dropped them. He could hardly drive well without them but perhaps listening to Beethoven on the journey home must have helped! On our return, his wife, who seemed to know exactly where they were, discovered them in his pocket! One of those absentminded professors then.

Chapter 35
Hungary – The Early Visits

Like my visits to other communist countries, most of my early visits to Hungary were in the early 1970s, such as a brief visit to Budapest in 1971 following a pharmacological meeting in nearby Vienna. This was at the invitation of Julius Papp, whom I had first met four years earlier at a meeting in Cambridge. Both Julius and his head of department in Szeged, Professor László Szekeres were present at the Vienna meeting and pointed out that Hungary was only a train journey away and that in Budapest, a few days after the Vienna meeting had finished, there was to be a meeting of the Hungarian Pharmacological Society at which I could be invited to speak. I took the opportunity to visit. Little did I know then, especially after that first traumatic visit in 1969, that I would, over the next forty or so years, make nearly seventy journeys to that country. Nor could I have imagined that two of our grandchildren would be born there.

Budapest is a beautiful city: I can never decide if it is Budapest or Prague that is my favourite city anywhere in the world. It depends which of the two I am in at the time! But, of course, Budapest then, in the communist period, was quite different to what it became fifty years later – swamped by tourists. No tourists in 1971.

I do not remember much about that visit, except how pleasant and attractive the city was, especially the area around Old Buda. And, how good the music was! The main outcome of the visit was a further discussion with László about a possible collaboration between his departmental research group in Szeged and my own in Glasgow. We decided that, in a year or two, I would again be invited to see the facilities in Szeged and make possible arrangements for some of his younger colleagues to come to Britain, as he and his deputy Julius had done in the 1960s working at Oxford University.

I have already written about the previous visit and the difficulty I had in leaving the country after which I (and my wife) said 'never again'! In fact, there were further visits leading up to especially significant ones in 1989. Indeed, Pam was persuaded to accompany me both in 1985 and 1987 following invitations for me to again speak at meetings of the Hungarian Pharmacological Society. Then, two years later, at a satellite meeting held in Budapest of pharmacologists following a IUPHR meeting held in Australia.

These meetings gave us the opportunity of seeing rather more of one of our favourite countries. We fell in love with it – and its people. Especially its people. On this particular trip there were a few days free so László and his wife Lenka took us to their holiday 'home' by Lake Balaton. This is where the Hungarian navy has its home. Of course, there are jokes about the Hungarian navy because present day Hungary has no outlet to the sea. However, before the breakup of the country after WW1, the seaport of Trieste, now located in Italy, was Hungarian.

At our first meal with László and Lenka in their holiday cottage we were told, to our surprise and Pam's horror, that 'mice' were on the menu. Of course, they were speaking German – maize in that language (with a Hungarian accent) can sound like mice in English! Hungarian food, including that particular meal, is we found, quite wonderful.

Lake Balaton (the 'Hungarian Sea') is the largest inland lake in Europe (over 230 square miles). The water is very shallow which means it warms up quickly, which makes it safe for children; indeed, the southern (Somogy) shore is like a seventy kilometre children's beach. László's cottage was at Balatonboglar near to a vast Trade Union house, a holiday resort for its members. If you behaved yourself you could have a cheap holiday there once every couple of years. From the cottage it was only a few yards to the lake itself. A delightful holiday destination which we were able to make use of on many future occasions. And a good venue for relaxing after strenuous scientific conferences! The eastern shoreline on the other hand is hilly, with attractive churches, often venues for music, and museums and palaces including the Festetics Castle (with a magnificent library) at Keszthély and nearby the warm spa baths at Héviz.

Balaton is a major venue for sailing and, when we were again there, in 1987 after a symposium in Budapest, I had been given a particular task. At one of the Paisley Baptist churches where I often preached, I met a member with a deep interest in the boats of the inland waterways of Europe; he was writing a book about them which was near to completion. He had come across a reference to a boat, last seen about fifty years ago on Lake Balaton either at Siofok or on the Tihány Peninsular, and was anxious to have a photo of it. Was it still in existence? I have forgotten the details but it was, for him, a very rare example of a particular kind of boat. So, Láci and I set about trying to find it among the hundreds of boats moored on that side of the lake. It was a mystery to be solved; I felt like Dr Watson to Láci's Sherlock! The director of the 'museum of the lake' was most helpful and gave us a guided tour. And, after a lot of searching we discovered the boat was still in existence, although in a sad state of disrepair. Its last function was as a restaurant. The photo was duly taken and published in the book about three years later; my only published photograph.

As one can imagine there are numerous restaurants around the lake. Some better than others. Advice – do not sit too near the gypsy band especially when the violinist attempts to serenade your wife! I was intrigued that at one of the BBC Scottish Orchestra televised concerts in Glasgow's City Halls, at which I was present, a real and famous group of authentic gypsy Hungarian musicians had been invited to participate. This was a concert linking a particular nation's folk music (in this instance Hungary) with the development of that nation's classical music, in this case the music of Béla Bartók. The biggest round of applause of the evening was that given to the fantastic cembalo player. He even outshone the BBCSO, our own wonderful orchestra!

László Szekeres was very proud of his country and its history and he has the (world?) record for taking us to the most museums in one day. Twelve, I think. We have seen much of Hungary through him. This is not a Hungarian travelogue but one visit to the traditional rural village of Zala, an outdoor museum, gave even Laci a surprise. At the lovely church we were welcomed by an elderly woman, in a dress of the time, who sang the gospel to us. Unsure what Laci made of that. I stopped at one of the wall plaques and Laci asked if he could translate it to me. Thank you I said, but there is no need and I 'translated' it into English for him! Much to his surprise. It was a text from the bible which I had often preached on; the reference was at the bottom! 'The foundation is laid already. No man can lay another. It is Jesus Christ himself' (1 Corinthians 3:10 in the Phillips version).

Another place we will never forget, because of the long, almost thirty year, association with one of our favourite composers, Joseph Haydn, was the beautiful Esterhazy Palace at Fertöd. Badly damage in WW2 it was being renovated at the time we visited. Whenever I hear a composition from Haydn's 'middle period' my mind returns to that place of beauty. I can visualise him composing it there.

At the end of the communist period, and at a time when the country was, following events in Poland, becoming more open, we began to make contact with Christian believers. How this happened is of some interest. It began with a lunch in Glasgow with friends from one of the Milngavie churches (Allander Evangelical Church) at which I had often preached. At that lunch the friend (George Russell) talked about a convoy of trucks that took clothes and food to Hungary and Romania, through an organisation based in Glasgow called Blythswood Care, which had begun operations as early as 1966. He gave us the address of a church in Budapest which was a key distribution point for these gifts. On our next visit to Hungary in 1989 we made contact. The following story gives some idea of the situation of just one of the Budapest churches at the end of the Communist period.

We took a bus to the church for the Sunday service and someone kindly translated for us. This was a 'Free Evangelical Fellowship' off Lumumba utca in Szuglo 35. The service was very busy, long and moving. I was asked to bring 'greetings' from my home church, an important part of most church services, especially in communist times. Visitors from another part of the country, or from another country, were invited to express to the local congregation the Christian fellowship and support of their own home church. We arranged with the wife of the pastor, Dr Mezés Ibolya, a cardiologist involved in heart transplantation who spoke good English, to meet us a day or so later. She took us back to the church and told us the story.

The building was originally a restaurant which the congregation was allowed, a year or so earlier, to convert to a church. This took one year and three million forints to renovate. The permission to renovate had been given by a communist party member who had been impressed by the work the church members were doing among the disabled. The member's daughter had seen a marked change in the life of her own disabled daughter who attended the church and who had become a Christian.

Much of the money involved in the construction came from the members; the rest came from the legacy of a Hungarian lady living in Switzerland. This took three years to reach (and be cleared by) the Hungarian bank. This clearance came just a few weeks before the payment deadline required by the authorities. During the reconstruction someone 'had a word from the Lord' requesting especial prayer for those working on the roof. This 'word from the Lord' was not understood by the church until the discovery in the roof of an unexploded second world war bomb. After it was defused the authorities responded 'great luck'! To which the church responded 'great God'!

In the years following the fall of communism there have been many stories of buildings being given approval for conversion into churches, including restaurants, but this approval was unusual in communist times.

The Szuglo church had an extensive basement, once the restaurant kitchen, which was used to store materials for refugees, especially from Romania, a venture supported by Tear Fund. On a later visit we again made contact with the church and happened to sit next to a student from the university in Szeged – our first student contact in a city that became our home. Although over the years we were in Budapest for several Sundays, almost always I had been invited previously to 'serve' (which is what preaching is called in Hungarian churches) in other Budapest churches so sadly we lost touch with that vibrant Szuglo fellowship. I wondered, over thirty years later, how they were doing – then I heard from Dora that the church was doing well with a church plant in another poor part of Budapest.

How was it that we were able to make these contacts without the gentle 'surveillance' of our good friend László Szekeres? Simply by arriving at times when he was out of the country: and because by then we could manage quite well by ourselves!

In November 1989 we had other contacts. Christian work among students in universities and colleges had been allowed to recommence; it had been quite active during the inter-war period but had to close during the communist period after the end of WW2. We had been given the names of the first staff workers and got in touch; coffee in one of the international hotels was a safe place to meet. This began a long friendship with Anna Marie Kool (from Holland but still living years later in Budapest) and especially (Dr) Dóra Bernhardt whose brother-in-law (Dr Kornél Herjeczki) was greatly involved in the beginnings of what in Britain we would call the UCCF, and also in the Hungarian Christian Medical Fellowship. Kornél became the prime mover in the setting up of the publisher Harmat, which is still active today in publishing Christian books.

Our first meeting with Kornél was when we called at his Budapest flat. His father, a former President of the Hungarian Baptist Church, opened the door to us because Kornél was out visiting his wife in hospital following the birth of their first child. This sets the date of our initial meeting with him pretty accurately!

We became very interested in the growth of Christian witness among university students in Hungary, Magyar Evangéliumi Keresztyén Diákszövetség (MEKDSZ) and later became involved in the beginnings of a Christian Union at the University of Szeged; and as a speaker at meetings of former MEKDSZ members.

Another eventful meeting also took place during those few days in Budapest in the absence of Professor Szekeres! I had been asked by the Scottish Lay Preachers Association, of which I was at that time President, to bring with me to Hungary a gift towards the establishment of a lay college for would be preachers. This meant contact with the Hungarian Baptist Union at their headquarters in Budapest. Very few spoke English in Hungary at that time but fortunately the then Secretary and President did! When I said we were going to Szeged they told us that the Baptist pastor there spoke English and gave me his telephone number. We phoned when we reached Szeged and a subsequent meeting started a deep and significant friendship. This friendship had huge repercussions, not only for ourselves but also for our family. But that is another part of our story!

Budapest friends – Dora, one of the original staff workers for MEKDSZ is on the far left, and Kornél of Harmat is on the far right.

Chapter 36
'And the Wall Came Tumbling Down'

We made several visits to Hungary during the communist period mainly because of my links with the Hungarian Institute for Drug Research situated in Budapest. For example in May 1989, when we were well looked after by George R from the Institute; yet another Hungarian home we visited with much talk about the prospects for political change in the country. George took us to the wonderful museum featuring the ceramic work of Kovács Margit in Szentendre,[1] to the cathedral at Esztergom on the Danube bend and, on another occasion, to the Kodály Museum at Kécskemet. On that occasion we then drove to have lunch with the 'famous' Puszta (meaning deserted, bare, abandoned) peasant artist Polyak. This lunch consisted of pork (or rather the fat of pork, it was 100% fat) together with bread and jam! A rather interesting culinary experience. In honour of our visit, I was given (at some cost to George) a huge wall plaque which, as it was not to our taste, we were fortunately able to 'offload' onto László Szekeres. During a car journey on another occasion George had music on which I was unable to recognise. It was by Purcell – King Arthur. Good music for driving across the 'Great Hungarian Plain'.

On this Budapest visit (there was some work done!) we heard a concert in the Vigadó by the brilliant Franz Liszt Chamber orchestra and saw opera from the balcony of the Opera House for 40 forints (about 15p!). Long-playing records were more expensive (the equivalent of 60p). Regulations at that time were still tight with regular visits to the police station. There was still the hassle of renewing our visas; the office was crowded and only open at variable times each week. However, although we had forgotten to 'attend' the Szeged police station we were simply waved through at the airport for our journey home. Something was beginning to change in Hungary.

---

[1] P. Brestyánszky Ilona, *Margit Kovács*, Képzömüvészeti Kiadó, 1982.

In Szeged the collaboration continued, I did an interview with the local radio station and was 'introduced' again to the Baptist Church by Árpád and invited to 'serve' at a special service for the anniversary of the excellent church choir. For some reason I noticed that there were only three tenors present; they were later renamed after another rather more famous 'three tenors'!

Another visit in 1989 coincided with the day (June 16th) of the reburial of the former executed Socialist Prime Minister Nagy Imre, who had resisted the Russian invasion in 1956. This was a moving, crowded occasion in Budapest at which two of my Szeged colleagues participated. It was clear that things were really changing. Later that year I was awarded an honorary degree (Doctor of Medicine honoris causa) by the Szeged Medical University, an impressive ceremony beginning with the National anthem and held in what had been, in pre-communist times, the main hall of the Theological Faculty. Many of our Szeged friends and colleagues were present, including the families Szili and Juhász and Nagy Sándor. Many gifts of flowers – and other things. After a long lunch the honorary graduates (three were from other faculties) gave lectures. Notice this was after receiving the degree and after a copious lunch. Some of the lectures were incomprehensible! Although not mine. Of course! We stayed on in Szeged for another week or so and it was during that period that news came through on November 12th of the collapse of the Berlin wall. Much celebration. Dancing in the laboratories!

As I write over thirty years later, I realise that it is difficult for many people today to understand the historical significance of that event. It is, after all, 'old history'. It was the fall of communism in most of Europe and the reunification of the two very different Germanys. What is also not appreciated is the part Hungary played in this. It was the decision by the Foreign Minister to open the border between Hungary and Austria, so allowing residents of the DDR (the German Democratic Republic or GDR) to pass freely to the West; this was a trigger for what was to happen later. This exodus through Hungary was soon blocked by the DDR, but this led to mass demonstrations in Berlin and Leipzig demanding the reform of the one-party state and to allow its citizens to leave the country if they wished. The regime then announced that it would allow citizens to apply for passports to travel to the West. When asked when this measure would take place a Party spokesman replied (mistakenly!) 'immediately'. This led to thousands of East Berliners arriving at the checkpoints. The outnumbered guards simply let the huge crowd pass through! The wall was rapidly demolished and quickly disappeared. The wall came tumbling down!

To have been in Hungary when all this was happening was for us one of life's most significant events. And, being in Eastern Europe (Poland, Czechoslovakia, Hungary) during the events leading up to November 1989 (the part played by the Church and Solidarity in Poland and of musicians and the Church in the DDR) was to give me an exciting, dangerous feeling that the world I knew was turning upside down. I was in Prague that year with my friend Frank Kolar standing near to the National Theatre and listening to a political open – air speech about freedom! Frank had tears in his eyes as he said 'This freedom of expression. I can hardly believe. To think this is happening in my lifetime!' Later, in June 1990 he with his wife Libuse and small son, drove in their small car all the way from Prague to Glasgow for the ISHR meeting, their first time out of Czechoslovakia as a family. And I had only arranged accommodation for Frank!

I saw on the TV today the joy of the reunion of families after a fifteen month separation due to lockdown; sadly, however not yet for us. The emotional welcome at Glasgow airport! Think what it was like then for the many, like George Krause in Berlin, of the first family reunion in over thirty years! The first meeting of a grandmother and her grandson ever!

There were for us as family significant consequences arising from that event in November 1989. First, it led to stronger ties with Hungary and a feeling of oneness with its people and a deeper desire to be even more involved in scientific collaboration with friends in Szeged. This led to my spending my sabbatical year there.

Second, it had consequences for the meeting in Glasgow in June 1990 of the International Society of Heart Research (ISHR) the organising committee of which I chaired. This meeting, of course, took several years to organise but a year earlier I had insisted that we build into the budget enough money to bring to Glasgow a hundred scientists (of the five hundred who attended) from the former Eastern bloc. I could foresee, from my many visits to these countries, that there would be the possibility that scientists from communist countries would be free to travel to Scotland. All these places were taken up.

Third, it led to our elder son and his family working in Hungary teaching English literature. I write shortly how this happened and why it is that we have two Hungarian born grandchildren. However, before they arrived in the old Roman city of Pecs, we had been taken there by our friends the Szili family to investigate accommodation for them. This was on the Sunday when, at long last, the last Russian soldier left the country. It was June 30th 1991. At the end of the church service the congregation stood and sang the National anthem. Not a dry eye!

Chapter 37
On Becoming a Millionnaire

A decision was made to explore ways to continue to work in Szeged after I had retired in 1998 from Strathclyde; I had already spent my sabbatical year (1989) in Szeged. We knew future Hungarian collaboration would only be possible with some kind of external financial support. Now, although Strathclyde had kept funds for me to use for overseas travel and subsistence, this would be insufficient to support the work we had in mind. I should emphasise that these 'Strathclyde funds' consisted of money coming from fees I had earned as a consultant in cardiovascular pharmacology – there was much interest at that time, including from me, in the development of drugs used in the treatment of cardiac failure, in the suppression of the life-threatening disorders of cardiac rhythm and in ways of protecting the heart against ischaemic damage. These 'Strathclyde funds' had accumulated over the years as a result of working in these areas with a number of drug companies both in the UK (there were several of these) and in other countries, for example as a long-term consultant for companies in Japan, Germany and Holland and, for shorter periods, in Switzerland, France and Italy. However, for a further long-term collaboration with the university in Hungary we would require sources of income from elsewhere. This kind of support became available.

The first of these sources was the Leverhulme Trust, who each year or so awarded a limited number of grants to allow recently retired senior academics to continue their research collaborations. These were known as Emeritus Fellowships and were highly competitive. Two 'supporters' were required and I was fortunate to obtain the agreement of two Nobel Prize winners (James Black and John Vane) to act in this way. This must have helped because I was given a Fellowship for the usual one-year period.

One day, when working in Szeged, my colleagues noticed an invitation by the Hungarian State Government to apply for Research Fellowships named after the distinguished Hungarian scientist Albert Szent-Györgyi. These were designed to bring senior scientists from the 'west' to spend time to collaborate with those in Hungarian universities. With help from my friends and colleagues I applied and, much to my surprise, this was successful. Indeed, we learnt from the newspapers that our application came top of the list! That there was already a history of joint ventures probably helped, as well as the fact that in 1989 I had been awarded an honorary degree (MD) by the Szeged University named after Szent-Györgyi.

Perhaps a few words about Albert Szent-Győrgyi are appropriate. He was before the war the Professor of Biochemistry in Szeged and whilst there discovered vitamin C: the story goes that the vitamin was discovered in a meal, cooked by his wife and full of peppers, that he had taken to his laboratory for his lunch! Perhaps the meal was too hot for him and he had plenty left over. For this discovery he was awarded the Nobel Prize in Medicine which perhaps he should have shared with this wife! Later Szent-Györgyi narrowly missed a second Nobel prize for his work, in the United States, on muscle proteins. Quite a scientist then. Apparently, in 1944 whilst still living in Hungary he made, at a secret venue in Turkey, an attempt (unsuccessful) to make a pact with some members of the UK Government to bring Hungary on to the side of the Allies. He emigrated to the USA after the end of the war and later the University in Szeged was renamed after him.

It turned out that this Szent-Györgyi Fellowship was a very generous prize to have won; indeed, it made me a millionaire. In Hungarian terms of course! The rate at that time was about 370-400 forints to the pound sterling. It covered travel and living accommodation during the year long period of the grant as well as financial support for the host university. In practical terms it enabled my wife and I to live in Hungary for a period of eighteen months because the Fellowship covered the rent of a flat. This enabled us to return some of the wonderful hospitality given to us in previous years by our Szeged friends and colleagues. It turned out to be a most eventful and quite wonderful period of our lives. Indeed, those years from 2003 to the middle of 2004 became very special. It was the culmination of years of scientific collaboration with my Hungarian friends lasting over thirty years.

So it was that in December 2002 I made a short visit to Szeged to view a flat selected by Gabi, the departmental secretary, in order to meet the flat owner, a solicitor and to open an account at the bank. This third-floor flat was in the 'ironing house' (Vasalóház) an attractive 'art nouveau' building about a fifteen-minute walk through the park to the university department. It had two bedrooms, thus allowing guests to stay; one bedroom could be converted into a substantial dining room allowing us to entertain on a larger scale. There was a small balcony which overlooked a memorial to a Szeged student who had been murdered during the Budapest uprising in 1956.

The department had given me as my office the old room belonging to the former now retired departmental head, our friend László Szekeres. This had a view of the Dom, the impressive city cathedral. So, surrounded by László's many books, I could continue to write up the results of our experiments in comfort with frequent visits along the corridor to the office of my collaborator Vegh Ágnés for numerous cups of strong coffee, always accompanied by discussions about how the experiments were going, which scientific journals to send the results to and future plans.

These studies were about the mechanisms of preconditioning; we were the first to show a role of nitric oxide in this means of protecting the heart. There were also questions regarding the protection of the heart by exercise – how much exercise is needed, how long can the protection last, and how can this protection be prolonged. Is nitric oxide involved? If so, what happens if we prevented its formation? Does it block the protection? Well, yes, it does! More coffee required to work the answers out! Then a wander back to my own 'den' to continue writing up our results in preparation for publication – always in English. So really my task.

Back in the flat Pam did wonders in entertaining and nearly every day someone called for advice, discussion and prayer.

We continued to be surprised with what Szeged had to offer, especially musically. The main Concert Hall housed orchestras from other parts of Hungary (especially Budapest and Pecs) as well as the local Szeged Symphony Orchestra which was of a good standard. Good pianists (such as Kocsis Zoltán and Schiff András) came. There was an Academy of Music in Szeged with a chamber orchestra and I was able to introduce the conductor to the music of Vaughan Williams, not well known in Hungary. At the attractive Opera House we saw operas like Tosca, Don Carlos, Eugene Onegin and Hungary's national opera Bank Ban by Ferenc Erkel. Erkel, who died in 1893, also composed Hungary's very moving national anthem. There was even more opera in Budapest which we visited several times on route back to Scotland.

Whenever we were in Budapest we continued to make contact with our friends in MEKDSZ and at Harmat for meals, prayer and fellowship. Harmat is a main Christian publisher in Hungary and we discussed how we could support them financially because translating and publishing is an expensive business. A perusal of the Harmat web site available today illustrates the variety of good Christian literature in Hungarian. Simpler, more basic literature is also available from '4H' a ministry of our (as yet unmet) friends Dr Eric and Rosemary Barrett through their frequent expeditions to 'greater Hungary'.

The climax of our stay in Szeged was the marriage of our young friend Juditka, the daughter of Imre and Judit Juhász, one of our earliest Christian contacts in the city. Both doctors, they were involved in student work, in the Christian Medical Fellowship and in carrying bibles into Romania – a very risky business in the 1960s – some 'hairy' incidents. On some occasions 'the Lord told them' to turn back once they had reached the border. There were serious consequences for carrying bibles.

One way to learn English was to travel to Scotland! The young Juditka stayed with us in our Bearsden home, worshipped with us and worked with children. We became firm friends. Soon after she returned to Hungary (with goodish English) her father Imre died. Later, during the time we lived in Szeged, she became engaged to be married and I was asked, as her Uncle Jim (Jim bácsi) to escort her down the aisle at the wedding ceremony, taking the place of her father. Wonderful privilege. I had done this before but with a different lady – my own daughter. However, this was somewhat different as the custom in the Hungarian Reformed Church was for the parents of the bride to give the couple, during the service, encouragement and 'advice' about Christian family life. This I managed to do in well-rehearsed Hungarian. She and her husband Lájos now have two lovely daughters moving into their teenage years; we are their somewhat distanced auntie and uncle.

Over the period of living in Szeged we became friendly with two 'missionary' couples. An American couple, Ed and Enikő Jordan had been sent out by the Southern Baptist Convention to work with the local Baptist church; Enikő's parent were originally from Hungary but Ed had to learn Hungarian from scratch. He made valiant attempts at this! The other couple had an interesting background story which I attempt to recount in 'Hungarian Portraits'. Les and Jill Szabady were from Canada but, as his name signifies, Les (László) was originally from Hungary. He left in 1956 after the revolution and when he returned, and spoke his mother tongue, it was obvious that he was one of those who had left the country over fifty years ago; his vocabulary was fifty years out of date! I had never realised before how language can change markedly over time and that the differences are not difficult to pick up. I wondered whether my own language also changes so markedly over the years and can be noticed; do I know of anyone who has returned to the UK for the first time after fifty years out of the country? Is the way they speak also fifty years out of date?

Jill together with Pam were involved in teaching English within the church, albeit Jill with a strong Canadian accent. This was a means of introducing folk to the gospel of Mark and the life of Jesus. I was also involved in an English language bible study in one of the Reformed Churches led together with a Lutheran theologian from the United States stimulated by our musical friends Péter and Esther Szerdahélyi.

We made especially deep friendships with folk in the Baptist Church; it was a rare Sunday when we were not invited to lunch with the family Szili, whose eldest son Barnabás had stayed with us in Glasgow back in the 1989. Indeed, we managed to invite almost all of our Szeged friends to stay in Glasgow with us and to explore something of the wonderful Scottish countryside.

Having our own accommodation also allowed us to host friends and family from Scotland. For example, our then pastor Mark came for a week to see where we were functioning, supported as we were in prayer by our own church. He spent time with Revész Árpád who, at that time, was also supported by our church family. Mark also made a visit with Árpád to Ukraine, a real eye opener for him. This example illustrated the value of ministers paying pastoral visits to their church members working in another country in a missionary or tentmaking capacity. From our own experience such visits are much appreciated.

During our stay in Szeged we ourselves also made visits to Árpád in Szombathely where I was always asked to preach; two sermons for the price of one I was told!

Of course, during this period we also had commitments in Scotland so short visits had to be made back home to Glasgow where our friend Krisztina was still 'house sitting' for us. I was still Interim Moderator of a local church and the Chairman of Interserve Scotland, then going through a period of change. Memorably, there was also a family celebration of Pam's 70th birthday.

Chapter 38
'Miracles are Normal'

This is really the story about grandparents, so if there are any of our Scottish or Viennese greatgrandchildren reading this (unlikely perhaps) they should talk to their own grandparents because what follows is really about them. They are the principal actors of this story; we simply had walk on parts!

It really begins with a visit Stephen made with me to Hungary in early September 1990. I had shared with him about the vision Árpád had about putting English teachers in the schools around his church since now, after the events of 1989, Russian would no longer be the main foreign language taught. Were there schools in Szeged willing to have a 'native' English teacher on their staff and financed by the local authority? Stephen had fruitful conversations with Elizabeth Abrahams about possibilities and discovered that there was a bi-lingual school in Pécs who wanted someone to teach both English literature and philosophy.

This happened and Stephen was appointed. The next problem was where to find accommodation in Pécs. On our next visit to Szeged later in September something quite remarkable happened. In Australia we had met with a former SUM missionary, then the pastor of a Baptist Church in Brisbane, who had published a book about his work in Sudan among the Nuba people. The book was called *Miracles are Normal.*[1] I believe that this is true. As Christians we should be on the lookout for them! One weekend, whilst staying in Szeged, we were invited to join with our good friends, the family Szili, for a few days by Lake Balaton. Numerous games of table tennis outdoors with the younger son and a lot of swimming. We were there for a Sunday and, after attending the morning service at the local Baptist church, who had just appointed a new minister, Mihály and Etelka Szili asked, 'Where would you like to go for the evening (really afternoon) service? We left this for them to

[1] Roy E Conwell, *Miracles are Normal*, Bethel Ministries, Mitchelton, Queensland, Australia 2000.

decide and they said – 'why not Pécs?'. Now Pécs was about sixty or seventy miles away.

Of, course they knew of Stephen and Fiona being appointed to a school in Pécs. So, we drove there. Imagine our surprise when the preacher was the same pastor we had heard in the morning! It turned out that he had previously been the pastor in Pécs and had a home there in a small village a few miles outside. After the service we were re-introduced and he suggested we went to see his home, now lived in by two of his children who remained there in order to complete their school education in Pécs. The top level of the house was available and the rent would help with the family finances. Would our family like to share the house with their two children? As soon as we saw the family home, we knew it was provision for them. And so it proved, although it took Stephen a journey involving two buses to reach the school where he taught. Even the fact that many in the village spoke German was part of the provision since no one knew English and Stephen and Fiona then had no Hungarian but both had studied German at university.

The second example was also one of the 'miracles of timing'. After two more daughters were born in Pécs (making four!) It proved difficult for the family, now of six, to survive on a single Hungarian teacher's salary equivalent of about £100 a month; in most Hungarian households both parents needed to work. Although there was support from their home church house group there were times when they did not know where the next meal was coming from. At one such time a gift arrived with exactly the correct amount of Hungarian currency (forints) for their needs, no more and no less. On another occasion a local Christian family left on their doorstep sufficient food for the next meal.

As 'tent makers' there were many opportunities for Christian witness. These included a weekly bible study in Hungarian for women in the flat, to which they had moved earlier in order to be nearer the schools where Stephen taught and where the two eldest girls (Sharon and Ailsa) commenced primary education; after Hungarian, German was then the second language – begun in Primary 1! There was also a weekly children's meeting in the flat and Stephen led bible studies in English for students from his school.

How did such studies start just a year after the fall of communism? Well, before the first Christmas Stephen had asked his class if they knew the Christmas story? Only one or two did so he explained what the coming of Jesus meant. Afterwards he invited those who would like to learn more to come to his home to study the bible. When the headmaster heard he invited Stephen to come and see him. Ominous! 'Stephen, it is not fair that you should be teaching 'religion' in English out of school hours; let's make it part of the school curriculum' to be taught during school hours! This same headmaster even offered to ferry children to a relay in town of the Budapest Billy Graham meeting. The bible studies continued throughout their time in Hungary.

The school where the two girls studied was one that specialised in ballet and folk dance (there were other primary schools that specialised in music) and later Sharon had an audition for the Royal Ballet in London. Eventually she studied for a time at the Scottish Dance School in Knightswood and later became a primary school teacher near Edinburgh as well as a teacher of ballet. She is now married with two children. Her parents, Stephen and Fiona had introduced Scottish Country Dancing to South West Hungary!

Of course, since we too were in Hungary for much of the time the family were living in Pécs, we often visited them, although some distance from Szeged, or they would come through to stay with us. Then, after over six years, they returned to Scotland and stayed in Milngavie. Another wonderful provision – and another story. Being so close to where we stay we have had the wonderful privilege – and joy! – of seeing the girls grow up from the time they were born.

Chapter 39
Five Hungarian Portraits

'Hungarian Portraits' is actually the title of an orchestral piece by Béla Bartók, although this dealt with 'pictures' of Hungarian village life rather than people. 'Portraits' (the Tudor ones) is also the title of a choral suite by Vaughan Williams for which he selected five characters from a series of poems by John Skelton (who died in 1529) a 'man of vigorous personality whose career was as stormy as his verse was lively'. There are 'portraits' of 'the raffish Eleanor, pretty Bess, a cantankerous clerk and an imaginative schoolgirl'. Elgar's 'Enigma Variations' are another example of musical portraits, this time of his unnamed friends 'pictured within'.

Perhaps nearer to the present series of 'portraits' would be a piece written by Bartók in 1938 for the clarinet virtuoso Benny Goodman and called 'Contrasts', although again these too are pictures of village scenes rather than of individuals, real or imaginary. My 'portraits' are of real people; these are memories of a few of my Hungarian friends. There are many other such friends but I know somewhat less about their lives, especially of the period before I met them. As in the Hungarian language, the family name comes first followed by their personal (Christian) name.

1 Juhász-Nagy Sándor

Sándor was one my earliest Hungarian scientific friends and, although he worked in Budapest and we only met at scientific meetings, I greatly enjoyed his company. Science can be fun and an early memory, I think from 1971, was standing up to our waists in the warm waters of Lake Balaton and discussing (arguing, debating?) about an unusual idea he and his much more extrovert colleague Szentiványi Mátyás had about receptors. These are areas on the surface of cell walls which respond specifically to endogenous substances, that are found in the body. In this case the particular receptors (there are two main types) were those that responded to adrenaline and noradrenaline. The question was whether they could interchange or transform from one receptor type to another. A somewhat unusual concept and there was much leg pulling! It should be pointed out that in those days such receptor typing was at quite an early stage.

Like me he was born in 1933 and he was a professor at the renowned Semmelweis University in Budapest working on coronary vascular responses linked to changes in cardiac metabolism. He was concerned how his experimental studies related to practical problems that arose during cardiac surgery. He was a brilliant teacher and is well named (it means 'great shepherd') a teacher who tended his students with great care; not that his students could ever be regarded as sheep!

He was a true Hungarian polyglot and patriot and was never tempted, like many others, to leave his home country for an easier life elsewhere. His was a life characterised by humility, humour, kindness and self-sacrifice. Towards the end of his life (he died of cancer in 2007) he wrote his 'memoirs', and near to his demise, quoted one of his favourite poets Weöres Sándor – 'death is like the sound of a distant violin'. His belief? 'Jesus is the Lord of life and that is enough for me'.

2 Szabady László (Les)

Les and his wife Jill came to Szeged from Canada in 2003 to work as 'tent makers' with the Baptist Church. Born in Hungary into a large God-following family, he could never remember whether he was one of eleven or twelve children. His family were persecuted because they were Christians; it was especially hard for 'non-conformist' church members in the early 1950s. He was baptised at the age of twelve. There was much harassment (that was the word he used) both at school and when eventually he started university in Szeged. On leaving education he was 'let go' from all of his twenty-one consecutive jobs because of his parent's beliefs; his father was a 'marked man' in his village.

After the failure of the 1956 revolution against Russian occupation he wanted to leave the country. The border with Austria was across a river. This he had to swim because the border guards had blown up the only bridge. When he eventually got to the other side he discovered bullet holes in his winter overcoat. The Austrian guards were helpful and managed to pull him out of the water. At a refugee camp he was given the option of going to either Canada or Australia. The Canada allocation was 'full' so he opted for Australia – a boat journey which took thirty-two days from a port in the northern part of Germany to Melbourne.

Les was placed in what was, during the war years, a military camp north of Melbourne where eventually he obtained a job through his interaction with Hungarians already in the country, because of his participation in the local football team. After two or so years he decided with a friend to explore other parts of that huge country. They purchased an old truck and explored much of the country before running out of fuel and water in the desert region between Alice Springs and Adelaide. They were very poorly equipped – 'we were so naïve' he told me 'no compass, no maps and with temperatures over 50 degrees during the day and minus 5 or so at night'. Quite lost. Of course, this region is very dangerous, indeed a death trap; we were once invited to explore this same desert region by our good friends Joyce and Ron Kuhl but declined!

It was in this hopeless situation that something remarkable happened. Alone (the trucks headlights were on at night to attract attention before the battery failed), desperate and facing death. Then one night they were awakened by someone tapping on the truck window. Winding down the window a stranger asked in Hungarian (!) if they needed help. A 'man' who looked in his seventies declined to answer their questions – 'who are you'? 'where are you from'? He took them in his car to just outside Adelaide, gave them the exact train fare to return to Melbourne and disappeared. No one at the petrol station where they had been dropped said they had ever seen the vehicle or the man who had saved them. Les calls him 'our Australian angel'!

Eventually Les was given permission to go to Canada which had always been his first choice. He started a business, went bankrupt and lost everything. Then he had 'a deep experience of the Lord' during recovery from a heart attack and, at the age of 72, felt God wanted him to return to Hungary and (in his own words) 'tell his story'. Indeed, he was a great conversationalist, a 'personal worker' but still spoke his native language of fifty years before!

Jill and Les served in Szeged and later left for a church plant on the outskirts of Budapest where later we stayed with them. They lived by faith and had little money. After we had settled back in Scotland, they came to stay with us and it was on that occasion that I interviewed Les and recorded his story on tape. They both died a few years later in Canada.

3 Szekeres László (Laci)

It was a letter from Laci in the late 1960s that first introduced us to Hungary. A letter 'out of the blue'. This led to a very long association with that country. Indeed, almost fifty years. So much so that one Hungarian friend once told me 'Jim, you have half a Hungarian heart' ('*A szivem fele részben magyar*') although I'm not sure which side, left or right! Despite our contrasting views on life (he was an ardent communist) Laci became a quite special friend. I often wondered about the origin of his left-wing views. Jewish, he had a bad time under Nazi occupation but again, in his own words 'escaped'. Was it the arrival of the Russian army in 1944 that saved many Jews from the gas chambers - including Laci? For most of the war Hungary was on the side of Nazi Germany but the government was then 'taken over' by the Nazis in 1944. The consequence was that the anti-Semitic programme, very apparent in the rest of occupied Europe, was introduced into Hungary, once an ally, with devastating results for the Jewish community, remembered today on the memorial wall plaques in the synagogues of Szeged, Budapest and Pécs.

László was a very good painter and thought at one time of making it his career; he studied for a year in the studio of the distinguished academician Pandur József until his father (himself a doctor) advised him 'better to be an obscure physician than an impoverished artist'. A wonderful oil painting of his father was in a prominent place in his living room and, after he 'retired' he 'took up' his brushes again. He continued to paint until there was no wall space left in his flat! He never really retired from science; even in retirement he would often appear in the department laboratory with the opening remark '*Na mi újság?*' – what's new?

This is not the place to summarise his scientific achievements (his obituary in the *Bulletin of the International Society for Heart*

Research does that) but these were recognised in the many honours that came his way including honorary doctorates from the universities of Krakow and Tubingen. He was a true polyglot. Apart from art and music he spoke at least five languages: interesting that when he recovered from his first stroke late in life, he could remember the English word for 'yesterday' but not the Hungarian. He puzzled why that should be?

We met often, stayed in one another's houses, including on many occasions his cottage at Balatonboglar, and discussed and argued over many issues; but he showed little interest in the things of God. Soon after his first wife died in 1990, he stayed with us in Bearsden after a scientific congress in Glasgow. He was due to travel home on a Sunday lunchtime. I gave him the option of staying at home until I could take him to the airport, or come with us to church. He decided to come, the first time he had been in a Christian place of worship. We could only stay for the first twenty minutes or so because of his flight but he did hear the children's talk which was, as usual for our minister Keith Crozer, about sheep. A good, easy to understand chat about the 'great shepherd'.

I spent more time in his company than with almost any other scientist with the exception of Végh Ágnes (see below). Many long conversations in many different places. He was a very good friend despite our differences about faith. Isn't it important for Christians to have good friends outwith their beliefs and to be there for them in times of need? We were the first to hear, by a visit from him very early one Sunday morning in Szeged, of his first wife's death. We are *in* the world as believers. Albeit not *of* that same world.

László died in somewhat strange circumstances in 2012. He was on Skype to his doctor daughters in faraway Pécs and Budapest when they realised all was not well and that, to their clinical eyes, he was showing signs of another stroke. Diagnosis at a distance. They immediately phoned for an ambulance but by then it was too late.

4 *Végh Ágnes*

When I first went to Hungary in 1969 Ágnes was still at school! She retired last year (2020) at the age of 65. It was László's idea that we work together from the year of my Hungarian sabbatical in 1989 through to when I left the Szeged department in 2004, the longest collaboration in my life in science.

We had met Ágnes (we used the shortened form of Ágika – literally 'little Ági', a word implying a deep friendship) earlier when she came to work briefly in Glasgow in my laboratory on the roof of the old Royal College building. I am not sure how valuable this experience was for her, as her own laboratory in Szeged was better equipped than my own. However, she did learn English – or rather the Glaswegian version of it, and probably speaks it as well as I do. Useful then when I worked with her in Szeged. Those years were the most productive and enjoyable of my life in science.

During the early post-war days of the communist regime the Végh family lost their home. Later her father (Ferenc) always had a small bag packed for the annual visit of the police, then followed by a day or two under detention 'because he still allowed his wife to attend church'.

When they had been forced to leave their family house Ferenc wrote a note on the train, which was taking them away to an 'unknown destination' and dropped it out of the train window. This note was found and given to Ágnes' brother. It stated that a window of their house had been purposely left open so that her brother, and a friend, could 'break into' their old home to rescue some of their possessions.

Pam and I got to know Ágnes well. When we first met in Szeged she and her parents were living in a flat in a typical communist building. We remember her mother's outstanding cooking, their bookshelves – three-deep in books (especially about history) and our visits to the family garden a few miles outside the city. Here they attempted to produce a special family wine. On one occasion I helped in this, pressing the grapes by dancing on them with bare feet, hence the rather characteristic aroma of the rather special vintage that year! We had many conversations about faith, especially after the fall of communism and during a period when her mother became ill. Back home in Scotland we had many 'phone prayers' with her. During one phone conversation Ágnes said 'thank you for praying for my mother but I too now have a good connection with God'. What a difference it made to my working

With ProfessorVégh Ágnes – a good colleague

life to be able to share Christian fellowship! To help her spiritual growth we gave Ágnes the New Testament commentaries written by William Barclay, still I think, despite criticism from other parts of the church, most insightful and helpful.

Although Ágnes was brought up as a Roman Catholic, like her devout mother, her father Ferenc was of the Reformed Church background and, after his wife died, he began again attending the local church. When Ágnes tried to join him and asked for membership she was 'turned down'; she would have to undergo a strict period of 'teaching'. Not a good welcome to someone who had faith and a love for the Lord Jesus. Later, the pastor of another Reformed Church visited her home and for the last years of Ferenc's life he would come regularly for prayer, share God's word and take communion with the family. This is the church at which Ágnes now worships and their Pastor (Sándor) seems to me to be a real shepherd of his flock. I would have loved to have met him.

5 *Révesz Árpád*

We were introduced to Árpád as the 'English-speaking Baptist pastor'. Unusual in those days. This was the result of a meeting with the Secretary of the Hungarian Baptist Union in Budapest. When he discovered we were going to Szeged he said that there is a Baptist church there 'and furthermore the Pastor speaks English!' So, after we arrived there and checking into our hotel, the almost certainly bugged Hotel Hungaria, we made telephone contact and were invited to meet Árpád. A very tall man and a former handball player; when he drove his Trabant car, his knees were around the steering wheel! A big man with a big and warm heart. So began a deep friendship with a quite remarkable and wonderful man.

I see from my diary that I was 'introduced' to the church in Szeged on June 11th 1989. In those days it was very important to be so 'introduced'; often there were government spies (strangers) in the churches to 'check' what was being said and who was present. I was often asked to 'serve', a delightful word for preach, and in the early years either other dear friends Hájos Ilona, Buzás or Árpád himself would translate. It was said by those in the congregation who spoke both languages that they heard two sermons; this meant, I think, that Árpád's was quite a free translation. He had learnt English as a student for a time at Spurgeon's College in London. How, I wondered, did he manage to get there during a severe period of communist rule? This was his answer:

'I moved to Szeged in 1976 and for years it had been a desire, I believe put there by God, to learn English.' My problem was that I could only be available at one particular time of the week – on a late Friday morning. I discovered in the daily newspaper (Délmagyarörszág) an advertisement by an English teacher in Szeged who gave private lessons. This teacher lived in the street Pam and I were eventually to live in. However, this teacher was only available on Friday mornings. At the only hours Árpád could manage! He specified that, as an atheist lawyer, there could be no speaking about God. Árpád took these two-hour lessons for eighteen months. At the last one Árpád asked if he could translate the story of the Prodigal Son. At the end the translator exclaimed 'why did he give his inheritance to this young man; it is not the legal way!'. To which Árpád replied 'such a legacy is life itself, which God gives to you too'. No comment!

In 1983 some pastors were allowed to leave the country for some theological education at the seminary in Rüschlikon in Switzerland. It was there that he met the Chairman of Spurgeon's College in London who, two years later, invited him to study there for a Spring term. As his language improved, God put into his mind to translate into Hungarian Billy Graham's book on the Holy Spirit. This he completed in time for Dr Graham's first visit to Budapest in September 1985. As Árpád translated the book he came to the page where Billy explains, with a simple prayer, how to place your trust in Jesus. At that point Árpád prayed, late at night in his London lodgings, that someone reading his translation would do just that. Years later someone in Szeged came up to him in the street and asked if he was that Árpád who had translated Graham's book. When he replied yes, she said 'do you remember that page where it is explained how to put your faith in Jesus?'. Of course, he did! She told him that as she read that particular page she had committed her life to Christ. Later she was baptised in Szeged Baptist Church, together with her two daughters.

It would seem that travel restrictions were somewhat eased in the 1980s but fruit like bananas and oranges were largely unknown in Hungary. On his excursions 'west' Árpád would come back to his Szeged home with a bag of bananas, each of them was carefully divided into five pieces for, at that time, the five family members.

Lack of funds for example to buy theological books in the West meant he had to improvise. Szeged is famous for the salami produced at the 'Pick' factory and, whilst at Spurgeon's he auctioned his salami (cut into very thin slices) for a total of £40 which he used to buy a two-volume commentary on John's Gospel. The salami quickly disappeared but the commentary is still in use after thirty-five years. Improvisation! But then one definition of a Hungarian is 'one who enters a swing door behind you and comes out in front of you'.

Whenever Árpád left Hungary he was always 'invited' by the secret police to a 'session' on 'how a socialist man should behave in the West'! The story of how he returned to Hungary after one such venture reads like a spy thriller!

The most remarkable characteristic of Árpád was his deep concern that people should experience, and come to know, Jesus and there are various stories as to how these personal contacts were 'engineered' by the Holy Spirit. The only other similar example of such Spirit guidance that comes to mind is that of George Dempster and recorded in such books, published in the 1930s by Hodder and Stoughton and long unobtainable, as 'Finding men for Christ', 'Touched by a loving hand' and 'The love that will not let me go'. On one occasion whilst still in membership at All Souls I heard George speak of his remarkable Spirit-led, one-to-one experiences in London. The 'Andrew method' is the Divine one and for it we have the record of Scripture. Think of Philip!

Pam with Árpád and Ildiko in a Budapest garden, 2006.
Good place to pray – but a sad farewell

Árpád shared with us, during an early stage in our friendship, that he felt God had called him to be an evangelist – a gifting so badly needed in the church. Indeed, after pastoring churches in a poor area of Budapest (where you could still see the shell holes in the walls fired from Russian tanks during the 1956 uprising) and then in a former church plant in the very west of Hungary at Szombathély, which we visited often, he did become a full-time evangelist for the Baptist Church. He was happy to collaborate with other denominations, including Roman Catholics, in city evangelism street preaching and showing evangelistic films on the walls of buildings. When he was first appointed to the Szombathély church, he began by visiting the police in Vas county, introducing himself and giving out copies of Mark's gospel and the Jesus video. He also telephoned all those in the directory with his surname, introducing himself and offering to visit. Some interesting results! One tent crusade had the mayor as guest of honour.

An opportunist, a man of prayer (a weekly prayer alliance included ministers of all denominations) and a visionary. With the fall of communism in Hungary he realised that the English language rather than Russian, would be taught in schools. He had the idea of 'planting' Christian teachers in the schools surrounding his church and advertising an English-speaking Sunday service! It was this idea that prompted our eldest son and his family to teach in Hungary for several years as already recorded.

Árpád had this special gift of quite naturally turning conversations to spiritual things. Two examples. He had often to travel to Budapest by train and he would always pray about where he should sit. On one occasion the girl opposite was talking on the phone and using the expression 'O God'. When she had finished Árpád began the conversation by asking how she knew God! There were occasions when someone he started a conversation with had come to faith by the end of the rail journey. There were others when the other person made excuses and changed their seat!

A short time ago he shared about a recent rail journey from Budapest to Pécs which had to be halted and the journey continued by bus. On the train was a Chinese student who had only recently arrived in Hungary and who was overheard to complain that she had paid for a ticket by train and not by bus. Árpád sat next to her on the bus and spoke to her in English. She said she wanted to learn Hungarian and Árpád offered to teach her! He started by telling her the most important phrase in Hungarian which, translated into English was 'God loves you'! By the end of their journey he had invited her to visit him and his family; later she put her trust in Jesus. She now attends a church in Budapest. The 'strange' thing about that particular journey was that in Budapest she had asked for a ticket to Bécs not Pécs (Bécs is Vienna in Hungarian). Difficult at a ticket office if you have no Hungarian language for the official to distinguish between a B and a P, especially with a Chinese accent! She was on the wrong train! But, well met. It was God who put her on the 'right train' and the 'right path'.

This gift for evangelism is, for me, very challenging. Few people in my experience have this natural gift. How do we share our faith? How much do I know of the experience of what Árpád described as 'Spirit navigation'? Something I am still 'working on' so late in my own Christian life. Perhaps, as William Lane once wrote, men (and women) need to be 'graciously approached for Christ'.

Chapter 40
Farewell to Hungary

To be accurate, that title should read farewells because there were more than one. Indeed, five in all.

There are certainly some people, and some places too, where it is very difficult to say goodbye especially when you know you will never see them again on planet earth. Hungary the country and Hungarian friends in particular are very much in that category. After all, I did make nearly seventy separate visits over a period of over forty years. After packing up our flat in 2004, we were invited to return on five occasions. These included a wedding in Budapest, scientific meetings in both Pécs and Szeged, a 90th birthday celebration for our old friend László Szekeres and culminating in my final scientific meeting in Balatongyörök in 2014.

When you have lived in a residence for almost two years (with a balcony overlooking a memorial to the student martyr killed for his participation in the 1956 uprising in Budapest) and for which you had to provide everything needed to live for that period – apart that is from furniture – there is quite a lot of packing to do. Not easy especially in the July heat and when attempting to give away as much as possible, only to discover people did not particularly want what you so much wanted to give away! For example, cutlery, kitchen equipment, bedding and crockery. What surprised us was that our friends showed little interest in our wonderful ornate Kalocsa porcelain hand-painted tea and dinner services. Too old-fashioned perhaps; and our friends already had their own. So, we ended up bringing them home and using them every day! And, not even our children or grandchildren (including the two who were born in Hungary) seem interested in possessing them!

Several events stand out in the ten year 'goodbye period'. The first was the wedding in Budapest of our friend Krisztina who had lived with us in our Bearsden house. This was the year during which she was studying at the International Christian College. This College, near the University of Strathclyde campus, sadly did not survive for too long: it was basically the former Glasgow Bible College, itself renamed from the Bible Training Institute (BTI) Glasgow where I had studied and became a Board Member. BTI had existed for over a hundred years with many distinguished graduates, many serving in overseas situations or in the pastoral ministry. The former Principal Geoffrey Grogan wrote a history of the College for the centenary appropriately entitled *Shaping Tomorrow, Starting Today*.[1] Over this period Krisztina was really our 'home sit' for a year when we were mostly either in Hungary or Australia. This saved our so friendly neighbours opposite pulling, and opening, our curtains every day! It was their suggestion that when they were not 'in residence' we could pull their curtains each morning and evening and that they would do the same for us. Little did they know that we would, from then on, spend three months each winter in Australia!

Krisztina came from the western city of Szombathely and met her German husband Johannes, at the European Student Evangelism Conference in Györ in 2004. They were married in Budapest a year later and lived in Germany until she died of cancer leaving two delightful children. Whilst in Bearsden she attended our local church and was responsible, together with the pastor's wife, for starting a bible study group for those 'young in the faith' in English – with a delightful Hungarian accent.

The farewell meeting in Pécs in 2006 (when I walked out of the Bishop's Palace with his silver cutlery in my pocket!) was a reminder of the several visits to our family when they lived there and when we lived in Szeged on the other side of the country. This family saga has already been told. This 'farewell lecture' was followed by the comment that 'there was something terribly really wrong with your lecture'. Oh dear! And probably my last. So, after all those years and so many lectures in so many countries this is the final critique. Was it then all worth it? However, this 'criticism' was followed by '. . . that you are leaving science'! Maybe then the talk was not so bad after all. I think, and so people have told me, that my English when speaking, for example at scientific meetings is readily understandable and, apparently unlike some others,

[1] Geoffrey Grogan, *Shaping Tomorrow, Starting Today*, Christian Focus, Fearn 1992.

especially Americans, easy to listen to. Perhaps this is because my accent (if I have one at all) is 'soft' and because I speak slowly. This is also true (apparently) when I preach and others have said 'you are easy to translate' and 'speak beautifully'. When I think back to my schooldays and my difficulties in this area, I can only thank the God who can do wonders with such scant material! Of course, Moses is another early example. My helpful teacher of English at school would be very surprised both about my speech and more especially my writing. Who says that the Lord has no sense of humour! A disability turned into something useful. And, I write this without any element of pride; simply amazement and thankfulness.

This 2006 visit included another visit to Szombathély by cross-country train, a journey that took three and a half hours yet the distance 'as the crow flies' is only about 200 km. This was to see Árpád again and, so I thought, to say goodbye and to 'serve' in the growing church. I was given a great welcome. 'I still remember your last visit' said one 'and your deep teaching on communion' and 'you preached like a father to us'. Of course, those in the congregation who understood English told me 'we had two sermons today; one from Árpád and one from you'. Quite different! But said with a smile!

There was now a wonderful music group in the Szombathély church; this is not unusual in Hungarian churches. This 'orchestra' included a gifted violinist who had been asked by Kocsis Zoltán to lead the Hungarian National Orchestra of which he was chief conductor. I told them afterwards that, as they led the worship, I felt I could just reach out to them and touch the Lord. They said we felt the same during the sermon. Later, Árpád asked me to visit with him a 91 year old man (Imre bácsi) reading from the bible and praying with him. This is what the pastoral ministry should be like. Árpád had earlier suggested that I took another 'sabbatical' in Hungary and we could 'serve' together. Too late, because he had been asked to leave the church the following year when he reached the retiral age. Of sixty! We talked about 'what next' for both of us.

The previous Sunday I had 'served' in a quite different church. I have already written about another Laci who, with his Canadian wife Jill, we had first met in Szeged. Now they were involved in a church plant near Budapest situated in an old chemical factory at

Rákos. Jill took an English language class – a good way of getting to know the many folk who now wanted to learn the language especially if this included some Christian teaching.

In many ways this was a sad visit. László Szekeres tried very hard to persuade me to continue the link with the Department but both it and the city of Szeged had changed. The biochemical aspect of the research was getting beyond me and the atmosphere in the country too had changed. There were demonstrations against the government about the state of the country (then the poorest in the EU), the PM had admitted being dishonest about the economy and a good number had lost their jobs including our two friends Iren and Szusza. The budget was overspent, the finance minister was, in the opinion of many, incompetent and the socialist mayor was reported to be 'noting' the names of those who took part in the demonstrations – including two of my University Professor friends. It seemed just like the bad old times might return.

There were clear material benefits in belonging to the EU. The renovated old bath house looked beautiful after years of neglect but the old market square with the water tower had gone. The replacement could have been anywhere. So little of the old typical Hungarian character of the city remained. The old shops had disappeared and the new shops in the lovely main 'walking street' (Karász utca and Széchenyi Square) could have been seen almost anywhere in Europe. The typical Hungarian shops, many of the restaurants including the famous Virág our favourite ice-cream shop, the Reformed Church bookshop, wonderful for browsing, no longer existed. There were no music shops. The stationers at which we bought cards, calendars and my favourite pens and pencils had become a second-hand clothes outlet. The famous Pick factory, manufacturers of the best salami in the country (some would say in Europe) had closed, with many redundancies. All so very different to say, six years previously.

This really was 'goodbye' to our favourite Hungarian city. Or so I thought! But there were to be two further visits. I had been invited to participate in the celebrations for László Szekeres' 90th birthday. I had decided, with the great help of Ágnes Végh to start this in Hungarian. Afterwards Laci's son-in-law, a pharmacologist from Pécs was heard to say 'I did not realise Jim spoke Hungarian; his accent is from Eger'! The meeting itself was rather formal (somewhat stunted introductions from his two successors as Head of Department) and László spoke at length about his life in science and then showed a power point of his many paintings, some of which are really good. I have a couple. Sadly, László died a few months later of a massive stroke.

This was the year I really said farewell to the Baptist church and served there for the last time. Friends from other churches were present and I preached (again!) from 2 Samuel 9 well translated by a young man from the student church in Szeged, started soon after the fall of communism by folk from the United States.

Our last (and final!) visit was in 2014, again following an invitation to speak at a meeting of the International Academy of Cardiovascular Sciences at a hotel in the village of Balatongyörök near the town of Keszthely. This turned out to be my 'nearly last' scientific lecture; a year or so later I was invited again to speak in London for a special celebration of the British Cardiovascular Society of which I had once been President. This last Hungarian meeting was an opportunity to say goodbye to so many old friends from other parts of Europe who had meant so much to me for many years both before and after the fall of communism. At the end of the meeting Pam and I were driven to Szeged by Végh Ágnes and her father. This gave us the opportunity for the really last time to thank so many friends in a city we loved – despite the alterations in the city itself. The 'old friends' were the same – Judit and her enlarged family, the Szili family (those Sunday lunches!) Sándor and Gisi Nagy, Péter and Esther, Irén and George, the many friends at the Baptist Church and in Budapest, Dóra Bernhardt, Kornél and Anna and the team of friends at the pleasant small hotel (Orion) we had stayed in over so many years. No dry eyes!

Part 5 HOME AND AWAY

Chapter 41

Happenings – Chance or Planned?

To those readers who have persevered to this point in the story I firstly offer my congratulations (or commiserations) and secondly, I ask a question. Has there been anything in the story thus far that has been in any way unusual? Any accidental and unrelated but fortuitous concurrence of events? Did these events just happen by chance? I am not thinking so much of those that could have happened to anyone, place and time of birth, survival of the blitz and flying bombs for example, but events 'out of the ordinary', whatever ordinary is in this life. Unusual happenings?

For me, looking back, there has been in my life thus far a series of unusual threads; the events leading up to the beginning of my life of faith, my marriage to Pam (the M and P tale), the strange Brighton story, the quite unexpected opening up of our lives to Nigeria and then Hungary, the birth of our second child (a 'miracle' baby seemingly back from the dead). There have been so many things seemingly falling into place. Too many to be just 'chance'? A life seemingly 'planned' then? God planned? The apostle Paul for example many times in his letters emphasised that his life was certainly planned. So, why not the lives of other disciples?

For me then, indeed for us as a married couple, there has been throughout our lives a strong sense of 'providence', of God being in control of events concerning us, of 'His hand upon us'. Of course, any reader of Scripture would say that this is the biblical story. It is what happened in Old Testament history. Just one example. Writing about Joseph's brothers (Genesis 37) Robert Alter writes of 'events divinely contrived'.[1] I am not sure about the word 'contrived'

[1] Robert Alter, *Strong as Death is Love – The Song of Songs; Ruth; Esther; Jonah; Daniel: A Translation with Commentary*, W.W. Norton & Co, New York 2015.

meaning 'brought about cleverly': perhaps 'arranged', 'devised', 'lovingly planned' would be more appropriate? A situation of being in God's hands, his will being worked out through his children.

This is seen most significantly in the coming of Jesus and in all that happened to him. As Peter said of the crucified and risen Jesus on the Day of Pentecost 'this man was put into your power by the predetermined plan and purpose of God'.[2] A 'predetermined plan', a 'purpose of God'. Could not this also be true in my life? God's hand moving powerfully in us when we come to Him by faith, indeed, before that! Then a life of 'happenings', unexpected developments around the corner!

One of my favourite Old Testament stories is found in the book of Ruth. If any reader does not know this story I urge them to read, or re-read it. The particular word in question comes when Naomi returns home after losing her husband and two sons in the, for them, foreign country of Moab. With Naomi in this homecoming is her daughter-in-law Ruth, who had decided not to remain in the country of her birth (with the likelihood of remarrying) but to accompany her mother-in-law. In order to provide for herself and Naomi, Ruth goes 'gleaning', picking up grain left behind by the gleaners. We then read 'now it happened',[3] 'as it turned out', that she came to part of the field belonging to Boaz, who 'happened' to be a kinsman of Naomi's deceased husband, and who 'happened' to come to his field at the right time. The timing seemed perfect because it was God's timing.

This phrase in Ruth could well apply to my life many centuries later. It is described in the AV version delightfully as 'hap'; 'her hap was to light on a part of the field belonging to Boaz'.[4] God's intervention was in response to a problem, the deep need for Ruth to find enough food for herself and Naomi. There is an African proverb, from Malawi in the Chewa tongue, which translated[5] goes 'the one with diarrhoea opens the door first', meaning the one with an urgent problem goes fast to seek help! The situation in the Ruth

---

[2] Acts 2:23 (J.B. Phillips).

[3] Ruth 2:3 (ESV).

[4] Ruth 2:3 (KJV).

[5] Isabel Apawo Phiri, *Ruth, Africa Bible Commentary,* ed. Tokunboh Adeyemo, Zondervan Corporation, 2006.

story is a blend of human responsibility (and choice) and divine sovereignty; of need and of God's intervention. It just 'happened'. And, this story had a 'hap'py ending!

It is of course possible to mistake God's pattern for our life. F. B. Meyer, in a prayer of confession writes of the sin, for which he asks forgiveness, of mistaking God's plan for our lives – 'if I have marred the pattern drawn out for my life'. But, when we do fall in with God's purposes, when we are in the right place at the right time, then our seemingly insignificant individual 'story' becomes amazingly, part of a greater plan. Each one of us is irreplaceable in the full telling of God's story. We count, every last one of us, and what we do also counts.

I give four examples of God's pattern being worked out in the lives of four of my friends and in which I had a small 'walk on' part. Interestingly, all the examples are of friends who were active in missionary work, three of them in Nigeria. It is about God's plans being worked out for those concerned and of being lovingly 'used' to forward those plans. All the glory goes to Him.

The first example is about an interaction with an old friend Mike Richards, although in this case it was remotely; this time we did not actually meet one another. Mike, as I wrote about earlier, was one year ahead of me at university and was one of those who played a part in my coming to Christ. After doing his National Service in the parachute regiment, he and his wife Joan went to Thailand in 1958 as pharmacists with what was then the China Inland Mission (CIM) at their hospital in Manorom. In 1965, he successfully applied for a lectureship at the University of Bangkok and then, as a member of the university staff, he pioneered Christian work among students. Much later, during a very varied 'career', he was invited to re-join the Overseas Missionary Fellowship (OMF, as the CIM had become) as a short-term replacement for a member of the Home Staff at the Mission Headquarters at Newington Green in London. When this position was refilled, Mike decided to re-enter academic life and applied for the position of Head of the Pharmacy School, for which he was very well qualified, at Robert Gordon College (now Robert Gordon University) in Aberdeen. It was at this point that after many years our lives again overlapped.

I was, at that time the external examiner in pharmacology at Robert Gordon's and whilst in Aberdeen was invited to sit in on a staff discussion about the response to the advertisement for the position of Head of School. This had been offered to the preferred candidate who declined because he had obtained a position elsewhere, as had 'number two' on the list of possible appointees. The discussion was whether to appoint the third candidate or re-advertise. During the discussion I felt that Mike should have been interviewed and asked God in prayer (silently, like Nehemiah in the presence of the king!) to keep the position for him if it was 'from the Lord'. They asked my opinion. My suggestion was that they should re-advertise. In private I then asked why they had not called Dr Richards for interview as his qualifications (not only a PhD but also a DSc from London University) were better than those of the other candidates; perhaps they were wary of someone who had been a missionary! The result was the position was re-advertised and Mike was appointed. He made a splendid job of it and revolutionised the research in his particular area of expertise (microbiology). Mike later followed me as Chairman of the Scottish UCCF Council.

The next example is also of a 'returned missionary'. In the centenary year (2004) of the Sudan United Mission (SUM) all the work and property of the Mission was handed over to the church that had resulted from its many and varied activities (schools, hospital, veterinary work and the theological college at Bukuru). Many missionaries were made 'redundant', because their tasks had now been taken over by Nigerians. What would happen to those who had served with the now redundant Mission? Indeed, what would now happen to the Mission itself? Having so successfully completed their primary task should the Mission rejoice at God's goodness and, in their centenary year 'close'? Some felt so. What happened was that it became another mission (called Action Partners) and later 'Pioneers'. Many former missionaries stayed on as employees of the church, which decided to hand over to the civilian authority former areas of the work that became too expensive for the church to continue to support, such as the hospital at Vom. Other missionaries decided to return home especially for their children's education or to look after elderly relatives. Or both.

One of these was David Williams. An Oxford graduate in English, David and his wife Bridget had then been over twenty years with the SUM in Nigeria. David applied for forty teaching jobs back in the UK without any success. Some applications were not even acknowledged. This, for Christians was the 'real world'. One school he applied to was the High School of Glasgow. This old established and famous grammar school (where my eldest son was once a pupil) had been closed by the Conservative Government but had been reborn by some of its former pupils and housed on land previously the home of the extensive sports facilities at Anniesland. The school continued, also as the High School of Glasgow; two of my granddaughters later received scholarships to study there. The headmaster Eric Harle, 'happened' to be a member of the same church as my wife and I and, knowing of my time in Nigeria, he asked my opinion about David's application. Was it worth bringing him up to Glasgow for interview? Surely not? I knew David and strongly recommended they see him. David was appointed becoming known especially for the quality of the school plays he produced and for his Christian witness. He stayed until his retiral and became very active, with Bridget, in the life of the local church. David succeeded me as Chairman of the Scottish SUM Committee.

This third story is for me the most remarkable of all. It concerns an old friend called Ken Bennett who a short time ago went to be, at the age of 95, with the Lord he loved and served all his life. He always regarded me as his 'little brother': for me he was more a brother than a friend. We got to know one another when he was appointed by the Sudan Interior Mission (SIM) to the African Challenge Church on the road from Ibadan to Lagos. This became the venue for the student services mentioned in the account of our time in Ibadan. He succeeded an American missionary called Dan Truax well known for the power of his voice and his fondness for rabbit pie and cake. He and Ken could not have been more different! I remember one of my Christian colleagues having doubts about Ken because, so he thought, since he had never been to university, he 'was not quite suitable'. How wrong he was. Ken was the most caring person I have ever met and was much loved by the students – as well as by us.

Ken was several years older than I, old enough to have been in the Royal Navy during WW2. With a great sense of humour and a really good knowledge of the local Yoruba language he became much involved in the work of the Hospital Chapel and the witness among university students. How he helped us in our final days in Nigeria I have also recounted.

The time too came for him and his wife Phyllis (always known as 'Phyll') to 'retire' from the field and the question arose what next?

On one of my return visits to Nigeria (in 1971) I met up with Ken and Phyll and we spent a relaxing weekend together at a retreat. As we sat in the 'lounge', we noticed an old copy of a Christian magazine, I think 'Crusade', on the drinks table. On looking through Ken saw an advertisement for the position of Warden at the North Oxford Overseas Centre (NOOC) set up earlier by a group of Christian academics as a welcome residential centre for students from overseas. The final date for applications for the post had passed but Ken decided to apply; I could take the application with me to post when I got home. In case they wanted a UK contact we put my telephone number in with the application.

A day or so after I arrived home I received a telephone call from John (afterwards Sir John) Houghton who was chairing the appointments committee. I explained the situation and argued, I think quite strongly, that they should consider Ken's belated application. This they did and Ken was appointed. He and Phyll had a marvellous ministry there for many years, making 'many friends' in several different parts of the world. These 'many friends' they were invited to visit after they had retired; for some, such as those in Singapore, they became more than friends and indeed members of the Bennett family. What I only discovered in the last conversation I had with Ken, a few weeks before he died was that the committee had already appointed someone – a gentleman with a 'colonial background' who did not fit in. The timing of that late application was perfect!

The final example concerns yet another former missionary: Bill Roberts, one time Scripture Union staff worker in Nigeria who had arrived there towards the end of 1965. Bill had been on the team of the CSSM beach mission in Frinton during one of our home leaves and we had shared with him about SU in Nigeria. During the Nigerian civil war, which began in 1967 Bill was resident in the Eastern Region establishing the work of SU. At the outset of the war this Eastern Region became Biafra. During the war Bill became much involved, amid much suffering and poverty, in relief work. Later he told his story, and how he had to be airlifted out of the country, in a book published by Scripture Union and which became a best seller. It is quite a story. Somewhere on my shelves there is a copy. I seem to remember the book was entitled *Life and Death Among the Ibos*, I think!

'Blacklisted' and forbidden to return to Nigeria after the end of the conflict Bill worked for SU in Sierra Leone. Here he married an American missionary called Jan and together they were caught up in yet another civil war. In Sierra Leone they had a very fruitful ministry especially among young people. Bill worked for a time in London with Tear Fund before retiring to Devon 'on a missionary pension'.

We lost contact, apart from annual letters at Christmas, until out of the blue I received a phone call from him about a possible holiday in Scotland. Apparently, having booked a cottage belonging to a friend, he had been told it was closed for the winter. Bill asked me if I knew of any cheap accommodation in Scotland where they could stay. I was at that time a regular visitor to the Baptist Church in Bunessan on the island of Mull and, when I enquired of the church secretary about the dates Bill and Jan had booked for, at the now non-available accommodation, I discovered that these were free, as was the caravan alongside the church which served to put up visiting preachers. They could use the caravan as long as Bill was willing to take the church services on the two Sundays. Bill, of course, said yes.

Now, I knew it was unusual for Sundays to be vacant because both the accommodation and the island were very popular. Normally one had to book a year in advance! Bill and Jan enjoyed their stay on Mull so much that they talked about living on the island and continuing to help with the small church. I pointed out that winters in Scotland could be harsh and suggested they 'test their call' by coming to Mull during the winter, when few preachers from the mainland would be likely to make the journey and most Sundays would be free. I remember meeting them at the bus station in Glasgow to see them off. It was snowing!

They were not put off by the winter experience and despite doubts from me decided to make the move from Devon and settle in Bunessan. Later, they moved to Tobermory in part because, both having good voices, they had become very active in the Gaelic choir and in the local Free Church. But it had all started with that telephone call to me about a place to holiday in Scotland!

The point about these stories is about being in the right place at the right time for the fulfilment of God's purposes for his children. It is not about 'chance' but is about the loving plans God has for his people and how he can use the most unlikely people, being 'in the way', to achieve his purposes. It is about the Holy Spirit guiding lovingly. And, yet again for me, of the enormous privilege of having a very small part in these purposes.

Question for discussion! Could God have moved these friends to Aberdeen, Glasgow, Oxford and Mull without human participation? Answer. Yes, He could! If in doubt check the early chapters of 1 Samuel especially chapters 5 and 6 – 'God flying solo'. God can 'cope' without us. However, God does use us, not because He needs to, but because of His love and kindness, He wants to involve and work through us. All the glory goes to Him!

Chapter 42
'Go Make Disciples' – Pakistan, Egypt, India, Turkey, Korea

The first two churches I went to in my younger days as a Christian (All Souls, Langham Place, London and Gunnersbury Baptist) placed much emphasis on world mission ("Go therefore and make disciples of all nations"),[1] so it was to be expected that, as a young married couple, this too would be on our hearts. Indeed, Pam's interest went back to when she was a child in the Methodist Church. She was very active in the Junior Missionary Association which involved persuading church members to contribute to the Methodist Missionary Society on a regular basis. So, she was active each Sunday with her account book! Indeed, she was so proficient at this that she received a medal for her work with any number of 'bars' and ribbons to go with it. Did she ever dream of going herself? I think so; but then she also dreamed of one day marrying a tall minister. This certainly did not happen!

After graduation and during our first year of marriage we had discussions with the China Inland Mission to determine if they could use a couple with our particular qualifications. The response was no. They had just appointed two pharmacists (our friends Joan and Mike Richards who were even at the time travelling to Thailand) and did not need more. A 'glut' of pharmacists then, if that is the correct term. The story of how we ended up in Nigeria has already been told, not as 'missionaries' but as 'tent makers' which, in those days, meant working in secular employment but involved in God's work. True of course for all Christian believers.

When we arrived in Scotland we were, almost immediately, asked to become involved in aspects of Christian work with which we were familiar from our years in Nigeria – Scripture Union, the Sudan United Mission and the Sudan Interior Mission. All of these had committees in Scotland responsible for the home aspects of their overseas work, including prayer meetings, hosting returning

[1] Matthew 28:19.

missionaries and raising support. So, I became much involved in committee work and, as a couple, hosting returning missionaries in our home when they were in Scotland on 'home assignments' – visiting churches and speaking about their work overseas.

There were prayer meetings for each of these missions, always in the evenings, but as the participants became 'older' and with declining numbers, when we moved from the family home to our present flat in 2006, we made the decision to combine the two missionary prayer meetings and move them from an evening to an afternoon. It thus became an Africa Prayer meeting. This was a good move; folk were now able to travel and return home before dark. They came from as far afield as Callander, Muthill, Edinburgh, Dalry, Kirkintilloch, Milngavie and various parts of Glasgow and Bearsden; even, for the occasional gathering, from 'the north', and from Penicuik, Oxford and Peru. Readers will remember that at one time South America was joined to the west coast of Africa!

Another important aspect of home support for folk serving overseas was visiting them in their missionary environment. I was fortunate to be able to do this in the years following our return from Nigeria especially in 1968, 'touring' both the SUM and SIM fields.

Later, and this came as a surprise to me, came involvement in the work of Interserve. In Scotland there was always a strong involvement in the work of what eventually became Interserve, it having evolved out of BMMF (which I think stood for the Bible and Medical Missionary Fellowship) and even earlier the Zenana Village Mission, which worked predominantly among women in India. At a church in Helensburgh where I often took the services, there is an old stained-glass window depicting the work of the Zenana Mission.

This involvement in Interserve came as a result of an unexpected invitation from the Secretary, Revd Brian Ringrose, who became with this wife good friends; many stays with them in their delightful small flat over successive Edinburgh Festivals. The letter of invitation lay on my desk for the best part of a year under yet another pile of papers in my untidy study. When I eventually discovered this 'lost' letter I replied apologetically to say that although I had few links with the part of the world in which they were involved, I would be happy to join them. This belated reply came as a surprise to Brian and I think the vacant position on Council had already been filled. However, the invitation stood and later, when the incumbent chairman Alastair Morrice was 'called' to serve in Central Asia, I succeeded him. Because the Interserve office in Lenzie was near to our home, I enjoyed regular visits to the office, often joining in the staff prayer times.

The Council was 'indigenous' to Scotland and it was this that contributed to the relatively good number of Interserve missionaries that were sent out from Scottish churches. It 'so happened' that I had the opportunity of visiting a good number of them in the countries in which they served. I summarise some of the more interesting of these.

Pakistan

The Pakistan adventure occurred as one of a small team of cardiologists asked to introduce a drug (called oxyfedrine) to cardiologists in that country. The basic pharmacology of this drug had been studied by my Glasgow group and it was marketed in Europe as an anti-anginal drug. It was produced by a German drug company for which I was a consultant. In December 1984 the team visited Karachi, Lahore, Peshawar and Rawalpindi. Whilst staying in the first two places I had arranged to visit Interserve partners involved in different ministries. I met all the partners in Karachi, because I happened to be there at the time each week when they met for prayer, bible study and mutual encouragement. I gained insights into the work they did and the difficulties of working in a Moslem country. There were also several delightful meals and good opportunities for mutual sharing! I also met the leader of Pakistan SU to learn about Bible Note distribution (very encouraging) and to be challenged by his brave commitment to working among children. I also made a visit when in Rawalpindi to the minister of the Anglican Church and heard about his radio ministry 'proclaiming Christ and the atonement'. The forty minutes of prayer with him was an inspiration for me.

The well attended scientific meeting times were unusual. At all of them the projector broke down – usually after I had given my talk! A lot of thinking on your feet! Of course, we were entertained in each of the places we visited. One highlight was to be invited to take part in the celebration of the 'Prophet's birthday', being taken on the back of a Toyota truck around Lahore as part of the procession with thousands of people in the streets. We were cheered (not sure why!) given green scarves, garlanded and showered with rose petals. At times there were clearly fanatic elements in the huge crowd and it could have been ugly if it had got out of control, which apparently had sometimes happened. It was an amazing, if somewhat frightening, experience culminating in an evening gala reception made up of army officers and their beautifully clothed wives. I was made aware of the political influence of the army. One of the colonels later invited us to a 'preach' (it was really a harangue) by a passionate Saudi Moslem Imam, which was both embarrassing and somewhat frightening. Being forewarned about this I had the previous evening read the Koran in my hotel room and the references to Jesus, regarded as a prophet in Islam. In the Iman's break for breath during the 'preach' I asked a question about Jesus. This brought the meeting to an abrupt end! Would we have been as passionate in telling the Jesus story to guests in our own country?

Peshawar is on the border with Afghanistan and is part of the notorious North-West Frontier. A frightening place, men walking around fully armed. Compared to the audience in Lahore and Karachi there appeared to be few cardiologists in Peshawar! Apart from the fascinating and oriental market the most interesting part of this visit was to be taken to see the Khyber Pass, looking into Afghanistan, and also a medical mission at a camp for Afghan refugees. The next flight was to Rawalpindi set among beautiful hills and I was taken by a Colonel Rahman to the very top of one of them. Wonderful views. It was here that I had fellowship with the minister of the Anglican Church built for the British Army in 1852.

On the flight returning us to Karachi I had a remarkable experience. As guests we were given first class seats and I found myself separated from my colleagues with an empty seat beside me. Although all the passengers were aboard the plane we were kept waiting 'for an important person' who was eventually brought direct to the plane in a big car. The empty seat next to me was taken by a lady. Now in Pakistan you do not make conversation with a neighbour and especially with an 'important' lady. However, she started a conversation with me. She asked what I was doing in Pakistan and then told me she was with the Ministry of Health (I think she was in fact the Minister) with 4,000 people serving under her. She had schooled in England but was clearly apprehensive about her return to Karachi for a meeting and we discussed how to deal with 'stress'. As the aircraft made its approach to Karachi airport, she asked me if I knew Psalm 23. She knew it from her days at school in England. Would I quote it for her? I did, as she clutched my hand whilst we came in to land. Of course, she was the first passenger off the plane; a black Mercedes on the tarmac was waiting her arrival. I often wondered what happened to her and what effect, if any, that strange conversation had, whilst sitting in that first-class Pakistan Airways cabin. It was simply put into the Lord's hands.

Egypt

Another visit with the same medical team was to Egypt in May of the following year. Once again, I had arranged to meet Interserve partners whilst there. After the usual (by now) airport delays, this time (due to 'engine failure'!) we arrived (late) in Cairo. The hotel where we were accommodated was on an island in the middle of the River Nile. There were the usual tourist tours (Pyramids, Tutankhamen's tomb, the old Jewish synagogue (associated with Jeremiah) a papyrus factory, the bazaar and an old Coptic church said by some to be on the site of the place where Jesus, Mary and Joseph stayed during their time in Egypt. Being Sunday I took a taxi to the Cathedral in time for a lively service in which an Interserve couple were leading the worship. It was good to have conversations with the Interserve team over numerous cups of coffee and also to meet up for lunch by the river Nile with an ex-student who had done her PhD at Strathclyde partly with me.

Next day we were taken to Alexandria on the Mediterranean coast. I tried to imagine it in the days of the early church: that was not difficult. Then a very long meeting that did not finish until after eleven that night. Someone had spoken for far too long! Next day was rather special. A drive through the desert along the coastal road to El Alamein, now a small village but the site of crucial battles during the second world war. The huge cemetery we all found intensely moving. I could not help remembering that my father's regiment would have been there; my father could have been there too if he had not been injured at Dunkirk and thus prevented from taking part in the 'African campaign'. Back in Cairo for a meal with other Interserve workers, learning how to present the Gospel in such a spiritually dark place.

India

My adjacent fellow PhD student at the Royal Veterinary College building in Camden Town during 1956/7 was a medical doctor from India – Dr R K Sanyal. At the time of my visit to India he was an important person in the State Government Medical Service. His unenviable task was concerned with how drugs could remedy the overpopulation problem and how they could be introduced – highly controversial. On meeting up again after several years there were many reminiscences of student days in London in a laboratory where we each had about two feet of bench space. 'RK' had taught me some pathology and introduced me to curry.

A Glasgow visitor to my own laboratory Dr H Siddiqui, always known as 'Sid', was often my host in India. On the last occasion I was invited as the British Pharmacological Society's 1990 Official Visitor. This involved a lot of travelling, giving lectures in the major places of medical education.

India is a fascinating country with a huge population from the highly educated (and rich) to the very many extremely poor. The single adjective to describe it would be 'colourful'; if a second is allowed it would be 'odorous', although some of the smells were hardly pleasant! Perhaps one story illustrates both the colour and the poverty. I was taken to visit a carpet factory. In it was a room where small boys, around five or six years of age, were concerned with weaving a small portion of a carpet. This was only possible for children with small fingers. Once their fingers, now badly disfigured, were incapable of doing the task in hand they were removed from the factory and many of them had to survive on the streets. They only ever saw the very small portion of the carpet on which they had been working. They never saw the whole finished carpet. This is, I think, a picture of spiritual life. We see only that small part, colourful and adventurous though it might well be, but here on earth we never see the whole picture. Here we see dimly, 'through a glass darkly' but there will come a time when the Lord allows us to see the whole – or that part of the 'whole' that concerns us; including the 'why's' of life.

I went three times to India. On my first visit, in January 1985, I was met at Delhi airport by my old friend 'Sid' and by Michael Roemmele. Michael lived for a time in Bearsden and was then General Secretary of BMMF, the Headquarters of which were at that time situated in Delhi. I spent Sunday with Michael and Betty and the other partners in the BMMF Office and learnt so much about the work in India, about which at that time I knew very little.

The reason for going to India on this occasion was to accept an invitation to speak at the Asian Pharmacological Congress. Previously I had welcomed a number of Indian pharmacologists to Glasgow including Dr Siddiqui. I think he was keen to repay our hospitality to him in Glasgow and he was very kind during the whole week-long visit. I met his family and he arranged visits to some of India's many historical places such as Agra and the Taj Mahal (somewhat disappointing) and later that week to Jaipur, the fascinating 'pink city', then to Amber, where there is a magnificent fort perched on a hill overlooking a lake. This is where I rode an elephant for the first – and last – time. The journeys to these places of interest by coach from New Delhi were very long – five or six hours – and, although we had an early start (05.00h) it was well after dark before we returned. I was reminded that on roads in India elephants (and bullocks) do not have rear lights. A collision would have had severe consequences – and not only for the elephant.

After a Sunday service at the Central Methodist Church adjacent to our hotel, Sid drove me to the airport for the flight to Lucknow where I was to give lectures at the Central Drug Research Institute and at the Asian Congress. On this one-hour flight, if you were fortunate enough to sit on the right side of the plane and had a window seat, as I did, there were glorious views of the Himalayas in the distance. I liked Lucknow, especially the campus of the Institute for Medicinal Plant Research, set in lovely grounds where the aroma of the garden was almost overpowering in the tropical heat. A tour of the city took in Imambada (a maze where, it is said, one could get lost in two minutes) and the Residency which, in 1857 was the centre of resistance during the siege of the city, the women and children sheltering in an underground chamber. It was interesting that during this visit and especially at the Congress I renewed contact with Indian scientists who had come to Glasgow and even some who had visited our home during the overseas student fellowship meetings.

The next visit was to the historic and cultural centre of Varanasi, on the Ganges. Here I renewed contact with Professor P.K. Das who had also spent time with me in Glasgow. A deeply religious man who showed me the place, about ten kilometres from Varanasi (Benares), where the Buddha had apparently preached his first sermon. This is now a lovely garden with a lake containing crocodiles, pelicans and cranes and surrounded by many ornate temples. Here PK tried to explain to me the intricacies of Buddhism. Later there was a trip on the holy but polluted Ganges river, the longest in India.

My last visit to India in 1990 involved a good deal of travel starting from Bombay (as it then was, now Mumbai) which I describe in my diary for December 1990 'as the most depressing city I have ever been to'; apart perhaps for Manilla in the Philippines, to which I was also once invited. It was in Bombay (the Indian centre for commerce and for 'Bollywood') that I met one of the Indian BMMF workers, traveling to his home on the back of his motorcycle, hanging on to him for dear life avoiding chickens, the occasional cow and worst of all (as he said) women driving on the wrong side of the road. It was a joy to meet his family and to learn something about what his ministry involved; BMMF was now indigenous and in good hands. On the return journey to the city by train I was introduced to the 'joys' of commuter journeys Bombay style, trains with people on the roof and hanging on to the side. For some reason we were offered seats – a typical sign of Indian courtesy – and learnt the trick of leaving the train without being submerged under the crowds of people descending the train and competing with those wanting to board.

I also met up with John, the son of my good friend at Strathclyde Derek Nonhebel. John had just arrived in India and was 'finding his feet'; we had prayer and fellowship together in my hotel room. John was to stay in India for several years, working among the 'underprivileged'; he married a lovely Indian lady and now lives in Bearsden working for the Christian Prisons ministry.

Then to Madras to lecture at the famous Women's Medical College, the first (and only) time I have talked to an entirely female audience, the lady professors lining the front row. Afterwards I was taken to a restaurant where, I was told with many apologies, knives and forks were not available. The wonderful, and hot, meal was served on a banana leaf and eaten with the correct hand. Saves washing up!

The lady professors were very kind and put me on a train for Vellore where the Christian Medical College is situated. It had a good reputation in India. Through an invitation from a friend and former missionary in Vellore Dr John McArthur, I had been invited to preach at the St John's Anglican church on the College compound at both early services; the first was at 07.30h; my first at such an hour. This College is a centre for Christian witness in a predominantly Hindu area and where there are many temples, the 'mobile' gods being carried around the town squares to enable the priest to bless as many as possible. I was asked if I would like to return to teach physiology to the medical undergraduates which, after the experiences in Ibadan would have been interesting. My schedules (and my family) did not make this possible, but I was impressed by the vision of the College to reach the disabled, the leprosy patients and the mentally ill. Then the return to Madras by the 'West Coast Express' (thirty minutes late).

I learnt much from my visits to India. Such a colourful, friendly, noisy, dirty, crowded country. Wonderful hosts (and food). And, so good to make contact with those who had visited us in Glasgow both as students and colleagues. My last impression, as I waited for newly found friends to take me to the airport for the return Air India flight to London, was of a relaxed attitude to everything. I would have allowed more time to catch a long-haul flight but my friends turned up happy, with just enough time to check in!

A country then which after so much Christian missionary activity over such a long period remains in need of the Gospel and, from us, much prayer.

Turkey

Over the thirty or so years that my laboratory was on the roof of the Royal College building I received, as guests, many scientists from other countries. These came from as far afield as China, Japan, Australia and Turkey as well as from all over Europe. As a result, I received invitations to visit them in return. One such post-graduate student (later a post-doctoral Fellow) was Oz Guc from Ankara. He and his delightful wife were frequently in our home; hence invitations to visit Turkey. These were usually combined with scientific meetings, for example in Antalya, a resort on the south coast. This gave us the opportunity of meeting up with Interserve workers from Scotland in Istanbul which we did on at least two occasions.

Both Jonathan Blythe (a lawyer) and Philip Clark (a pharmacist, whom I once taught) went out with Interserve as 'young men'. They spent the first year learning Turkish and then remained in Istanbul for very many years; indeed, Jonathan is still there, having set up a law firm employing Turkish lawyers. Both married and had children whilst there. Fully involved then! Including in the local churches. And, a rarity these days, they were long-term; there for the long-haul.

Another Interserve'er in Istanbul was Dr Helen Belford. Sadly, Helen had to return home through illness. I was with her in hospital, reading and praying, just a few hours before she went to be with the Lord she loved and served.

Korea

This is a misnomer. I have never been to Korea. However, a few years ago a couple from South Korea, with their two children, rented one of the top flats in our own block. On their first Sunday and as Pam was preparing to be picked up for church (I was taking a service elsewhere) there was the clatter on the stairs and this family came downstairs dressed 'in their best'. Pam asked where they were going. To church they said. 'Which one?' 'We do not know, we are just going to look for one'. 'Would you like to come with me'?' 'Yes please!'

This began a lovely friendship. Roy and Hannah were welcomed by the church fellowship, took part in the weekly bible study held at that time in our home and later they hosted it in what they called 'the upper room'! I learnt so much from them about daily living as a Christian, their kindness, gentleness, prayer life, living each day in the presence of Christ. Even though conversation was not easy because of the language. You do not need talk to reveal Jesus! We still keep in touch ten or so years later.

A Korean gift from Hannah and Roy. This is how we think of them – servants of Christ

Chapter 43
Further Afield – Saudi Arabia, Japan, United States

Of the many (over thirty) counties I have visited as a scientist, to give lectures or take part in conferences, in only a few have I not met up with Christian believers, perhaps partly because of the limited time spent in them (Brazil, Philippines). In other countries the meetings have been planned (to visit missionaries) but in others the contacts with Christian believers have been quite fortuitous – probably not the right word! Two such were Saudi Arabia and Japan. Here are the stories.

Saudi Arabia

I had been invited to examine (in pharmacology) at the medical school based in the capital, Riyadh. My task was to examine the students orally (in English!). These were long sessions, from 8 to 13h for the men and from 17 to 19h for the women. Never the twain shall meet. Not only examined separately but taught separately, mainly by staff from India and Pakistan. No mixing. The women got the worst of it; I learnt that for practical pharmacology the women had to wait until the men had finished (leaving a mess behind) before they could enter the laboratory to begin their own classes.

The first year I visited (June 1980) there were 57 men and 24 women. Of course, the women, in the presence of two male examiners, were heavily veiled except for one attractive candidate who attended in a mini skirt! Was this, I wondered, to influence us examiners? Somewhat taken aback, after the oral I asked who she was. She was a princess, a member of the Saudi Royal family! In general, the standard of their knowledge of the complexities of the subject, and of the English language, was quite good. The women better than the men. Of course.

At the end of the examination process (over two or three days) I was taken to meet a senior member of the faculty, together with the treasurer, to be paid. This was in the Saudi currency, riyals, several thousand of them in big bundles. As this currency was useless if taken out of the country (anyway forbidden) it had to be exchanged by a back street money changer. On handing these bundles over they were counted (automatically, it would have taken all day by hand) and thrown into a large cardboard box. I then knew the origin of the phrase about 'throwing your money away'. The exchange was in traveller's cheques, sterling or dollars. I examined for two years but declined further offers. I had little contact with the few Saudi academic staff except for one invitation, apparently unusual for a 'westerner', to a Saudi home. But he had trained in the UK!

I had heard that there were some Christians in Saudi Arabia but they were not allowed a church; except for the large (several hundred) working immigrant Korean community. As for other Christians, I had the names of a couple (I will call them simply Howard and Nora) and spent some time with them. I learnt much about their witness to the expatriate community. Many restrictions and potentially dangerous. I left with great admiration for those who had chosen to witness for Christ in such situations. And confined; no woman was allowed to drive.

Japan

I had doubts about accepting my first invitation to speak at a meeting in Japan. This was partly because my wife's favourite auntie and her husband had died in separate WW2 Japanese internment camps in Sumatra following the capture of Singapore, where they had lived. In the end I was to make five or six separate long - term visits over the years, including a period as a consultant for the large Chugai Drug Company.

Japan is a very long country; 1500km from 'top to bottom' and made up of many islands. The largest Honshu, is the size of the UK. My first visit, to Tokyo in 1978, was unforgettable. The flight time was very long and via Singapore, Taiwan and Hong Kong! I had been invited to speak at the International Congress of Cardiology and, although my travel was paid, I had to sustain myself once there. This meant staying in the smallest hotel room imaginable, all I could afford, and living on green tea, free at the Congress site, and pizza.

The meeting itself was held at the five-star New Otani Hotel and when I registered was given a conference bag giving details of the programme. However, also inside (strangely) was an invitation for any Christians present to meet in the hotel Japanese garden for morning coffee. I accepted the invitation! Was it the free coffee? Of interest to me was the presence at coffee of some British colleagues who I did not know were believers; this was to lead to interesting later contacts. Among those present on most days was a Japanese cardiologist called Hiroshi Shinoda from Osaka. Over forty years later we are still in contact.

How did this interesting arrangement for coffee in the garden come about? Because the hotel had arranged for a suite on the top level to be given (?) over to a Christian missionary from the USA, I think to 'lure' Americans to the hotel as tourists. Maybe the thinking was that all Americans are Christian. Certainly, in my experience, not the case. During the week of the conference I got to know this couple quite well. Dan Maddox (his wife was called Ruth) was a pilot during the war and had been captured and interned by the Japanese. On his release he went to bible school and decided God was calling him back to Japan. They had a great ministry. Over fifty years later I wonder if the arrangement still exists. Probably not.

I had arrived in Tokyo on a Saturday night and on the following day decided to find my way to an English-speaking church. I had the address and decided, with map, to attempt to find my own way there. One major problem was that the map did not give the names of streets; I learnt that this is usual – locations are given as, for example, 'the street with a shoe shop on the corner'. Undaunted I took the metro (packed because Sunday in Japan is the big shopping day) and exited at the nearest station, only to find it was in the centre of a large and busy department store. I could not find my way out to the street. All signs were, of course, in Japanese. Going down an escalator a man was waiting, apparently for me. He had seen me going up and down on various escalators and that as a lost European I was in some difficulty. He introduced himself as a cardiologist at the conference and guessed I was at the same meeting. Could he help? Yes please. I explained where I was going and that I was sure I would be able to find my way to the church once I was in the street. He questioned this! He suggested I take a taxi, waited with me in the longish queue and explained where I wanted to go to. The driver did not know where the church was so my friend, who did know, came in the taxi with me, declined an invitation to come to church and would not accept my attempt to pay the fare.

I tell this story to give some impression of the courtesy and kindness of Japanese people I found wherever I travelled in the country, which over the years, was often. A later visit illustrates another Japanese characteristic. Efficiency. I had been invited to visit Hiroshi Shinoda in his home and meet his family. At that time, I was speaking at a meeting in Osaka, a commuting distance from where he lived. He told me the time of a suitable train and to get out (after several stops all with Japanese names I could only guess at) at a particular time. There he was on the platform. Trains keep time to the minute. I could not give similar instructions to a visitor to my home on a ScotRail commuter train to Bearsden; he or she could have landed up anywhere! The trains are special. The ultra-fast 'bullet' trains have places marked on the platforms telling you where your reserved seat is and the doors open precisely at the right place. I have tried this on British rail trains; the marks on the platform are usually for carriages well away from your seat.

I visited most of the big cities including Sapporo on the northernmost island of Hokkaido reached by ferry and famous as a ski resort and venue for winter Olympic games. Here, I was entertained in a typical Japanese home. Very simple, little furniture (no chairs), sliding doors, meal served by the wife in her kimono. But this is not a travelogue. If any reader wishes to understand Japan and its people and culture, I recommend one of my favourite travel books.[1]

Impressions of Japan? Being in a multi-story hotel during an earthquake. Room swaying from side to side. Quite frightening. A few years later that same city was almost completely destroyed by

---

[1] Alan Booth, *The Roads to Sata, a Two Thousand Mile Walk Through Japan*, Penguin Books, Harmondsworth, 1987.

yet another quake. The quiet peaceful shrines and temples of the ancient city of Kyoto in cherry blossom time. A typical formal tea ceremony, green of course, with two kimono clad geisha 'ladies' or 'women of art'; not much conversation despite a friendly interpreter. Eating lean thin slices of Kobe beef (from cows said to be fed partially on sake, the national drink) cooked by dipping them into boiling water. The long eight course official dinners and the sore knees afterwards. The long flights, eleven or twelve hours if the non-stop direct flights were over the pole. But especially the courtesy, efficiency and kindness of the people.

United States

This could be entitled 'small notes from a large country', a poor attempt at something akin to Bill Bryson's classic best seller *Notes from a Small Island*;[2] without his expertise and wit of course.

I made about a dozen, often extended, visits to that very large country[3] partly as a consultant to drug firms but more often as an invited speaker at international meetings on heart research and on shock. Indeed, the Shock Society was founded in the US before then spreading to Europe. I could summarise these many visits in two words - hospitality and dangers.

My first visit was in 1976, not long after my arrival in Scotland. This visit was concerned with coronary blood flow. My final visit was in 1999, the year after I retired. The initial invitation came from Martin Winbury, the doyen of drug effects on the coronary circulation. Despite the fact that we had never met, I was invited to stay with him and his wife Blanche, my first experience of American hospitality. He lived not too far from New York to which we made a day trip by train. It was Martin who introduced me to the customs of eating breakfast (hash browns) on the way to work at a roadside café and then travelling to work by plane! Flying then is the equivalent to us going to work by train or bus. Compare that with my daily commute to work; a ten minute walk, twenty minute journey by train from Bearsden station to Queen Street and a three minute amble to the department.

---

[2] Bill Bryson, *Notes From a Small Island*, Black Swan, London 1996.

[3] Alistair Cooke, *America*, British Broadcasting Corporation, London 1973. My favourite book on this great country.

Another example of hospitality was during a visit to Evansville, a smallish town in Indiana to speak to a group of scientists working for another pharmaceutical company. This was on a Friday and my next appointment was elsewhere on a Tuesday. So stuck for a weekend. Yet another invitation to stay, again with a family I had never met. 'Come and stay'. On the Sunday I was asked what I would like to do. I said to go to church. A surprise for them. They looked up the nearest church, took me to it and came to collect me when I estimated the service would be finished. When I arrived back at their home, it was filled with people – neighbours and friends come to meet this stranger from far away Scotland. Elaine, the wife, in a loud voice posed a question to the assembled company – 'where do think Jim went this morning? No response. 'To a Baptist Church!'. Rather, indeed very, unusual in that location! But it did give me the opportunity to explain my faith, feeling like Paul must have felt speaking at the Areopagus in Athens. And later when she took me for lunch at her country club. It was later that particular trip I revisited old friends from our days in Nigeria and now in Canada the Rees's, Trews and my old boss John Grayson. Again (of course) invited to stay. Then taken by David Trew to see the Niagara Falls. In Miami another invitation led to my first (and last) baseball match and a drive down the Florida Keys. Hospitality and kindness in a 'foreign land'.

'Christians in science' are everywhere, as I discovered when spending a few days in the laboratory of Lerner Hinshaw in Oklahoma. This part of the US is prone to typhoons and Lerner took me to investigate the 'cave' in the garden in which they took shelter. After we discovered we both followed Christ their minister came for a pastoral visit. At 10 at night. I did not get to bed until 2am, five hours before I was booked to fly on to the next destination. I discovered from these visits that there is a worldwide and close 'fraternity' among scientists working in the same areas, with genuine friendships made.

There is however also a dangerous side to living in the USA. There are 'no go' areas which are really dangerous and I received several warnings not to leave my accommodation after dark. Before that warning came, I almost discovered the possible dangers for myself. Another invitation was to visit Washington and this time staying in a hotel; the headquarters of US Naval Research were concerned with the clinical problems associated with sepsis, shock and of hyperbaric medicine. These scientists were naval officers under an admiral! I discovered that a concert was being performed at the central Concert Hall; the conductor was the Russian cellist turned conductor Rostropovich and the orchestra was playing Shostakovich. Easy to get there by taxi but after the concert had finished taxis were soon taken. Nothing for it but to walk – with the aid of a map. I found myself in one of these 'no go' areas and being followed on the opposite pavement. Quite frightening. A taxi coming in the opposite direction came to my rescue but on relating this next day my host was concerned about what might have happened to me whilst 'in his care'. There is a genuine fear of what might happen on the streets – and not only at night. And the US is the only country where I have given a lecture in a university department surrounded by a high wall with barbed wire along the top.

Pam was able to join me on some of my American visits and the highlight was a visit to Boston for a conference, after which we took the opportunity of hiring a car and driving up the Appalachian trail through Massachusetts and Vermont to Montreal during the 'fall' of September 1997. I had seldom driven an 'automatic' and certainly not a car as large as a Buick Le Sabre 9. After many attempts to find the right exit out of Boston we arrived at our initial destination near the summer home of the Boston Symphony Orchestra at Tanglewood. It was here I practised my conducting 'skills'. In my imagination: the BSO were, sadly, not present.

The place we stayed in Lennox was called 'Apple Trees', welcomed at the door by chipmunks and where steps were needed to get into bed. Next day we drove to Sturbridge and Stockbridge, the main street immortalised by the illustrator Norman Rockwell.[4] We spent much time at the Rockwell Museum and some of his prints still decorate some of our walls at home. There was also a visit to the Mission House where John Sargent had first ministered to the Mohican Indians over two hundred years ago.

---

[4] Norman Rockwell, *My Adventures as an Illustrator*, H.N. Abrams, New York, 1954.

This part of the US at this time of year is a delight and a top tourist route. Green covered mountains, the trees beginning to turn, signs warning us of the bears (despite many places to buy honey!) especially when we took a walk in the woods (the title of yet another book by Bryson). And, yet again everyone we met (including a chief of police who gave us his card 'in case of difficulties') were so friendly and helpful. And then to Montreal and the same route back to Boston where we were sorry to have to say 'goodbye' to the Buick!

My visits to the US took me from 'coast to coast' from San Francisco (and the redwood trees in the Muir national park) and Santa Barbara, to New Mexico, to the 'deep south' of Alabama (where an elderly couple I met had never heard of Scotland and thought I came from outer space!) Duke University in South Carolina, where the concept of 'preconditioning' had been discovered. Even a place called Kalamazoo. And everywhere hospitality, kindness, friendships – and, in places, danger. Could I have been tempted to live there as some of my European friends have done? Certainly not.

Chapter 44
'On the Far Side of the Sea' – Australia

We have a great love for this huge island! This is mainly of course because of family; our daughter Debbie lives with Phil in Warwick in Queensland and our three grandchildren are also Australian citizens. Joshua, married to Samara, is in Adelaide, with a delightful daughter called Ziva, whilst Daniel and Rebecca, are in Melbourne. Our more recent visits were of course made after the family emigrated to Australia in 1999; however, we had visited Australia before, both of us in 1986 and again the following year and I also visited in 1996. So, we are not strangers to 'the far side of the sea'.[1]

The first visit was in February 1986 when I had been invited to speak at the world meeting of the International Society of Heart Research about the cardiac arrythmias that result from coronary artery occlusion, and which are a major cause of sudden cardiac death. We left in the snow (it took about an hour to de-ice the wings at Heathrow) on a British Airways flight via Abu Dhabi, Singapore and Adelaide to Melbourne. A long flight, but this was over thirty years ago; we left at 17.15h on Wednesday February 5th and arrived in Melbourne on Friday the 7th at 09.00h. Apart from the meeting itself, there were invitations to attend the Victorian Committee of the Sudan United Mission, and evenings with Willie Mackay, who had taught me at the Bible Training Institute (BTI) in Glasgow, with Dr John Upton of the Australian UCCF, with the parents of the Scottish painter Pam Carter, as well as with Australian colleagues from my own department in Glasgow, where they were once occupants of the laboratory on the roof of the Royal College building called 'kangaroo valley'.

Thinking this would be our 'one and only' visit 'down under' (how wrong we were!) we were anxious to also visit Sydney, only a short flight away, as Australian distances go. Here we were met at the airport by Stan and Iris Motherwell, Stan being at that time

[1] Psalm 139:9.

Chairman of SUM Australia. This was the beginning of one of the most wonderful friendships of our lives. We have stayed with them on numerous occasions in their ground-floor flat at Burleigh Heads on Queensland's Gold Coast. Stan died a few years ago but we are still in regular contact with Iris and phone her often. Some friends become very special.

A day or so later we met with SUM missionaries (who were in both Sudan and Nigeria) Keith Black and his wife Betty. With their daughter Christine and her two children, we were taken on a cruise of the harbour, with a lunchtime picnic at Watson's Bay, followed by a visit to the Sydney Tower with wonderful views over the harbour. We spent both our evenings at the Sydney Opera House (Verdi's *Falstaff* and then Mozart's *Magic Flute*). What a great city Sydney is! Magnificent, especially at night.

From Sydney we flew to Adelaide because an old friend and former colleague in Glasgow, Bill Dryden was at that time working along the South Australia coast in a research establishment which had a particular interest in the toxic effects of heavy metals. We too had an interest in their cardiovascular effects, because at that time most of the water pipes of Glasgow were of lead: we had already published our own research on the effects of lead on the heart.

With a few hours to spare next day before our flight home we explored this delightful city with its riverside walks, and visited the famous Adelaide Oval, where we saw part of a Sheffield Shield cricket match; no admission charge and we were almost the only spectators in that huge ground. Strange for us that the play we saw (*Taking Steps*) at the Adelaide Theatre that evening was by Alan Aykbourne.

Because we, again mistakenly, thought this would be our last journey to the 'other side of the sea' we had decided, on our journey home, to visit Singapore at the invitation of one of my former students. We lunched at the famous 'Raffles' Hotel and were then taken for dinner to a fish restaurant where you could choose the fish you wanted to eat from the fish tank! Singapore is a city where you can be measured for a suit which would then be ready for you to pick up on your way to the airport next day. This is what I did. In my diary I write that Singapore airport is the most modern I had ever seen and that this visit to 'the lands on the other side of the sea' was a 'most wonderful once in a lifetime holiday'. Little did we realise that this would be repeated the following year.

A second invitation came just after we had returned home. This one was to speak at a meeting of the International Union of the Pharmacological Societies (IUPHAR) in Sydney in August 1987. Perhaps someone had listened to that Melbourne talk. This one was about how those early cardiac arrhythmias could be modified by drugs. Again, thinking that this would be our really final visit 'down under' Pam came too: and we decided, as I had also been invited to speak at a satellite meeting in Auckland in New Zealand, to go home by flying around the globe, which was actually cheaper than returning home by our outgoing route.

This time we broke our outward journey since another former student Arunee Suraya, had invited us and stay with her in Bangkok, where we found we had been given the only airconditioned room in the house (her bedroom) to sleep in. On that same day our daughter Debbie, by then a medical student in Manchester, flew to Kenya in order to spend an assignment at the Kijabe Medical Centre, run by the Africa Inland Mission.

Bangkok is one of the most congested cities in the world. The traffic was horrific. Next day, after a visit to the Royal Palace, where the creaky floorboards were to warn the king of any approaching danger, we were also taken, to various other palaces and museums and on a river cruise by yet another former student who then took us to eat at a restaurant on the other side of the city, a journey that took over an hour by taxi. The restaurant was so large (it seated 3000 people) that we were served by waiters on roller skates. Very efficient, but what if they collided at speed?

We were to see the huge difference in Bangkok between the rich and the very many poor. On one evening we were taken to meet Arunee's brothers. The route took us through one of the poorest areas in the city to a huge mansion entered by a metal security gate where I was shown into the snooker room. Coming from Britain I was expected to provide strong competition to the various brothers and guests, especially assembled for the occasion. I was beaten by everybody; they were all much too good for me. Next day came the long drive through the paddy fields to Pattiya which was full of tourists and other hangers on. The beach home where we stayed the night really was on the beach! Not much sleep that night with the expectation of being carried away by the tide. Just as well the water was warm!

Next day we flew to Sydney where we were again met by our new friends from the previous year, Stan and Iris Motherwell who invited us to stay in their home along the coast at Hornsby. Australians are proud to show visitors their great country and we were taken to various places outside Sydney including the Hawksbury River (where there was a bible teaching camp) and the spectacular Blue Mountains, including the 'Glorious Leap' and the 'Three Sisters' (nothing to do with Chekhov). The most striking thing for us was the steepness of the limestone cliffs covered with eucalyptus trees so that the 3000-foot mountains were covered with a film of green, the lower slopes a haven of orchards; lemon, cherry and peach trees covered with blossom. When we stopped for coffee there was a line of cheeky parrots waiting for us to finish, at which they flew down, perched on the rim of the cups and ate the sugar at the bottom!

As in the previous year we again attended the Opera House (Medea by Cherubini and Wagner's Lohengrin) and we had a tour of the House and dinner before the performance. Then, next day the flight, longer than we expected, to Auckland.

There was something unusual about this particular long trip to Australia. Being a meeting (a 'gaggle') of pharmacologists from all over the world, it was more like a 'gaggle of guinea-pigs', since the British component (well over a hundred) had been asked to be involved in a clinical drug trial of melatonin, reputed to prevent or alleviate the symptoms of jet lag. I was one of those who took part and felt no problems after travelling such a long distance, feeling fine on arrival 'at the other end' despite having only five hours sleep. So, I thought, I must be on this 'wonder drug'. However, when the code was broken and the results published, I discovered that I was on placebo; this accounts for the small blip on the published graph (in the British Journal of Pharmacology). That's me, there for posterity. Certainly. In my case, the placebo, whatever it was, seemed to be highly effective. Who says there is no such thing as a placebo effect! Of course, those with a scientific bent might well offer an alternative explanation – maybe the 'Bangkok effect'? Perhaps I should point out that melatonin was not available at that time in the UK (except to certain pharmacologists!) but could be bought 'over the counter' in Singapore. As far as I am aware that potent placebo, whatever it was, is not available anywhere. But what was it? If I knew I could have been onto something and have retired early.

Although it looks only a small distance from the Australian east coast, in fact New Zealand is a considerable distance, several hundred miles. It gave us the feeling of being on the edge of the world. No wonder New Zealanders (and Australians too) feel the need sometimes to spend time in Europe and sometimes even stay there, like Clive James. Isolation is a problem and accounts for the fact that about half of those who emigrate from Britain to that wonderful country of New Zealand return home.

It seems as though we have friends all over the world. Certainly we did, in New Zealand. Francis and Marjorie Foulkes were such; from our time in Nigeria where Francis, a CMS missionary, taught both in Akure and in Ibadan. He is the author of several helpful bible commentaries, Ephesians for IVP and several others for the African Christian Press, with which he was heavily involved. Good to meet old friends!

I think we really had no intention of revisiting New Zealand but, as sometimes happens, an opportunity came many years later to explore rather more of the country. We were glad to take it and I write about that visit elsewhere.

From Auckland we continued towards home with the first stop in Fiji; Nadi is a three-hour flight from Auckland. We stayed at a travel lodge, in idyllic surroundings surrounded by palm trees – and more cheeky birds. Everyone we met was so friendly with the greeting of '*bula bula*' and big smiles. After a swim, a walk among the sugar canes and a meal served in a coconut shell, we were serenaded by an orchestra of guitars. As I wrote in my diary 'this is certainly a place to come to stay again if we ever got the chance'. Sadly, we never did. Next day we flew on to Honolulu, at this point feeling rather groggy. The journey took us across the international date line and, as it was September 3rd, our daughter's birthday, we sent her two birthday cards from either side of the date line. So, she had two birthdays or, at least two different cards sent on the same day!

Hawaii was rather a come down after the relaxation of Fiji although we came to like Waikiki and the swims in the Pacific. Thence to Vancouver and Victoria Island to stay with more old friends, Stewart and Evelyn Dunlop who were neighbours in Bearsden and with whom we had worked with Scripture Union Scotland. We watched the many yachts, the seaplanes coming in from Seattle, the big liner offshore – the 'Princess Margaret' – built on the Clyde, we had a picnic by a river watching the salmon leap, drove the spectacular coast road, visited a 'frontier town' and celebrated our fortieth wedding anniversary at a fish restaurant. Home next day through Seattle and Vancouver. Not like a Michael Palin world tour but for us an adventurous and once in a lifetime experience. Never to be repeated. It is an indication of my busy schedule at the time that the day after arriving back from this 'world tour' I had to fly to Paris for a meeting on quite another topic – and then preach somewhere away from Glasgow two days later.

I made one more visit to Australia, the only time solo. This was in October 1996, following a telephone invitation to speak at a meeting of the Australian Society for Emergency Care Medicine in Melbourne. I went via Perth and discovered that this reduced jet lag (Perth is in the same time zone as Singapore). After resting for a few days, I then flew to Melbourne. One thing that struck me about this meeting was that, unlike Britain at that time, doctors and nurses met on the same footing. Indeed, it was the nurses who did much of the organisation and who made excellent speakers. During a few hours away from the meeting I attended a chamber music concert nearby and heard, for the first time, a quartet by the Czech Jewish composer Erwin Schulhoff, whose music the Nazis had labelled '*entartete musik*' (degenerate music). A communist, he was arrested in 1941 and died later that year. I found his music not at all degenerate but had a creative imaginative freshness. Interesting to discover a new composer so far from home.

It was on this visit that I first made contact with Adam and Helen Brown, once of Bearsden. They later became wonderful hosts on our many subsequent Australian journeys which took us into and out of Melbourne. They became very good friends and we owe them much. We keep in touch by phone with Helen, now a widow; always a source of information – and laughter.

The return journey was again through Singapore where I had been invited by an old student Matthew Gwee, to speak at the pleasant and impressive university. Also in the city were the headquarters of the Overseas Missionary Fellowship (the former China Inland Mission) and I was asked to discuss with the Director my views on 'tent makers' which that organisation had at first been slow to take up. Friends, with whom I stayed, were fellow members of my home church in Bearsden!

Chapter 45
The Family Move 'Down Under'

Our daughter Deborah (Debbie) studied medicine first at St Andrews University, one of the youngest students to do so, and then in Manchester for the clinical studies. After working in that area in various hospitals (one of our granddaughters followed her to these same hospitals many years later) she became a GP in Lytham St Anne's. Then in 1999 she and her family (by then three children) moved to Australia. She was interviewed (remotely) for two jobs, one near Brisbane and the other in South Australia in a small town called Mount Gambier. I remember her phoning to discuss this move and, having been three times to Australia, I was enthusiastic despite the fact that we would, or so we thought, not see much of our growing grandchildren. She chose, rightly I think, Mount Gambier. Climate wise much better than the very hot Gold Coast.

They left in May, the beginning of the Australian winter. The journey must have been horrific with three young children (7, 5 and 2) and much luggage. Then, when they reached Adelaide (the nearest international airport) they had a six-hour bus ride to the Mount. They were not the first of the family to arrive; Beth, their much-loved dog, had been sent on ahead for six weeks quarantine during which period she lost her bark. Some arrival then in a totally different country. It is hard enough moving house in Britain let alone a move involving a journey of several thousand miles. Fortunately, Australians speak a kind of English!

Mount Gambier is a delightful small (population 30,000) and well spread town (Australia is not short of land!) near the Limestone Coast and was at one time the second largest town in South Australia. It lies some 280 miles south east of the capital Adelaide (and a similar distance from Melbourne in the neighbouring State of Victoria) and is the centre of some of the richest pastoral land in the country with soft-wood forestry areas, dairy produce, meat, wool and cereals. And, for wine; around Penola, just twenty miles from the Mount, the volcanic soil is the base for one of the oldest wineries in Australia, the world-famous Coonawarra vineyard. Half an hour's drive south from the Mount is the Limestone 'crustacean' Coast, the 'rock lobster capital of Australia' at Port MacDonnell. This coast has good beaches and the powerful seas of the Southern Ocean have sculptured the soft rocks into weird and wonderful shapes. Just off the road, is Mount Shank, an extinct volcano with superb views of the surrounding countryside. Perhaps though not so extinct; the last significant earthquake caused the crosses on two of the Mount's churches to crash to the ground. This was however a century ago.

Mount Gambier is built on the slopes of, hopefully still extinct, volcanos. There are three crater lakes, the largest (3 miles round and containing 36,000 million litres of water) and deepest (average depth 70m) is the Blue Lake, where the water changes colour dramatically around November from winter steel blue to an intense turquoise blue, the colour changing back in March. The two smaller crater lakes ('Leg of Mutton' and 'Valley') are tree lined and favourite recreation, walking and picnic areas. Near the town centre are a number of extensive limestone caves, the home to families of possums. Some of these cave systems, such as the one at Naracoorte, are World Heritage listed; famous for fossilised animals.

The centre of the town has several good restaurants and cafes, a cinema, good library (with compact discs), some very good shops such as 'Bakers Delight' and 'She's Apples', which is Aussie slang for 'it's all right', 'ok' or, for individuals, just 'good'. There were, as in almost all small Australian towns, second-hand bookshops and charity shops. Some good bargains at these!

From what has been written above then an almost perfect environment in which to live and bring up a family. Good medical facilities, schools and so many open-air sporting facilities; both boys became keen footballers and cricketers, with coaching from the South Australian State team in Adelaide, from whom our youngest grandson won the 'spinners' cup. There were tennis courts and a large swimming area. Debbie chose well when they decided on Mount Gambier!

Apparently nearly half of all British emigrants to Australia return to the UK after three years, which was the term of Debbie's first appointment to the GP practice at Hawkins Medical Centre. Good that they all decided to stay and become Australian nationals. They are still there over twenty years later. Both boys have made trips to explore Europe (including a tour of Lord's cricket ground in London) whilst Rebecca, our granddaughter, spent a period at school in nearby Milngavie together with Stephen and Fiona's youngest.

Debbie later became involved in the training of young doctors wishing to practice in rural communities, a great need in the country. This was a scheme from Flinders University in Adelaide. Later she became involved in work among 'native Australians' in the Northern Territory, including islands off the north coast, and more recently, in New South Wales.

We visited the family every year except one from 2000 to 2016 for periods of about three months during the Australian summer (the Scottish winter). After 2016 it was, with age, becoming more difficult for us to travel. The weather in the 'Mount' is unlike much of Australia. Being not far from the coast, and with no landmass between there and the Antarctic, the temperature could be quite low even in summer; on more than one occasion even lower than in Glasgow. However, it could also be hot; on Pam's 80th birthday in 2014 the celebration party had to move indoors with the air-conditioner on full blast with the outside temperature well over 40 degrees.

Staying in Mount Gambier on so many occasions was for us an immense and unusual privilege; to see so regularly the three grandchildren growing up, from their entering primary school right through to their time at university. It was great collecting them from school and later from work, watching them playing cricket and soccer, walking the dogs with them, taking them to cafes and the cinema whilst, in their early years, there were those bedtime stories! And, of course for us, wonderful and prolonged summer holidays in the middle of a Scottish winter.

How did we spend our time? Relaxing, reading (about thirty books each visit), helping with shopping, visiting the weekly market (wonderful cherries and apple juice) cooking meals, making jam and marmalade, even playing the piano – all in the warmth of an Australian summer! But, of course to stay for two to three months is a long time – for the hosts! And, where for such a prolonged period would be stay? For the first visit, when the family were in rented accommodation (opposite to the lovely home of Jim and Natalie Wilson, who became good friends) we did stay with them in a large bungalow. Then, for the next two visits, we stayed in accommodation provided by neighbours (who were also friends) at a time when they were away in Europe or in a pleasant garden 'granny-flat'.

This gave us the idea, after the family had moved into their own property in Power Street, of converting a disused stone shed into accommodation for us to use on future visits. We talked to a neighbour, an architect, about what would be involved, drew up plans and discussed the cost. The following year the 'garden residence' was ready – one large living room, air-conditioned (essential) with an adjacent shower room and just a few yards from the decking of the main house. Comfortable and ideal, as the accompanying photo shows. We had a television, good for watching the humiliation of the England Test cricket team on their visits 'down under', and there were also the means of playing music and preparing meals. We usually joined the family for the main evening meal.

We even had a guard dog! The family always had a dog or two. Beth, who emigrated with them from England, sat at my feet when, as usual, I read in the garden and was hyper-excited whenever we arrived, circulating around us at increasing speeds. After, through age, she had to be 'put down' the family went to see the pups of a border collie. They could not choose between the last two in the litter so took both! Molly and Lucy were quite different; Molly was the football playing, extrovert guard dog, sitting outside the 'residence' all night to keep us safe from marauding wallabies and snakes whilst Lucy slept inside the main house. When the family sold the house in 2017, they went to look after other sheep on a nearby farm. Would they still remember us? I think so.

As for Mount Gambier churches, we 'tried' four of them at different times, were always made welcome, but failed to 'settle 'in any one of them. The peripatetic Parratts then. However, we did make good friends in all the various churches and even made pastoral visits to one or two whilst our relaxed 'timetable' enabled us to study God's word in some depth; the garden in an Australian summer was a good place for this!

Australia is subject to terrifying bush fires and, during an early stay in Mount Gambier, and from a vantage point in the garden, we could see the signs of one approaching, moving slowly towards us. Then, although some of the outlying residents needed to be evacuated from their homes, the wind suddenly changed just as the fire got near the airport and it changed direction. A day or so later our neighbour and friend Jim Wilson took us out to see if his calves were safe. They were, but as we drove back the roots of the burnt trees were still smouldering; months later there were signs of new life.

As mentioned, three months or so is a long time to stay with anyone. Perhaps especially family! We, at their suggestion, tried to 'get away' from the Mount at various times and explore other parts of this great country. We made several trips, often by bus, to Adelaide, the very relaxed State capital, where there were even better restaurants and shops, a delightful area around the River Torrens, the attractive cricket ground and an arts centre with a bi-annual music festival. The journey to reach Adelaide is of great interest if you take the coastal route through the beachside towns of Robe and Beachport then along the Coorong. This is a forty mile series of fresh water lagoons separated from the sea by huge sand dunes. It is the home for over a hundred species of birds, with pelicans breeding on the islands. However, keep a watch out for snakes on route to the observation hut! When going by car, another attractive small town not far from Adelaide is Hahndorf, first settled by German emigrants in the early nineteenth century; it is like stepping back into time. Surprisingly, more recent occupants are the owners of the 'Scottish restaurant', saltire blowing in the breeze and with haggis on the menu. Excellent food! We discovered the couple who ran it, with great success, came from the Maryhill area of Glasgow, just two miles from where we live!

There were family holidays too. The first one was to Tasmania reached by plane from Melbourne. It is like Australia packed into a much smaller island; the Tasmanians refer to their bigger neighbour as 'our northern island'! It is the only place where one of us (Pam) saw a platypus in the wild and where I held up the traffic on our way to the former convict colony at Port Arthur to allow a wombat to cross the road. Maybe Port Arthur was home to one of my descendants because we passed a small village with a name suspiciously like my surname. We thought it unwise to stop and investigate.

Other family holidays were to various parts of the Fleurieu Peninsula south of Adelaide, to small coastal towns like Goolwa (good for an exploration by boat of the Coorong) and Victor Harbour. We once took a bus from there to the ferry point to Kangaroo Island, much of which was devastated in 2020 by a bush fire. The island has some remarkable rock formations (appropriately called 'Remarkable Rocks') and an impressive colony of sea lions. The main other inhabitants are kangaroos (being an island there are no predators) and 'Little Penguins'.

We also explored further afield. Always on our itinerary was a visit to Burleigh Heads on Queensland's Gold Coast, the retiral home of our good friends Stan and Iris Motherwell. Australians are a friendly people (lots of 'g'days' to strangers) but some friends are very special. What makes one person 'click' with another? Common experiences (they were both involved with the Australian Branch of the Sudan United Mission) and especially, for us, a shared Christian faith. We have non-Christian friends too of course, but most of our closest friends in different parts of the world are, like us, Christians. Each Sunday we travelled with them to a Brethren Assembly at which, after a trial run, I was always invited to preach whenever we visited.

On our various visits to stay with them (I think there were eight or nine in all) we were taken to various places both north and south of Burleigh, north to the Sunshine Coast (so called, it was often raining!) as far as Noosa and as far south into New South Wales as Coffs Harbour where we just manage to 'escape' before the road out of the town was flooded. But, of course, there was sunshine! There is an interesting mountain range between Grafton, with its lovely jacaranda trees, and Byron Bay, the most easterly tip of Australia, with peaks higher than any in Scotland and looking, from a distance, like a man sleeping. Renamed Mount Jim by Iris!

On one particular trip with them we stayed with their friends on a somewhat isolated farm with a resident koala and with snakes under the decking; is this, we wondered, rather like Debbie's one time home near Young! Our hosts led a 'remote farmers' church meeting but, because of the distances involved, the regular meetings were 'on line'. Rather like us during lockdown.

There was also a significant visit to the Mount Coot-tha Botanic Gardens in Brisbane with impressive views from the top. Here we met up with an old friend Keith Black (once in Nigeria with SUM) and with Pioneer missionaries from South Sudan, Rhys and Rhondda Hall who showed us something of their work on a tablet, then a new invention for us, in the Japanese Garden. And in the rain! The Halls became folk for whom we regularly prayed in the monthly Africa Prayer Group which met for many years in our flat.

There were two particularly special 'holidays from the family' that should be mentioned, although this is not meant to be an Australian travelogue! One was to the Queensland coastal region around Cairns at a wonderful resort called Palm Cove. An ideal and most relaxing place (and highly recommended!) with access to both the Great Barrier Reef and the Kuranda scenic railway, one of the greatest engineering feats of the nineteenth century and made, by 'fortitude, sweat and bare hands', in order to move gold from the Barron River to the coast past the spectacular Barron Falls (a drop of 265metres) and finishing at Kuranda, where there are fantastic views over the Pacific Ocean. The route down is by a strengthened glass lift through the dense rain forest.

Cairns was at one time the headquarters of the Flying Doctor Service, formed to bring medical help to the very remote cattle farms of the whole of Northern Australia.

The other major holiday from Mount Gambier was to New Zealand. A most helpful travel agent Ian McDougall, a patient of Debbie's, arranged for us to go on a two- week coach tour taking in both North and South Islands. A holiday of a lifetime and also recommended to any readers who are still left. We were the only non-Australians on the coach and, when we arrived at the Maori sulphur fumed town of Rotorua, I was 'elected' coach captain, to be welcomed by the local Maori chief and to take part in a ceremony which included nose rubbing and the traditional warriors dance, the haka. I was complimented on the length of my tongue! The drivers on the Grand Pacific Tour were superb; certainly, I could not have attempted driving those hairpin bends with huge drops on both sides, especially on the South Island's west coast. Other highlights were a climb up the Mt Cook glacier, the amazing scenery around Milford Sound, visiting Christchurch, the centre of which was demolished a few years later in an earthquake, being held up by thousands of sheep on the road, and a Scottish evening in Dunedin, where for the first and only time in my life I played (briefly) a Steinway piano. The host of the Scottish evening, also originally from Maryhill, had haggis substitute on the menu; too far away from source for the real thing.

We grew to love Australia and, as with our other grandchildren in Hungary, despite the distances from home, things 'worked out' for us to spend time with each of them over many years. If I write another book it will be not for them but for the generation that follows; some of whom perhaps we will never see.

Postlude:
The Sense of an Ending

Many substantial pieces of music, some symphonies for example, attempt to 'round things off' with a 'coda', a kind of summing up of what has gone before, pulling the threads together; or sometimes, so it seems, unravelling them further! Some even introduce new material, perhaps as though to say that there is more to come! Just you wait for the next composition! It is certain that how to finish is more difficult than how to begin, which is perhaps why many musical 'last movements' are disappointing. What follows here is not a coda, a synopsis of what has gone before, but just a few words on the ageing process. This is simply because I am now nearly five years older than when I first wrote about 'old age'.[1]

So, what difference have those additional five or so years made to my thinking on ageing?

(1) I am slower in both mind and body. Names, for example, are more difficult to extract ('download') from the memory hard drive. Also, there is an increasing sense of my own spiritual weakness, how often I miss the spiritual mark and how wonderful God's forgiveness is!

(2) I think I am more adventurous in my faith. My faith is becoming 'more simple' and God is somehow more 'real' to me – 'if our faith could be more simple', as the hymn goes. The essentials of faith matter more – the person and work of Christ, his daily presence, how God continues to speak through his word. I also find that some things that I was passionate about in my younger days do not seem to matter so much now. I will not elaborate! There is also more thinking 'outside the box' or, as our present minister put it, more waiting until 'the penny drops'.

(3) Relationships within the family have become increasingly more meaningful and closer; whereas sadly some of those relationships with the fewer old friends who remain seem to become more distant; contact is less often than it once had been.

[1] In: *Marvellously Made*, Handsel Press, 2017

Of course, there are sound reasons for this but nevertheless they are missed.

The last memory that I would leave with my readers is this. That I have found it true that 'in all things' (and that 'all' includes my science) there has been a sense that my life has been God-directed. There has been a pattern to my life and, like those small boys in that Indian carpet factory, I can only see at present a part of that pattern. How for example, my life has impacted, if at all, on 'the lives of others'. On my last birthday I received a card, on which the words read that 'age is merely the number of years the world has enjoyed you'; to which the writer has added after 'world' – 'and us too'. The point is, whether or not that could be true of me, we all 'touch' the 'lives of others'. Could it be that we might be like a 'scent of water' to those living around us? After all, this is God's plan, purpose and pattern for each one who are in his family. We are to carry around with us, as Paul wrote, an 'aroma', a scent, of the Lord to whom we belong.

At family gatherings we end by singing the following. And, with this I really conclude:

> How good is the God we adore,[2]
> our faithful unchangeable friend;
> whose love is as great as his power.
> And neither knows measure nor end.
>
> Tis Jesus the first and the last,
> whose Spirit will guide us safe home;
> we'll praise him for all that is past,
> and trust him for all that's to come.

[2] Some versions have, 'This, this is the God we adore' (Joseph Hart, 1712-68).

Appendix 8
Adventures in Music

I think it was Plato who said, or wrote, that 'music gives soul to the universe, wings to the mind and life to everything'. I believe this is true but wonder what kind of music he was listening to all those years ago. Perhaps the music of wind and water? It is, as John Logan said, 'the medicine of the mind'. It was certainly Francis Schaeffer who said that one of the things that made him sad was that for so many people, Christians included, classical music is a complete vacuum, robbing them of one of the very rich areas of joy in this world. This echoes the words of the Hungarian composer Zoltán Kodály that music is not only a 'source of spiritual energy' but must be available for everyone. His concern was that music is not just a 'diversion for private individuals' but that it belongs to everybody.

Apparently, according to the BBC, very few people in the UK have any interest in classical music; last year, and in lock down too, there were only ten such programmes on TV, almost all from the Proms. And, not one opera. Much more on radio of course. So, it seems that those of us that love classical music are a small, but enthusiastic and (largely) knowledgeable minority. Happily, indeed joyfully, I fit into this group; classical music is for me an integral part of my life.[1]

Further, Schaeffer continues, ignorance of classical music is a hindrance in our communication with many with whom we wish to speak about the faith we believe. Interesting in this regard is that copies of my two previous books have found their way into the homes of a few of my fellow concert goers. One couple even sent a copy to their own home in Sri Lanka! This is one advantage of the 'same seat syndrome', booking the same place every year for concerts at the two Glasgow concert halls for concerts by the SCO, the RSNO and especially for the BBC SSO and getting to know your musical neighbours.

---

[1] Jim Parratt, *Highways of the Heart (M is for the Musical Heart)*, Handsel Press, 2019.

But where did my love of music come from? Is a deep love of the music of Bach, Haydn, Mozart, Beethoven, Schubert genetically determined? Does this, in part, account for the fact that both my brother and I have a deep and active love of music? My mother spoke of a relation who was famous for his playing of the Jew's harp and she certainly loved some music. I once made a tape for her of some of her favourite music. This included the intermezzi from Wolf-Ferrari's opera *The Jewels of the Madonna*, and 'The Three Elizabeths' suite by Eric Coates, and much piano music; whenever, as a widow, she stayed with us in Bearsden she would ask me to play. Was a dormant inherent interest in music the reason why she wanted both of her sons to learn an instrument?

My early musical experience then was through learning the piano, Handel (suites) and after a while the Beethoven sonatas; I even tried part of the third concerto with my teacher playing the orchestral part. The other early influence was, on our battery-operated radio, and heard over the air waves, a Bruckner symphony (the fourth). My first concert was in the Royal Albert Hall (right up in the gallery) looking down on the keyboard with Julius Katchen playing Tchaikovsky 1 and someone singing the Letter Song from *Eugene Onegin*. This was probably in 1948. Then so many concerts at the Royal Albert Hall and after the 1951 Festival of Britain, the Royal Festival Hall where I had a season ticket. John, my brother and I went quite often to the 'Proms' all, in those days, played by the BBC Symphony Orchestra with just three 'resident conductors', Malcolm Sargent, Basil Cameron and Adrian Boult. There is a photo we found in one of the London newspapers with the two of us at the barrier and Sargent conducting. How different the Proms are today with many different orchestras and conductors taking part. Certainly, London was a wonderful place to hear music, at one time the musical capital of Europe. Followed closely now by Glasgow? Certainly pre-lockdown.

However, I think a major stimulus for music appreciation for many was seeing the Walt Disney film 'Fantasia'. I am unsure when I first saw this, presumably after the general release in 1942; so, when I was about ten or eleven. For those unfortunate people who have never seen this great film, a very brief summary of the contents. It begins with a symphony orchestra (the Philadelphia conducted by Leopold Stokowski) gathering together to give a concert. Then a series of cameos ('animatic segments') set to pieces of classical music, each introduced by the music critic Deems Taylor, by Tchaikovsky, Bach, Beethoven (from the 'Pastoral Symphony' with a highly effective storm), Stravinsky (from the 'Rite of Spring'), Mussorgsky ('Night on the bare [bald] mountain') and Paul Dukas (with Mickey Mouse as the 'Sorcerer's Apprentice'). Everything wonderfully well done. It should be compulsory viewing in Primary 6, with accompanying offers to learn an instrument. The film certainly did that for me.

As this book is headed 'adventures' here are some of mine – in music. When I was still at school, I went to a concert conducted by the inimitable Thomas Beecham. During the interval someone talked to me, very enthusiastically, about what was to be performed in the second half. It was the first symphony by the Russian composer (one of the five Russian composers known as the 'mighty handful') Mily Balakirev, who died in 1910. I knew nothing of him and, indeed had thought of leaving the hall during that interval. I am so glad I didn't! If I had to choose my favourite ten pieces of music (impossible) this would be on it. What triggered my love for it was an enthusiast who took time to talk to me, then a young person!

The second incident was just before we moved into our first Scottish home in 1967. The house was empty. I was there to welcome our furniture coming from storage. I had with me a battery-operated radio which, over fifty years later, is still functioning. A Roberts of course. I had it tuned to the predecessor of BBC3. Over the airwaves came music I did not know at all. It was the 'Sinfonietta' of Leos Janacek. An ear and eye opener. I may even have pretended to conduct it! The next door neighbour could see me in the kitchen (no curtains) and must have thought, with some dread, that a mad family were about to move in.

Janacek became one of our favourite composers. We have seen all the operas and Jenufa is still our top favourite of all operas; the Scottish Opera production was the best of all. We have been to the Janacek festival in Brno welcomed by old friends and where we saw one of our favourite conductors Charles Mackerras receive the Janacek medal. The last time we saw him conduct was in London at the Royal Opera House conducting another Janacek favourite 'The cunning little vixen'. Delightful! Here is a photo of me in the Janacek Museum 'playing' the composer's piano with the composer looking on. But would I have listened to any Janacek if I had not tuned in to the radio in that empty house?

The third example came as a result of our stay in and love for Hungary. As it happened, we were in Budapest for a children's choral competition in the lovely Vigadó concert hall overlooking the Danube. We were greatly moved, not only by the singing but by what they sang. Again, unknown to us. The choral music of Bardos and especially of Zoltán Kodály.

Playing Janacek's piano under the watchful eye of the composer

It is in his writing for choirs, particularly for children's choirs, where surely his genius is most clearly demonstrated – 'See the gypsies eating cheese' (!), or 'The Aged', to words by Weöres Sándor and, this to words by Ady Endre, 'Too late' (*Mi mindig mindenröl elkésünk* . . . 'we're always late for everything our steps are tired, our gait is sad'.) A picture of old age to challenge Gustav Holst's 'Saturn' (The Bringer of Old Age) in 'The Planets' Suite.

Best of all for me the beautiful folk song called 'Evening Song' – 'Esti dal' (*Erdő mellett estvéledtem* . . . 'I put my hands together and asked the good Lord for a good night' (*úgy kértem jó Istenemet*). If there is a thanksgiving service for my life after I have been 'called home' I have asked that a recording of that Kodály song be played. And sung by a children's choir:

'*Én Istenem, adjál szállást, már meguntam a járkálást, a járkálást a bujdosást, az idegen földöd lakást.*'

'My God give me shelter, I have had enough of wandering, of wandering and of hiding, of living in a foreign land.'

The point of the 'adventures' described above is that we should be open to the music we do not already know. We have friends whose musical taste appears to stop at Beethoven or Schumann. They miss the delights of Rubbra, Stenhammar (try the orchestral Serenade Opus 3), Tubin (introduced to me with a performance of his eighth symphony by the RSNO conducted by Naeme Järvi, but perhaps better to start with his fourth symphony); Suk, Novak or Shostakovich (the tenth Symphony or the Piano Quintet a good place to start).

My introduction to chamber music was, whilst I was still at school, on Sunday evenings at one of London's museums near the Albert Hall where the Amadeus Quartet were in residence. It was there I first heard the Schubert String Quintet, for me the music I love most of all. At present my favourite venues for chamber music are at the lovely historic Merchant House in the centre of Glasgow (the Westbourne lunch time concerts) and the East Neuk Festival each June/July at various venues around the coastal villages and churches centered on Crail.

Another adventure was hearing my first musical. This was 'Guys and Dolls' at the National Theatre with Imelda Staunton as 'the' Miss Adelaide. A wonderfully versatile actress; the next time I saw her was in Ibsen's Uncle Vanya as a very moving Sonya. I may have seen the NT production of 'Guys and Dolls' about a dozen times and have taken most of my family to see it too. I have both the libretto and the Guys and Dolls book! My favourite part is called Adelaide's lament. She has a cold. This what she sings:

> The flu! A hundred and one point two. So much virus inside
> that her microscope slide looks like a day at the zoo

There is a Christian message in Guys and Dolls, perhaps the greatest of all musicals, which includes 'an all night prayer meeting' a number of 'respectable sinners' giving their testimonies and it ends with the marriage of a reformed (?) gambler and a Salvation Army girl. I have seen other musicals but nothing compares . . . as they say.

But my musical adventures are most evident with my attempts to continue to play the piano and the discovery of music I never knew existed and yet which is delightful (and challenging) to play. They are now categorised as 'playable now', 'still working on' and 'too difficult for now'. I am returning to the music I started with despite problems with my left hand and less nimble fingers.

When I started to learn I was given the choice of going through the various Music College grades or just playing for my enjoyment. I chose the latter. There was at that time a series of 'pieces', mostly easy to play, which served as introductions to the music of the great composers and published by Keith Prowse (edited and arranged by Ernest Haywood). The factory where they were printed was a short walk from my home in Chiswick. Of the 'Home Series of the Great Masters' I can still find those concerned with Bach, Handel, Mozart, Schubert, Mendelssohn and Tchaikovsky. Much later, I think in the 1980s, I discovered the Pianist Magazine, each issue of which contained a number of scores ranging in difficulty. Some real discoveries here such as Liadov and Scriabin Preludes, a Nocturne by Paderewski and a Suite by Borodin. Then there was the rediscovery of 'A Bach Book for Harriet Cohen'.

Other discoveries came through hearing music on disc or over the radio such as the music of the Spanish composer Mompou, the improvisations of Francis Poulenc (bought in France) such as 'Hommage à Schubert' and 'Hommage à Édith Piaf, some (just a few!) of the transcriptions by Stephen Hough, late Brahms and Bach-Busoni Choral Preludes and Schubert Tänze.

I still find listening to old long-playing records bought years ago bring back memories of when I first heard them. Many were brought back from the former Eastern Europe, labels like Supraphon, Eterna, Hungaroton (of course) and Russian records, with titles written on the sleeve in a script I cannot fathom. I am still trying to guess the name of a composer born in 1939. Clue? Seven characters. It is good to discover new things and to rediscover old ones.

It would be too difficult to list my best loved music (that would mean another book) but to close, this is a short list of my favourite books on music. Many found in second hand book shops especially in Australia; such shops are another of my delights!

(1) Henry J Wood, *My Life in Music*, Victor Gollancz, London 1938 and reprinted many times. Wood was responsible for introducing so much, mainly 'new' music, a list of which is included in his book. Hardly any is played today eighty years later. A warning perhaps for certain contemporary composers. 'Will it last'?

(2) HC Robbins-Landon, *Mozart's Last Year*, Thames and Hudson, 1988. And *Mozart the Golden Years*, Thames and Hudson, 1989. This was given to me by 'friends at a Drumchapel Church'.

(3) Karl Geiringer, Haydn, *A Creative Life in Music*, George Allan and Unwin, London 1964.

(4) Susan Tomes, *Beyond the Notes*, Boydell Press, Woodbridge, Suffolk, 2004 and *Speaking the Piano*, Boydell Press, 2018. This is the fifth and almost latest delightful book by this Edinburgh based pianist, mainly about performance.

(5) Bernard Levin, *Enthusiasms*, Jonathan Cape, London 1983. Indeed, anything about music by Levin or by the provocative Norman Lebrecht.

(6) Anthony Storr, *Music and the Mind*, Harper Collins, London 1993.

(7) Edith Schaeffer, *Forever Music*, Thomas Nelson and SPCK, 1986.

(8) Jim Svejda, *The Record Shelf Guide to Classical CDs and Audiocassettes*, 4th edition, Prima Publishing, Rocklin, California 1995. Full of both insight and wit!

Appendix 9
About Jams and Red Herrings

This story, like several others, starts in Hungary. It is a marmalade story. However, there is a preface to this (and subsequent jam stories) so we should 'begin at the beginning'.

I have in the distant past made many kinds of soups for the family and my meat loaf, an idea planted by the gift (for my wife), during a visit to the United States, of 'American Cookery' by James Beard; a heavy tome to carry home. This recipe, well remembered by some in the family, is broadly based on an old American recipe, much adapted by *'secundem artem'* and probably stimulated by my limited experience as a pharmacist. However, it was only an extended stay in Szeged Hungary (2000 – 2003) that led me to try my hand at formulating 'preserves'. This was probably stimulated by the Hungarian liking, which I too shared, for all things sweet. As my dentist observed, during a recent survey of the inside of my oral cavity – 'you certainly have a sweet tooth'. Indeed, more than one. This, and the fact that marmalade is not usually available in Szeged and that the word 'marmalade' was not known by my assorted friends, led me to attempt (I put it no stronger than that) to make a special Szeged marmalade. Incidentally, I find that in my favourite Angol-Magyar diakszoltar, sweet preserves (for putting on bread or toast) are usually called, as elsewhere in Europe, jam. Thus, marmalade is narancs dzsem (literally 'orange jam').

Marmalade is defined, in my favourite dictionary, as being concocted by boiling a pulp of citrus fruits with sugar. I concocted my Szeged 'jam' in the kitchen of our delightful flat in Szeged with a secret ingredient – Szeged water.[1] The result was then given away to friends – as they then were – despite somewhat quizzical and even suspicious looks. Indeed, some after tasting a microscopic

[1] For non-residents of Szeged I should explain that this water comes from the river Tisza on which the city stands. There are some rather rude Hungarian ditties about the state of this water which are not to be repeated either in Hungarian or in English.

amount, even asked for the 'magic' recipe, still available from me. I should add that we even tried some ourselves with no harmful effects. So far! So, we are all probably safe; it was, after all, nearly twenty years ago.

The real jam making came later. After I retired and before attempting to write. Not concurrently. Are there any tips for any potential first-time jam makers? I have two. First, jam should always be made when any wife is out (banned?) of the kitchen. Second, it should always be accompanied by music. This depends on the particular jam being made and suggestions, well tried, are given below. The Brahms double concerto had a particularly soothing effect on the marmalade made in Szeged.

At one time, so popular did these home-made jams become, that I thought this could become a full-time occupation. Rather like a young jam maker called Fraser Doherty who comes from Dundee, the Scottish home of jam and marmalade making. His method of jam making, called 'super jams', is interesting in that he uses grape juice rather than sugar, a method I have yet to try. The apparent success of my own jams, recommended by several well-bribed friends, led to thoughts about a suitable trademark so that, in superior stores (not supermarkets) they could be distinguished from lesser varieties. So, 'Pimjam' became both a 'trademark' as well as an email address for ease of contact if the demand for 'Pimjams' went viral. This is not as far-fetched as it might seem since it was in Australia (or a very small part of it) that the most successful Pimjam for several years was made. This was cherry jam, which is notoriously difficult to set because cherries are very low in pectin. Pectin is required for a 'good set'. To make this jam required much experimentation (and frequent washing of the kitchen sticky surfaces and floor). The ultimate result was highly recommended by the owners of the farm from which the delicious cherries came.

Not many readers will know of the world jampionships, the Olympics of jam makers. I read about this competition in the Glasgow Herald where it was a major news item because, for the first (and last) time they were to be held in Scotland. This was in Arbroath, of all places, more famous for fish, beach holidays and the Declaration (of Arbroath) than as a world jampionship city. I decided to enter. Could my jams beat off opposition from countries like South Africa, Australia, the USA and even, perhaps surprisingly, from other European countries. Well, the short answer to that question, giving the game away before describing what happened, was no!

Being on a train route, along the attractive east coast of Scotland, I decided to take my entries physically to the venue and spend a day in Arbroath, a place previously unknown to me, for my first (and last) visit. The jam entrants for the competition were held until the 'big day' in the 'cold room' of the art gallery at Hospitalfield House, an impressive building a bus ride from the town centre. There were entries from all over the world and all, except my own, sent by post and mostly well wrapped. All to await tasting and the judge's verdict. I am sure with baited breath.

Before coming to that (no peeping to the end!) there was an unexpected consequence of this visit. I had alerted the folk in the gallery of my coming and they welcomed me with coffee and then a private viewing of the many paintings because, as I was informed, 'there is one painting here that will certainly interest you'. So, I was given a private guided tour. It did. Surprise me that is. Included in the collection was a painting of a distant relation, a rather unattractive lady called Elizabeth Parrott, apparently the mother of my grandfather William Parratt. I do possess the family bible dating back to the end of the eighteenth century which records his marriage. In fact, there were in the gallery three paintings of members of the family, all women. The first, by a painter called Peter Tillemans (sounds Dutch; dates 1684-1734) the other two are of Elizabeth Fraser nee Parrott, painted in the early 19th century. The artist(s) unknown. This would explain the Fraser connection and, presumably their place in the Hospitalfields gallery. I did not follow up the Fraser connection further.

Later, after the visit, I did send an email to the gallery requesting further information about the origin of the two later paintings of this supposed relation by marriage. This was mainly because of the lady's appearance. Could this really be an ancestor? What is known about the artist concerned? No response. I think the reason for this is that the gallery owners might be worried about a possible claim on their property by this previously unknown family member. A fortune seeker?

Now, when I first went to Hungary the first phrase I was taught and which later came in very useful was 'I am a very great detective' (in Hungarian of course) and this particular skill, if it is one, should have been useful in Arbroath. Those of you who read closely will have concluded that the lady in the paintings could not have been my great-grandmother. Firstly, the resemblance (no one in my family could possibly have looked like that) secondly, the lady in the paintings, or so I was informed, came from Liverpool, an unknown and remote city as far as my family is concerned. Thirdly, and here we have an even more important clue, the surname is not the same. When does an o become an a? These are clearly two distinct, albeit not particularly distinctive, families. The paintings are red herrings. No need to revisit Arbroath then. The Parrotts are not the Parratts.

For those of you who have been eagerly awaiting to read of the results of the world jampionships, here they are. I discovered that I had narrowly (I think) missed the bronze medal position – mainly due to 'appearance' and 'labelling'. Note not the taste. However, I did appear on the front page of the Glasgow Herald. Announcing the winner, who appropriately came from the city of jam (as well as jute and journalism) was a young man in his teens and who clearly must have a bright, if sticky, future, there was also the statement that the competitors 'ranged in age from teenagers to a man in his eighties'. Unnamed (sadly) but that really was me!

Now for my favourite jams made through several years of experimentation. Here they are.

1 Elderberry jam

Apart from that Aussie cherry jam mentioned above and still spoken about in South Australia, my number one favourite jam, last made in September 2018, is made from elderberries combined with apple and pear. The quantities are:

Elderberries 650g

Apple or pear (from the garden at St Germain's where we now live) 225g

Juice from two lemons

Sugar 875g

Heat to soften the fruit then add the lemon juice and sugar and boil for about twenty minutes. Delicious! Colour very dark. For music to make by, I suggest Dvořák's 'Serenade for Strings'. If you are still stirring before it has set try his 'Serenade for Wind' to finish the jam on a joyful note.

Sadly, birds are also very fond of elderberries so, at least for me, these lovely berries are hard to come by. But well worth the effort if you can get there first. Before the birds that is.

2 Mirabelle plum jam

In the garden at Saint Germains there is a tree that usually only has copious leaves on it. That is until one year (2018) when it was suddenly laden with a small yellow fruit. Because nobody knew what the tree was, the fruit was left, although some birds seem to enjoy them. Poisonous? Until the resident guinea-pig jam maker took the plunge and turned them into something resembling a cherry jam. We later, through the expertise of the resident gardener Neil, discovered that it was a Mirabelle plum tree which rarely fruits in the West of Scotland. This led to many other potential jam makers taking the plunge and the 'village' was awash with plum jam. In fact, we had discovered a liking for Mirabelle fruit preserves when staying with our good friends Jean-Claude and Janik Stoclet in Brittany. Good to have some on home soil, although the tree has not borne fruit since July 2018 until briefly, and with little fruit, this year. This conserve is just right to put on toast for breakfast. Try the following:

Mirabelle plums (stoned) 1000g

Sugar 1000g

Juice from one lemon

Water - about ten tablespoonfuls

Elderflower essence eight drops (add at the end)

Heat to soften the fruit and then boil until set.

The stirring music (as this is an uncommon jam) could be music not often heard but which fits with a less common jam. So, perhaps Suk ('Serenade for Strings') or Janacek ('Taras Bulba' or the Suite from *The Cunning Little Vixen*).

Here is an unsolicited recommendation from Neil, the resident gardener: 'thank you very much for the plum jam. I shared it with Joyce James and she agrees with me the jam is special – sweet but with a fruity tartness that delighted the palate. Lovely consistency, spreads easily on Rich Tea or Digestive Biscuits'. As I have not seen Neil around for several days I am wondering if he is ok.

3 'Hamlet' jam

No prizes for guessing the constituents of this family favourite jam! 'To be or not to be'? That becomes two (2) b. That is blackcurrant and blueberry jam. Easily made.

Blackcurrants 650g

Blueberries 600g

Water 600ml

Juice of one lemon

Sugar 1200g

Heat the fruit to soften with the water. Add the lemon juice and then the sugar, stir until dissolved then heat until set. This takes about twenty minutes.

No guesses about suitable music to stir by. Tchaikovsky's tone poem Hamlet or the last movement of his fifth symphony - for extra vigour.

4 White currant and raspberry jam

My younger brother, who lives in Cumbria, grows beautiful white currants and brought some up for me to try. Very good with raspberries although the currants need to be crushed as they can be rather 'pippy'.

White currants 750g

Raspberries (must be Scottish and from Perthshire) 250g

Juice of one lemon

Sugar 1000g

After softening this takes about twenty minutes to set. Try listening to Dvořák's Symphony number eight, especially the final two movements to give it a rhythmic stir.

Of course, there are more traditional jams such as strawberry (with rhubarb or cranberry) gooseberry or raspberry. These I make to give away to friends. BUT of course, all jams should carry a health warning. All that sugar! Go carefully. And run before and after – but not too soon after!